21st Century Common Sense
A Bold Reform Agenda for our Broken, Gridlocked, Dysfunctional, and Boring Politics

By Bob Spear

Contact info:
    Email: drbobspear@gmail.com
    Website and blog: 21CommonSense.org
    Like my FaceBook page: 21st Century Common Sense
    Follow me on Twitter: BobSpear8

Illustrated by Carrie Tazbir:
    Email: carrie.tazbir@gmail.com
    Portfolio: www.wix.com/carrietazbir

© Copyright 2019 by 21CommonSense LLC. All rights reserved.

This book or any portion thereof may not be reproduced or used in any manner whatsoever without the express written permission of the publisher except for the use of brief quotations in a book review.

Printed in the United States of America

First Printing, 2019

ISBN-13: 978-1-7330976-1-1

21CommonSense LLC
190 South Shore Road
Swanton, Maryland 21561, USA

Please report any typos or errors to
21Blogger@21CommonSense.org

Acknowledgments

Thanks to all those who advised, critiqued, edited, and otherwise contributed to the creation of this book. Some of you agreed with me, some disagreed in whole or in part, but all offered useful advice and suggestions. The most important contributor throughout was my advisor and editor Steve Herman. In addition to Steve, this list includes Susan Mezey, Michael Mezey, Kevin Faley, Jessica Josephson, Patrick Hunt, and Mark Stutzman. The list also includes several members of my family, especially my mother Idamae Spear, my brother-in-law Michael Fargione, and my wife Mary Helen Spear.

This book benefits greatly from the contributions of Carrie Tazbir, my illustrator. Please visit her portfolio at www.wix.com/carrietazbir.

Mary Helen was not only a valuable critic of various drafts but also the long-suffering spouse who put up with my preoccupation with this work for the last several years. I thank her forever and from the bottom of my heart.

Note: All of the many state and county maps, as well as maps of existing and previous Congressional Districts (CDs), are taken from official state sources in Maryland, Pennsylvania, North Carolina, Louisiana, and Minnesota. Maps showing proposed CDs were drawn by the author and are superimposed on official state maps.

Executive Summary

THIS BOOK IN FIVE MINUTES

Full realization of democracy in America is a work in progress. We've come a long way, but still have a long way to go. This book discusses 21st century challenges to our democracy and proposes fixes to meet those challenges.

Part I. Challenges

1. Presidential Selection Challenge: The Presidential election season is way too long, the candidate selection process is overly complex and undemocratic, Vice Presidents (our likely future Presidents) are appointed rather than elected, and the electoral college is obsolete.

2. U.S. Senate Challenge: The Senate is not representative of the people. Voters in the least populous state have 66 times more power to choose their Senator than voters in the most populous state. That is hardly a democracy.

3. Gerrymander Challenge: Both major parties have become quite sophisticated and effective at drawing legislative districts that unfairly favor themselves.

4. Other Election System Challenges: First-Past-The-Post (FTPT) voting; the entrenched two-party system; caucuses, conventions, and closed primaries; single-member congressional districts; interminable electioneering; voting rights restrictions; unlimited money in political campaigns; and lack of transparency and financial disclosures by candidates and officeholders all detract from the proper functioning of our democracy.

Part II. Fixes

1. Ranked Choice Voting (RCV)

    a. After selecting their 1st choice for each office, voters may also select a 2nd and a 3rd choice.
    b. For single-winner-contests, if the top candidate has less than a majority of the 1st choice votes, then the candidate with the fewest votes is eliminated, and votes for that candidate are reassigned to each voter's next highest choice. This process continues until someone has a majority of the total vote.

2. Two-Party System

    a. Open primaries are mandated for all federal elected offices. In an open primary, all candidates compete against each other, and all voters select among all candidates for that office regardless of party affiliation. All voters can vote in every primary. Open primaries replace all closed primaries, caucuses, and conventions.
    b. Eliminate legal preferences for the two-party system. Repeal all laws which mention or favor political parties.
    c. Political parties will still exist. They can hold meetings, caucuses, and conventions at their own expense. They can endorse candidates and adopt platforms. But no party or group has a legal advantage over any other party or independent candidate.

3. Empower Citizens to Amend the Constitution

a. Citizens and states can propose a constitutional amendment. (Congress can also propose a constitutional amendment, as at present.)

b. Voters have the final say: Voters must approve a Constitutional amendment in two general elections separated by another general election and a new President. In both of these amendment ratification votes, ratification requires approval by a majority of all votes cast, including a majority of the votes cast in 60% of the states containing 60% of the U.S. population.

4. Presidential Selection Fix

    a. Shorten, simplify, and democratize the process of choosing Presidential candidates:

        i. Adopt three rounds of Presidential primaries, including four states in round 1 (held in August), ten states in round 2 (in September), and all other jurisdictions in round 3 (National Primary Day, in October).

        ii. Tabulate primary votes by Congressional District (CD). The winner of each CD receives the "Nominating Vote" from that CD.

        iii. Candidates who receive at least 15% of the total Nominating Votes qualify for the general election, which takes place in December.

    b. Hold a primary election for Vice President on National Primary Day.

    c. Alternative: Replace the position of Vice President with a new Chancellor of the Senate. Elect the Chancellor for a four-year term of office in even-numbered years not evenly divisible by 4 (that is, the years when we currently have mid-term elections). The Chancellor presides over the Senate, is first in line to succeed the President, and makes all judicial appointments.

    d. Provide for the direct election of the President and Vice President/Chancellor. Adopt the Local-State-National (LSN) Voting System. Under the LSN Voting System,

        i. One electoral vote goes to the winner of each CD;

        ii. One electoral vote goes to the winner of each state; and

        iii. One electoral vote from each state goes to the winner of the national popular vote.

    e. Implement the LSN scheme either through the LSN Interstate Compact (bypassing the electoral college without a constitutional amendment) or through a constitutional amendment (eliminating the electoral college altogether).

5. U.S. Senate Fix: By constitutional amendment, reconstitute the US Senate as a representative body. Each state gets one Senator for every five seats in the House, but every state gets at least one Senator.

6. U.S. House of Representatives Fix

    a. Mandate a rule-governed process for drawing congressional districts without human decisions concerning any CD boundary, eliminating the gerrymander forever.

    b. Adopt multi-seat CDs while using a proportional voting scheme.

7. Other Election System Fixes

    a. Compress the political campaign season to run from Independence Day to the general election in December.

    b. Automatically register all voters at age 18. Establish a National Voter Registration Authority to maintain all voter rolls.

    c. All elections shall last nine days, beginning on a Saturday, giving voters two full weekends to vote in person. Allow mail-in ballots without justification. Announce election results at the end of each day of in-person voting.

    d. Campaign finance reform: Limit who can contribute, how much, and when. Limit fund-raising by candidates. Provide public financing for all general election campaigns.

    e. For candidates and elected officials, require transparency and full financial disclosure, and prohibit nepotism.

Part III. A Revised Constitution

The proposed Constitution II would replace the existing 1787 Constitution. This new constitution incorporates all previous amendments to the 1787 Constitution, all the fixes proposed in Part II, and additional fixes that ought to be considered as long as we are rewriting the whole document. Part III also includes a procedure for ratification and transitioning to Constitution II.

The additional challenges and fixes included in Constitution II include these:

1. Congressional Rules Challenges: Congress follows rules which promote gridlock, preventing necessary legislative action. Presidents step into the resulting power vacuum, creating the imperial presidency.

2. Congressional Rules Fixes

    a. Reform the filibuster. Reestablish majority rule in both chambers of Congress.

    b. Reform the Senate's "advise and consent" procedure. Allow the President to make temporary appointments if the Senate fails to act within a designated period.

    c. Give Congress both advance notice and veto power over Presidential executive orders.

3. Bill of Rights Challenges: The Bill of Rights in the Constitution is incomplete. Some implied rights lack specificity or clarity. Some citizen rights and some states' rights are missing entirely.

4. Bill of Rights Fixes:

    a. Some implied rights should be clarified, such as privacy; freedom from discrimination and torture; the right to bear arms; and the rights to life, liberty, and the pursuit of happiness.

    b. Some citizen rights missing from the Constitution should be included, such as the definition of citizens, voting rights, initiative and referendum, and approval of constitutional amendments.

c. Some states' rights should also be included, such as the right of states to work in concert with each other without ceding power to the federal government, a limited right of states to supersede federal law, and a limited right to secede from the Union (with concurrence by both the state and the Union).

I offer Constitution II as a starting point for debate, not as the final solution. I am raising issues that Americans should discuss; others will certainly offer different and perhaps better solutions. I only ask that we judge each proposed solution by these measures: Will it make us more free? Will it make our democracy more representative, more democratic? Will it unify us or better bring us to consensus? Will it help us govern ourselves?

Table of Contents

Acknowledgments iii

Executive Summary iv

Table of Contents xi

Preface 1

    Democracy Works Best When We All Participate 1

    The Original Common Sense 5

    Common Sense for the 21st Century 6

Part I. Challenges 9

    Introduction to Part I 9

        How We Got Here 9

        Progress in Democracy 15

            Expansion of democracy through constitutional amendments 15

            Expansion of rights through Supreme Court decisions 16

            Expansion of rights through federal laws 16

        Remaining Electoral Challenges 17

    Challenge 1. Presidential Selection 18

        ...Too Long 18

        ...Too Complicated 19

        ...Undemocratic 20

        VP Candidates Appointed 22

        [Interesting sidebar: Election of 1788] 25

Obsolete Electoral College	26
Challenge 2. Senate Structure	**31**
Proportional Representation	32
Iterative and Perpetual Characteristics of the Senate's Undemocratic Imbalance	36
Provenance of Structural Unfairness in our Constitutional System	37
Previous Fixes	39
Challenge 3. Gerrymanders	**41**
Decennial Reapportionment	41
The Practice of Gerrymandering	42
Disenfranchised Voters	44
Worst Cases in Practice	46
Worst Case in Theory	48
Why and How We Need a Fix, and What Clearly Will Not Work	52
State Legislative Districts	54
Challenge 4. Other Election System Deficiencies	**55**
First-Past-The-Post (FPTP) Voting	55
The Two-Party System	57
Caucuses, Conventions, and Closed Primaries	61
Single-Member Congressional Districts	64
Electioneering Forever	65
Voting Rights Restrictions	67

    Congress for Sale 69

    Financial Disclosures, Transparency, and Nepotism 70

Part II. Fixes 72

  Introduction to Part II 72

  Three Big Fixes 74

    Big Fix 1. Ranked Choice Voting 74

      Relevance 74

      Restating the Problem 75

      What is Ranked Choice Voting (RCV)? 75

      Ranked Choice Voting Procedures 76

      Expected RCV Results 77

      Additional Rationale 80

      Critics and Costs 81

      RCV in the US and Around the World 81

      Congress's Power to Act 82

    Big Fix 2. Restrain the Two-Party System 84

      Open Primaries 84

      Party Caucuses and Conventions 87

      All Other Laws, Regulations, and Practices 87

    Big Fix 3. Empower Voters to Amend the Constitution 88

      Amendment on Amendments 90

  Election System Fixes (Challenges 1-4) 93

    Challenge 1. Presidential Selection Fixes 93

      Shorten, Simplify, and Democratize the Process of Choosing Presidential Candidates 94

xiii

Let Voters Select Vice Presidential Candidates 101

Better Solution to the Vice-Presidential Selection Challenge: Replace the Vice President with an Elected Chancellor of the Senate 102

Provide for Direct Election of the President and Vice President 106

Challenge 2. U.S. Senate Fix 114

Article V Provision 114

Proposed Makeup of the New Senate 116

Terms of Office for the New Senate 120

Senate Elections 121

Conclusion 123

Challenge 3. Gerrymander Fix 125

Redistricting without Gerrymanders 126

Multi-Seat CDs Combined with Ranked Choice Voting 148

Challenge 4. Other Election System Fixes 159

Fixes Previously Addressed 159

2 Compressed Election Season Schedule 160

Voting Rights 163

Campaign Finance Reform 168

Candidates and Elected Officials: Financial Disclosures, Transparency, and Nepotism 170

Summary of Electoral Fixes by Method of Realization 171

Fixes Through State Laws 172

Fixes Through Federal Laws 176

Fixes Through Constitutional Amendments 182

Fixes Through Cultural Change 186

Portrait of Future Congressional Elections 188

Single Constitutional Amendment Concerning Federal Elections 192

Amendment on Federal Elections 193

    Section 1. Composition of the Legislature. 193

        1.1   The Legislature 193

        1.2   The House of Representatives 193

        1.3   The Senate 194

    Section 2. General Provisions on Federal Elections 198

        2.1 Voter Eligibility 198

        2.2 Automatic Voter Registration 199

        2.3 Voting Procedures and Ranked Choice Voting (RCV) 200

        2.4 Primary Elections 203

    Section 3. Elections for President and for Chancellor 204

        3.1 Elections and Terms of Office. 204

        3.2 Primary Elections for President and for Chancellor 205

        3.3. General Elections for President and for Chancellor 206

    Section 4. Elections for Members of Congress 207

    Section 5. Dates of Primary and General Elections, Convening of Congress, and Inauguration 208

    Section 6. Continuance in Office 209

    Section 7. Transition to the Reconstituted Congress 210

Part III. A Revised Constitution 211

    Introduction to Part III 212

        Authority and Necessity 213

- Why Do We Think We Have the Authority to Do This? 213
- Why Do We Need to Do This? 216
- Guidelines for the Contents of Constitution II 217
- Additional Challenges and Fixes Addressed in Constitution II 219
  - Congressional Rules Challenge and Fixes 221
  - Bill of Rights Challenge and Associated Fixes in Constitution II 230
- Convening the Constitution II Convention 249
  - First Approach 250
  - Second Approach 251
- Constitution II Convention Procedures 253
  - Consent of 60% of Us 254
- Formatting Notes in Constitution II 255

Constitution II for the United States of America 257

- Preamble 257
- Stipulations 259
- Article I: Bill of Rights 261
  - Section 2: Bill of Rights of Natural Persons 263
  - Section 3: Bill of Rights of Citizens 265
  - Section 4: Bill of Rights of States 270
- Article II: The Legislative Branch 275
  - Section 1: The Legislature 275
  - Section 2: The House of Representatives 276
  - Section 3: The Senate 278

Section 4 - Meetings 282

Section 5 - Membership, Rules, Journals, and Adjournment
.... 282

Section 6 - Compensation 284

Section 7 - Revenue Bills, Legislative Process, and Presidential Veto 285

Section 8 - Powers of Congress 287

Section 9 - Limits on Congress 292

Section 10 - Powers Prohibited of States 294

Section 11 - Transition from the 1787 Constitution to this Constitution II 295

Article III: The Executive Branch 298

Section 1 - The President 298

Section 2 - Civilian Power over Military; the Cabinet, Pardon Power, and Appointments 302

Section 3 - State of the Union, Convening Congress, and Executive Orders 304

Article IV: The Judicial Branch 306

Section 1 – The Judiciary 306

Section 2 – Judicial Power, Original Jurisdiction, and Jury Trials 308

Section 3 - Treason 310

Section 4 – Misconduct by Public Officials 310

Article V: Debts, Supremacy, and Oaths 313

Article VI: Elections 315

Section 1. General Provisions 315

    1.1 Voter registration 315

    1.2 Ranked Choice Voting 316

    1.3 Conduct of elections 318

    1.4 Open primaries 319

    1.5 Fundraising and transparency 320

Section 2. Elections for President and for Chancellor 321

    2.1 Direct Election of the President and of the Chancellor 321

    2.2 Primary Elections for President 321

    2.3. Primary Election for Chancellor 323

    2.4 Local-State-National (L-S-N) general election voting system for President and for Chancellor 324

Section 3. Elections for Members of Congress 325

Section 4. Dates of Primary and General Elections, Convening of Congress, and Inauguration 326

Section 5. Continuance in Office 327

Article VII: Citizen Empowerment; Constitutional Amendments 328

    Section 1. Enacting and Repealing Federal Statutes 328

    Section 2. Proposing an Amendment 329

    Section 3. Constitutional Convention 330

    Section 4. Ratification 331

Appendix 1. RCV Procedures 332

    RCV Categories 332

    RCV Voting 333

    RCV Counting of Ballots...333

    FairVote.org's Procedure for Multi-Winner Elections............336

Appendix 2. Maryland Redistricting..340

    Maryland Congressional District 1 342

        Partitioning LAST County..345

        "Partition" and "Left Over" Definitions...................................346

        Could the LAST ZCTA in LAST County Be Too Large? 347

        Subdividing LAST County for This Demo 348

    Maryland CDs 2 Through 8..348

        MD CD 2:..349

        MD CD 3:..351

        MD CD 4:..352

        MD CD 5:..355

        MD CD 6:..356

        MD CD 7 358

        MD CD 8:..359

    All 8 Maryland CDs 360

    Avoiding Future Gerrymanders...360

Appendix 3. Pennsylvania Redistricting...362

    Pennsylvania Congressional District 1 364

    Pennsylvania Congressional District 2 365

    Pennsylvania Congressional District 3 367

    Pennsylvania Congressional District 4 368

    Pennsylvania Congressional District 5 370

Pennsylvania Congressional District 6 371

Pennsylvania Congressional District 7 373

Pennsylvania Congressional District 8 374

Pennsylvania Congressional District 9 376

Pennsylvania Congressional District 10 377

Pennsylvania Congressional District 11 379

Pennsylvania Congressional District 12 380

Pennsylvania Congressional District 13 382

Pennsylvania Congressional District 14 383

Pennsylvania Congressional District 15 385

Pennsylvania Congressional District 16 386

Pennsylvania Congressional District 17 388

Pennsylvania Congressional District 18 389

All 18 Pennsylvania CDs 390

Appendix 4. North Carolina Redistricting 391

North Carolina Congressional District 1 392

North Carolina Congressional District 2 394

North Carolina Congressional Districts 3 through 12 396

    North Carolina Congressional District 3 396

    North Carolina Congressional District 4 398

    North Carolina Congressional District 5 399

    North Carolina Congressional District 6 401

    North Carolina Congressional District 7 402

    North Carolina Congressional District 8 404

North Carolina Congressional District 9 405

North Carolina Congressional District 10 407

North Carolina Congressional District 11 408

North Carolina Congressional District 12 410

North Carolina Congressional District 13 411

All 13 North Carolina CDs 413

Appendix 5. The Rules in Excruciating Detail 414

General Principles 414

Summary Procedures 414

Detailed Procedures 415

Obtain your state's source data: 415

State summary data 415

County data 416

ZCTA data 416

Replicate these steps for each CD from CD 1 to CD N-1: ... 417

Draw the Reference Line 417

Select the Starting Point 417

Scan Line and Scanning 417

Build the Congressional District 418

Last CD in a State (CD N) 420

Resources and Tools 420

Data source: Missouri Census Data Center 420

Master Congressional District Workbook for <state name> using Excel 425

Create the Excel Workbook and Load Source Data 426

Appendix 6. Three-Seat CDs in Louisiana 436
    Louisiana Congressional District 1 (LA CD 1) 437
    Louisiana CD 2 439
Appendix 7. Three-Seat CDs in Minnesota 441
    Minnesota Congressional District 1 (MN CD 1) 443
    MN CD 2 446
    MN CD 3 448
Sources/Citations 450

21st Century Common Sense
A Bold Reform Agenda for our Broken, Gridlocked, Dysfunctional, and Boring Politics

Preface
Democracy Works Best When We All Participate

Underlying Principle of Democracy:

"All men are created equal."

Every citizen is born with the same rights and responsibilities, fully equal before the law with every other citizen; and every citizen has the same power to participate in the public debate, voice his/her opinion, recommend a course of action, and influence the outcome.

If we can point to one underlying principle of democracy, it is the bold statement in the Declaration of Independence: "All men are created equal." This single principle informs all our democratic institutions and every form of democratic government. In a pure democracy like ancient Athens, all citizens come together in a huge meeting place to make all public decisions together. In a representative democracy, people freely select their representatives who in turn come together to make decisions for the common good. Whichever form of democracy the people choose, the underlying principle remains the same. No single citizen should have an advantage in the public square over any other citizen based on financial assets, social position, inheritance, educational attainment, race, gender, sexual orientation, religion, political affiliation, zip code or city or state where he/she happens to reside, or any other irrelevant factor.

In practice, this pure, underlying principle often gets compromised for two main reasons. Honest brokers don't always agree on how to implement the underlying principle in the fairest way, or the competing parties do not enter the political discussion as equals.

In the American system of government, we have instituted a number of practices that undermine the all-men-are-created-equal principle, that is, practices which effectively make some citizens more equal than others. Some citizens have a built-in and unfair advantage over their compatriots. For example, in the original Constitution, a slave was counted as 3/5 of a person for purposes of determining the population of each state and therefore the number of seats that each state would have in the House of Representatives. Similarly, each state was awarded two seats in the Senate, regardless of the number of persons in that state. Both of these constitutional provisions contradict the notion that all of us are created equal. Though not directly stated in the Constitution, the Supreme Court has enshrined the notion that corporations have the same rights as people, which means that corporations have a voice in public debates. We tolerate many practices in the public domain that make some people more equal than others, especially the outsized influence of corporate lobbyists and of the political donor class. When it comes to drafting laws, selecting candidates for public office, or getting the attention of elected officials, lobbyists and major contributors have an inside track. Joe citizen may try to compete, but he does so at a considerable disadvantage.

The major purpose of *21st Century Common Sense* (21CommonSense.org) is to examine the practices that give some Americans an unfair advantage and to recommend adjustments that would tend to level the playing field. There is no perfect system, nor will any set of laws or constitutional amendments make for an ideal system. The fixes that we will discuss are imperfect, of course, but they could help make the existing system better.

From the outset, let me state that I accept without qualification or argument the underlying principle that all of us are created equal. Someone who rejects that principle might find little of merit in *21st Century Common Sense*. We will examine those practices which give some citizens an inherent advantage over others to see whether we can realize greater opportunity for all.

Unfair or unequal practices include provisions of the federal or state constitutions, federal or state laws (or the lack of applicable laws), judicial decisions, or just common or accepted or traditional social or cultural practices. Regardless of the provenance of the practice or the reason for its continuance, we will examine it with a view to making our public business more fair, open, and equal for all.

This mission is not pie-in-the-sky rhetoric. Rather, it is exactly what our Founding Fathers undertook when they signed the

Declaration of Independence, when they adopted the Articles of Confederation, and when they adopted the US Constitution. Our project will be a reappraisal of how we can better govern ourselves so as to make ours a more perfect union.

The Original Common Sense

COMMON SENSE;

ADDRESSED TO THE

INHABITANTS

OF

AMERICA,

On the following interesting

SUBJECTS.

I. Of the Origin and Design of Government in general, with concise Remarks on the English Constitution.

II. Of Monarchy and Hereditary Succession.

III. Thoughts on the present State of American Affairs.

IV. Of the present Ability of America, with some miscellaneous Reflections.

Man knows no Master save creating HEAVEN,
Or those whom choice and common good ordain.
THOMSON.

PHILADELPHIA;
Printed, and Sold, by R. BELL, in Third-Street,
MDCCLXXVI.

Thomas Paine's *Common Sense*, published in January 1776, inspired American colonists to adopt, by July of that same year, a completely radical idea: revolution against the government of King George III and establishment of a new and independent country based on the principles of liberty and self-government.

You can read Thomas Paine's original pamphlet, often called the most influential political tract of all time, at https://archive.org/details/commonsense00painrich

Common Sense for the 21st Century

21st Century Common Sense is a 21st century version of the same thing: bold proposals for reforming the American Government based on the principles of liberty and self-government. Unlike Thomas Paine's revolutionary tract, my ideas are bold rather than radical: Thomas Paine and his fellow revolutionists wanted to throw out the British Monarchy and everything associated with it; I on the other hand want to build on what we have achieved, preserve all that is good and valuable in our existing political structures, but boldly transform the broken pieces into something more democratic, more representative, more of a perfect union.

Let me briefly comment on my purpose, assumptions, and intended audience:

- My **Purpose** is to spark discussion, debate, and action. I am tired of hearing Americans grousing about our broken politics. We need to begin the kind of national conversation that leads to real political reform. Such reforms may include new federal and state laws and constitutional amendments, new political customs, and new social norms.

- **Assumptions**: As you peruse this volume, I assume that you will recognize and concur with the litany of ills we face. I am less sanguine about the prospects for general acceptance of the solutions I am proposing. These are all draft proposals – the best that this author is able to offer at the time of writing, but not necessarily the best you or all of us together can devise. Our political dysfunction today is analogous to the economic dysfunction this nation faced in the Great Depression. When FDR was campaigning for President in 1932, he famously stated, "The country needs and, unless I mistake its temper, the country demands bold, persistent experimentation. It is common sense to take a method and try it. If it fails, admit it frankly and try something else. But above all try something." [1] Perhaps that is a prescription worth remembering when we try to reform our politics.

- **Audience**: While political scientists and students of American government may find something of interest here, I do not offer my commentary as a formal academic work, building on the last two centuries of academic political science research. Rather, this book is directed at laymen, reasonably informed American voters, and anyone interested in improving the American political system.

21st Century Common Sense is presented as a series of interrelated essays:

---

[1] Franklin Roosevelt, Commencement Address at Oglethorpe University, May 22, 1932. *The Atlanta Constitution*, May 23, 1932.

- *Part I. Challenges* provides some historical context on how we got to our current democracy and on the challenges we face in maintaining and improving it.
- *Part II. Fixes* lays out the constitutional amendments, federal and state laws, and cultural/social behaviors needed to meet those challenges.
- *Part III: A Revised Constitution* incorporates all previous amendments to the 1787 Constitution, all the fixes proposed in Part II, and several other provisions that may as well be updated if we are going to create a whole new document. Part III also suggests a procedure for proposing Constitution II to the people and states for ratification and for transitioning to Constitution II.

In addition to this printed version, the online version appears at 21CommonSense.org, an online blog, an engine for new ideas, a forum for political discussion, and a jumping-off place for specific reformist campaigns.

Part I. Challenges

Introduction to Part I
How We Got Here

American democracy has been under development since Colonial times as settlements, villages, town, cities, and colonies experimented with various forms of self-government. They paid little more than lip service to what was going on in Europe. It's true that the King of England appointed royal governors for each colony. But England was months away by ship. An emissary had to cross the Atlantic twice to get a message or decision over and back, and so governors usually depended on the colonists themselves to implement the functions of government. Each colony had an elected legislative body (lower chamber) and a privy Senate (upper chamber) appointed by the governor but made up of colonists. Purely local matters were largely left in the hands of those localities.

In the mid-18th century, relations between England and their American colonies became increasingly bitter as the English King and Parliament began to intervene more directly and forcefully into Colonial affairs over the colonists' objections. England believed that it was only exercising its God-given right to rule; the colonists thought that England was usurping their rights of self-government that they had enjoyed for two centuries.

Hence a movement began among the Colonies to separate themselves from England, to declare independence, and to form a new nation.

Bitter argument between loyalists (or Tories) and separatists came to a head in 1776. In January of that year, Thomas Paine published *Common Sense,* his 48-page pamphlet excoriating the King and Parliament and indeed all autocratic governments. His essay was a forceful polemic in favor of American independence. Then, at a meeting of all the colonies in Philadelphia in July 1776, the American Colonies issued their *Declaration of Independence* from England. Before that meeting *Common Sense* had gone through multiple printings and reprintings, making it the single most successful political pamphlet in history. Before Independence, historians estimate that about a third of the colonists supported separation from England, a third wanted to remain a part of England, and a third were undecided. But Thomas Paine's pamphlet helped swing opinion in favor of independence.

To become and remain a new nation, America first had to fight and win a war against England, the American Revolutionary War

(1776-1783). Then America had to set up the mechanics of a new government. The colonies cooperated marginally well during the war, motivated by the urgency of facing a common enemy. But that cooperation was certain to falter once the war was over. For that reason, discussions/meetings/conventions took place from 1777 to 1781. Their purpose was to establish the post-war American Government, uniting the thirteen original states in perpetuity. These meetings finally produced the Articles of Confederation, which lasted as America's foundational document from 1781 to 1787.

While perhaps a good first step in creating a constitutional democracy, the Articles of Confederation was flawed in many serious ways. Because its authors mistrusted the kind of strong central government epitomized by England, they designed an exceedingly weak national government. The Articles of Confederation gave most powers to the states and gave the central government no enforcement mechanism to ensure that every state lived up to its obligations. The Articles created Congress, a unicameral national legislature that also exercised executive and judicial functions. The Articles of Confederation did not provide for the election of any federal official directly by the people. Rather, each state legislature appointed two to seven Delegates to Congress. All votes in Congress were taken by state with each state having one vote. Major decisions required the concurrence of nine states; lesser matters could be decided by a simple majority. Further, the Articles required unanimous consent of every state legislature in order to adopt any amendments to the Articles themselves.

Recognizing that the Articles of Confederation was not working, leaders throughout the states called for a Constitutional Convention, which convened in Philadelphia in 1787. Every state was invited to send a delegation to help write a new foundational document or to at least amend the original Articles. Every state except Rhode Island sent a delegation. That convention produced the 1787 Constitution of the United States, and ultimately all 13 states ratified it. Interestingly, the 1787 Constitution required only nine states to ratify it, after which it came into full force and effect among those states that had ratified it. The authors knew going in that they would probably not be successful if they required unanimous consent, so they decided to ignore that requirement of the Articles. (In this respect the Framers set a very good precedent for the solution to our current challenges presented in Part III of this work.)

While the 1787 Constitution corrected many of the faults of the Articles of Confederation, American democratic government remained then (and still remains) a work in progress. Among the most significant improvements of the 1787 Constitution over the Articles of Confederation are the following:

- A far stronger federal government with the power and authority to carry out its duties throughout the United States.
- Separation of the powers of the federal government into three co-equal branches – legislative, executive, and judicial.
- A federal system of governments, composed of a federal government separate and distinct from the several state governments, which remain sovereign within their own jurisdictions.
- A careful system of checks and balances, both between the federal government and the states and among the co-equal branches of the federal government.

- A bicameral legislature, the Congress, consisting of a more numerous lower chamber, the House of Representatives, and an upper chamber, the Senate. The people elect the House of Representatives directly, with the number of Representatives from each state proportional to the population in each state. Originally, state legislatures appointed the members of the Senate, with two senators per state.
- Election of the President by electors appointed by each state, with the number of electors from each state equaling the total number of senators and representatives from that state. (We now refer to the collection of electors from all states as the electoral college, even though the term "electoral college" does not appear in the Constitution.) Quite interestingly, the 1787 Constitution does not require that the people choose the electors from each state, though that is the case today. (In the first Presidential election, held from December 1788 through January 1789, only six states held a popular vote.)
- The Senate's "advice and consent" role in confirming Presidential executive and judicial appointments and in ratifying treaties as well as other limitations on the power of the President.
- A fairly detailed list of the powers of Congress, limitations on the powers of Congress, powers of the states, and limitations on the powers of the states.
- Jurisdiction of the federal courts.

While ratification of the Constitution was being debated, many critics thought the role of the federal government would be too powerful vis-à-vis both the states and the individual citizen. Therefore, a series of amendments were proposed to make the rights of the people and of the states more secure. These amendments would then be submitted to the states for their approval as soon as the Constitution itself was adopted. Ten of these amendments were ratified in 1791 and became known as the Bill of Rights. Many of our most precious rights as American citizens derive directly from the Bill of Rights. These first ten amendments are as follows:

Amendment 1: Freedom of religion, speech, the press, and assembly

Amendment 2: Right to bear arms

Amendment 3: Limits on the quartering of soldiers in private houses

Amendment 4: Limits on searches and seizures without a warrant

Amendment 5: Rights of defendants in criminal cases: indictment by a grand-jury; protection against double-jeopardy and self-incrimination; prohibition against the loss of life, liberty, or property without due process of law; limits on eminent domain

Amendment 6: More rights of defendants in criminal cases: speedy trial by an impartial jury, access to information concerning the accusations against them, confrontation of witnesses, compulsory evidence for the defense, and the assistance of counsel

Amendment 7: Right to a trial by jury in civil cases

Amendment 8: Prohibition of excessive bail, excessive fines, and cruel and unusual punishments

Amendment 9: Rights of the people beyond those enumerated in the Constitution

Amendment 10: Powers not given to the federal government by the Constitution are reserved to the states and to the people.

The original 1787 Constitution was less than perfect from the outset, and it did not create a most perfect union. Even the Framers themselves, or many of them, recognized that their work was incomplete – hence the insistence on the Bill of Rights, adopted as amendments to the Constitution during George Washington's first term as President.

Progress in Democracy

After 1791, the long course of American history bends in favor of the expansion of democracy, enfranchisement of wider segments of the populace, and giving more power to the people. Though some of these changes remain controversial, all of them expand citizen rights, empower individuals and groups, and/or ensure equality before the law. We have made major improvements through constitutional amendments, judicial decisions, laws, and customs. Examples in each category follow:

Expansion of democracy through constitutional amendments

- Abolition of slavery (13th Amendment, 1865)
- Citizenship rights (14th Amendment, 1868)
- Right to vote regardless of race (15th Amendment, 1870)
- Direct election of Senators by the people (17th Amendment, 1913)
- Women's right to vote (19th Amendment, 1920)
- Limit of President to two terms of office (22nd Amendment, 1951)

- Right to vote for President extended to the District of Columbia (23rd Amendment, 1961)
- Elimination of poll tax or other impediments to voting (24th Amendment, 1964)
- Right of all citizens to vote at age 18 (26th Amendment, 1971)

Expansion of rights through Supreme Court decisions

- Brown v. the Board of Education of Topeka, Kansas (1954): Made school segregation illegal
- Miranda v. Arizona (1966): Requires law enforcement to advise suspects in custody of their right to remain silent (right against self-incrimination) and of their right to an attorney
- Loving v. Virginia (1967): Banned laws which forbade interracial marriage
- Roe v. Wade (1973): Established a woman's right to an abortion before the third trimester of pregnancy
- District of Columbia v. Heller (2008): Established the Second Amendment right of an individual citizen to own a firearm for traditionally lawful purposes, such as self-defense within the home

Expansion of rights through federal laws

- Social Security Act
- Voting Rights Act
- Freedom of Information Act
- Right to organize unions

- Child labor laws, minimum wage laws, and laws concerning workplace health and safety
- Equal access to education for women, the disabled, minorities, and the poor
- Expanding access to healthcare: Medicare, Medicaid, Veterans Health Administration, and the Affordable Care Act
- Environmental protection laws – the EPA, clean water, and clean air
- Right to privacy

Remaining Electoral Challenges

Although we have made progress toward the achievement of "a more perfect union", much remains to be done. The balance of Part I of this paper discusses the principal election-related challenges we face today. Part II proposes constitutional amendments, laws, and procedures which would go a long way toward meeting those challenges. Finally, Part III proposes a rewrite of the 1787 Constitution, titled Constitution II, an easier and more straightforward path to meeting all these challenges at once, empowering citizens, making our country more democratic and more representative of its citizens, and "forming a more perfect union".

The principal electoral challenges are these:

1. Deficiencies in the manner of choosing the President and Vice President
2. The Non-Representative U.S. Senate
3. Gerrymandering of Congressional Districts
4. Other counterproductive characteristics of current federal election practices

Challenge 1. Presidential Selection

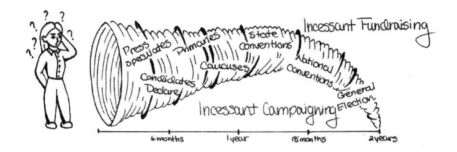

Most Americans agree that our Presidential elections last too long and are unnecessarily complicated and unrepresentative. Vice Presidential candidates are appointed rather than elected, and the electoral college is obsolete.

...Too Long

1. In the last several Presidential election cycles, we have been evolving into a perpetual Presidential campaign season. No sooner do we complete a Presidential election than parties and candidates begin jockeying for position in anticipation of the next election, four years hence. Since many of the potential Presidential candidates already hold elective office, they have limited time or patience for the mundane task of governance (for which they supposedly were elected to their current positions) and instead become focused almost exclusively on the next Presidential election.

2. Right now, the period of active campaigning extends at least two years. In January 2015, fully 21 months before the 2016 general election, pundits, insiders, and experts agreed that it was becoming almost too late for any additional candidates to get into the race. (Of course, the ultimate winner did not enter the fray until June, although lots of speculation about his potential candidacy surrounded him before he officially announced.)
3. These interminable campaigns are endurance contests, exhausting for both the candidates and the public. They do not necessarily show which candidates might have the requisite qualifications, experience, character, temperament, and wisdom to serve as Chief Executive. Rather, they show which candidates can survive the grueling schedule while committing the fewest public gaffes.
4. Interminable campaigning and lack of attention to actually governing frustrates the public and turns them off to serious political discourse. We hear sound bites and talking points *ad nauseam*. Rarely do we hear serious proposals or debates about real issues.

...Too Complicated

1. In addition to going on way too long, the process involves procedures and schedules established by each state, with no rhyme or reason for each state's choices (at least none discernible to the public) and certainly no national plan.
2. Some states have a primary, while others have a caucus. Why?
3. In most states, the primary or caucus is held on the same day for all, while in other states the Republicans hold their

primary or caucus on one day while the Democrats hold theirs on a different day. Why?

4. Several states have both a primary and a caucus. Why?
5. In some states, voters may choose which party's primary/caucus to vote in on election day; in other states, voters must be a registered member of a particular party in order to vote in that party's primary; and in a third group of states, Democrats vote in the Democratic primary, Republicans vote in the Republican primary, and independents can vote in either; and finally, at least in Nevada, Independents can vote in both the Republican and the Democratic primaries. Why?
6. Some states award delegates to winning candidates proportionally while other states have a winner-take-all rule. Why?
7. Caucuses are unrepresentative and basically unfair, contributing to the general perception that the whole process is rigged.
8. After all the primaries and caucuses and state conventions, national party conventions can still thwart the will of the electorate.

Conclusion: Presidential primaries should be simplified and standardized among all states. If this were done, public apathy would abate, enthusiasm engendered, voter participation increased, and confidence in the results restored.

...Undemocratic

How many times have you heard voters and pundits decry the choices available to them? Citizens are unhappy and frustrated with the process, which results, in their view, in two major party candidates neither of whom reflect the interests of the citizens these candidates purport to represent. Part of the problem here is that, during the primary season, candidates must appeal to the most radical, entrenched, vocal, diehard elements of their own political party – after all, that is usually the best way to win the party's nomination. The public be damned. Candidates who appeal to the majority of the electorate, rather than the majority of their own party, rarely succeed. As a result, we often end up with two major party candidates who are disliked by most of the voters who will choose between them on the day of the general election.

This might not be the only time that we need to remember the caution the Founding Fathers, especially George Washington, gave us against the formation of "factions", that is, political parties. Factions divide us; factions make it difficult for us to agree on a common agenda, a common solution, or a common candidate.

We do have political parties, and they are powerful, entrenched, and resilient against reform. Any effort to do away with political parties is probably doomed to failure. The two-party system is entrenched in every state, hallowed by tradition, and protected by myriad laws. It has served us well in many cases. For example, political parties make it possible for Congress to pass laws by insisting on some degree of party discipline in voting for a legislative agenda.

Yet we need to find a way to allow citizens to select candidates for President without respect to party labels. It's fine for citizens who agree on a common agenda to coalesce in order to elect candidates who agree with them – that is, it's fine for citizens to unite as members of a political party. Nevertheless, citizens in a true democracy should be able to select Presidential candidates who appeal to the nation writ large rather than to limit our choices to those who have won the allegiance of only their own political party.

VP Candidates Appointed

We leave the selection of Vice President entirely in the hands of one person, the Presidential candidate of each political party. How often have we witnessed this charade? The party's candidate for President, facing the camera with serious demeanor, announces solemnly that his choice of Vice President is not only his first important decision but also that he takes this responsibility very seriously. Further, the candidate states that he is choosing the one person most capable of fulfilling the duties of Vice President and also, if necessary (gulp and sigh), President.

Yet we know from long experience that these statements are poppycock. More likely, the person chosen as the Vice Presidential candidate is one who may unify the party, help the party win one or more key states in the general election, provide geographic balance to the ticket, or shore up some perceived shortcomings in the Presidential candidate.

Rarely is the Vice Presidential candidate the only or the best person to carry out the duties of that office: 1) serve as President of the Senate, 2) cast the tie-breaking vote in the Senate when the votes are evenly divided, 3) count the ballots for President and Vice President following the next Presidential election, and 4) inquire daily at the White House as to the President's health. It's this last responsibility, of course, which should be our primary concern.

Presidents sometimes use their V.P.'s in other ways as well, such as performing ceremonial functions as an adjunct to or substitute for the President, joining the President's cabinet, or serving as a Presidential advisor.

The Vice President occupies the second-highest position in our democracy and has a clear advantage when it comes to choosing a successor. Fourteen of our nation's Vice Presidents later became President, either through the death or resignation of the President or by a subsequent election. Think about that: 14 of our 45 Presidents to date (nearly a third) served earlier as Vice President. Only two Vice Presidents wanted the job of President but never got elected. So why should we leave the selection of Vice President solely in the hands of one person?

One can make an argument for the current custom: After their election, the President and Vice President should work together as a team, and for this reason the team captain should be able to choose his/her running mate. But that argument seems less persuasive than the argument that the voters should choose the Vice Presidential candidate, especially in light of the fact that V.P.'s so often later become Presidents.

We should not pretend that the voters get to choose the Vice President in the general election. Voters almost never make their selection for President based on who is running for VP. At best, that is a secondary consideration.

To summarize the argument: Presidential candidates select our Vice Presidents; we do not really elect them. Vice Presidents become Presidents (14 did so, and only two who wanted to, failed in that attempt). This outcome is hardly democratic. Hence we need a more democratic system of choosing our Vice Presidents.

We do have some leeway here: the constitution is completely silent on the question of how we go about selecting candidates for

Vice President. Recall that in the original 1787 Constitution, the electors (members of what we now call the electoral college) were required to vote for two people. The person receiving the most votes would become the next President, and the person with the second-most votes would become the next Vice President. With George Washington on the ballot in the first two Presidential elections, this procedure was not a problem: Washington was the unanimous choice for President while a plethora of candidates split the vote for second place. After Washington's tenure, political parties formed and began fielding a ticket consisting of a Presidential candidate running alongside his Vice Presidential candidate. If electors chose the party's ticket, the likely result would be a tie between the Presidential and Vice Presidential candidates. Indeed, the likelihood of a tie was a major issue following the elections of 1796 and 1800.

The 12th Amendment to the Constitution, ratified in 1804, solved this problem since it requires members of the electoral college to fill out two ballots, one for President and another for Vice President. Since 1804, political parties have contested every Presidential election. Each party nominates a ticket consisting of a Presidential and a Vice Presidential nominee, and voters in the general election are asked to choose among the tickets.

However, the Constitution does not mandate candidates for President and Vice President running together as a "ticket". If we choose to do so, could we not move away from Presidential and Vice Presidential elections controlled by two major political parties? Since the selection of Vice President is so momentous, shouldn't we let voters determine the nominees? Democracy is all about choice and especially about who gets to make the choices. When we think about improving the way we choose our next President, we should also consider ways of democratizing the selection of Vice President. Shouldn't we insist on a primary election for Vice President?

> **[Interesting sidebar: Election of 1788]**
>
> Only 10 of the 13 original states submitted electoral votes in the first Presidential election. Rhode Island and North Carolina could not participate because they had not yet ratified the Constitution. Only six states held a popular election to choose electors. Five states opted to let the state legislature choose electors, but New York's legislature became deadlocked and so it cast no electoral votes. George Washington was unanimously elected President with 69 electoral votes. Everyone knew that Washington would win, but after that all bets were off. John Adams, with 34 electoral votes, came in second and became our first Vice President.
>
> The Framers expected most elections to end up in the House of Representatives. That actually happened in 1801 and 1825, but we have avoided any subsequent occurrences. Because most Americans now believe that the people should select the Chief Executive, we would consider the notion of throwing the Presidential election into the House as a constitutional crisis.[2]

---

[2] United States Presidential Election, 1788–89. https://en.wikipedia.org/wiki/United_States_Presidential_election,_1788-89 [accessed on June 6, 2017.]

Obsolete Electoral College

The US Constitution established the electoral college system, which gives each state a number of Presidential electors equal to the states' representation in Congress – that is, the number of its Representatives in the House plus its two Senators. We currently have 538 electors (based on 435 seats in the House of Representatives, 100 Senators, plus 3 from the District of Columbia). The Presidential candidate that wins a majority of the electoral college votes (270) is declared the winner. The Constitution also provides that state legislatures have the power to determine how those electors will be selected, and the Supreme Court has adjudged that this power belongs exclusively to the state legislatures. The Constitution does not require participation by the people in any way: Although we have a public election for President in all 50 states and in Washington, DC, such an election is not constitutionally required. The legislature of Alaska or Maryland or (you name it state) could decide tomorrow that they will no longer hold a Presidential election, but rather, that state's Presidential electors (members of the electoral college) will be chosen by lot, or randomly by zip code, or by a committee of the legislature, or by any other means the legislature so chooses. About the only restriction placed on state legislatures is that they cannot appoint a member of Congress or any other federal officer to serve as a Presidential elector.

In 21st century America, it's easy to criticize the Framers of the Constitution for creating the electoral college and for not considering a role for the citizenry at large. But remember again that the Framers, while fearful of too much power in the hands of an autocrat or for those already in power, were also fearful of too much power in the hands of a mob. Hence they created this indirect Presidential selection method.

The Framers created the electoral college system for several reasons:

1. Ensure the indirect selection of the President and Vice President – that is, allow states to choose the electors but then allow those electors to choose whomever they want for President. Nothing in the Constitution suggests or requires that the electors will be pledged to support a particular candidate. In fact every four years we face the prospect of "faithless electors", that is, members of the electoral college who threaten to vote or who actually vote for a different candidate than the one to whom they are nominally pledged. "Faithless electors" have never altered the outcome of an election; the notion of independent electors making the Presidential selection has never worked in practice. [Note: If the system of indirect election of the President has never worked as intended, you might ask why, after two centuries, do we still have it? Why indeed!]
2. Balance large states versus small states and give an outsized influence to small states. This is why the number of electors in the electoral college assigned to each state equals the total number of Senators and Representatives for that state. Had the Framers not been persuaded by the fear of the small states being engulfed by the large states, then the electoral college might very well have been designed with only the number of seats in the House assigned to each state, rather than the total of the Senators and the Representatives. Including the number of Senators (two per state) gives an advantage to states with

smaller populations. Yet large versus small states has never been an election issue, so perhaps we could safely dispense with the inherent advantage to those states with small populations.

3. Encourage the selection of candidates who have a wide geographic following. The electoral college system makes it difficult for a candidate wildly popular in one state or region of the country to be elected President if that candidate has little or no support elsewhere. (Note that this design has not always worked perfectly: We elected Abraham Lincoln in 1860 with support from only the Northern states.)

Of these three reasons for the electoral college, only the argument for wide appeal across all regions of the country seems to have relevance today.

The Constitution also provides a procedure for choosing the President when no candidate receives a majority of electoral votes. In that case, the House of Representatives chooses the President, but every state gets only one vote. Just about all Americans agree that letting the House pick the President would be a disaster for our democracy, making it exceedingly difficult for the ultimate winner to govern, especially if the House chose a candidate without a plurality of either the electoral vote or the popular vote.

At present, in every state except two (Nebraska and Maine), the candidate receiving the most popular votes in that state is awarded all the electoral votes in that state. In most states, the election in any given year has not been expected to be closely contested. Since all the electoral votes go to the winner in that state, most states are ignored throughout the Presidential general election campaign. For example, in the general election campaign in 2016, what candidate bothered to campaign in Massachusetts (which Hillary Clinton won 61% to 34%) or Kansas (which Donald Trump won 57% to 36%)? Answer: no one. The voters in all but a handful of states were completely ignored.

In Presidential elections, the electoral college combined with the winner-take-all system makes most of the states and most of the country's voters irrelevant. Less populous states have an outsized influence on the outcome since every state gets exactly two electors for their two Senators, regardless of the population of the state. For many recent Presidential elections, only the so-called "swing states" matter. Many analyses of Presidential campaigns have been published, showing that the 8 or 9 swing states receive all or nearly all of the campaign visits by the Presidential candidates themselves during the last two months of the campaign, meaning that the other 41 states are ignored. This focus continues post-election: In their first year in office, the new President visits these same swing states most often.

The ultimate results of Presidential elections sometimes appear perverse: In five of our Presidential elections, the candidate who won the popular vote failed to win the Presidency.

After the 2016 election, a Pennsylvania political activist opined that the current electoral college system is just fine, observing that both major party candidates paid attention to Scranton and Harrisburg in the waning days of the campaign, and that they would not have done so if we had a system where the winner is the one receiving the most popular votes. The observation about the candidates paying attention to Scranton and Harrisburg is true, but the logic is backward: How about the citizens of Los Angeles, who received no visits or attention from either party in the run-up to the election? Don't those citizens also merit some attention?

The motivation to change the electoral college system is to make every vote count and to encourage candidates to attend to the concerns of voters in every state. National polls indicate that 70% of American voters would prefer a system in which the candidate for President receiving the most popular votes would be the winner of the election. But the best system would also encourage candidates to appeal to voters across the entire country rather than to voters in only one region.

By the way, I feel obliged to respond here to critics who have suggested that the winners of the 2000 and the 2016 Presidential elections are somehow illegitimate because they did not win the popular vote. This is nonsense. George W Bush and Donald Trump won their elections based on the rules of the game at the time the game was played. Any criticism about their legitimacy is like claiming that the losing football team should be awarded the victory because they gained more yards than their opponent. I would say, if we do not like the rules of the game, then we must change the rules, but amendments only affect future contests. What might have happened if the rules had been different in 2000 or in 2016? Maybe the winners – Bush and Trump – would have employed different strategies, maybe they would have campaigned in California, and maybe they would have won the popular vote too. Let us be clear: The challenge is to fix the rules going forward, not to re-litigate the elections of the past.

Challenge 2. Senate Structure

Consider this scenario. You are attending a high school reunion at a state park, and 66 of your classmates show up. You all agree to go on a nature walk but must choose between Trail A, an easy 2-mile stroll through the forest, and Trail B, 1.5 miles of steep, rocky terrain with little protection from the sun.

Jokingly, you all agree that, since we live in a democracy, this decision too should be made democratically. And so it is. The vote is 65 in favor of Trail A and one in favor of Trail B. Based on our time-honored democratic tradition, you all march off together – on TRAIL B!

The one lonely vote for Trail B outweighed 65 votes for Trail A!

Does that sound very democratic to you? Yet that is precisely how American "democracy" works in the makeup of the US Senate.

Let me explain.

Proportional Representation

The United States Senate is not a representative body. It does not represent the people of the United States and was never intended to. Rather, the framers of the Constitution designed the House of Representatives (the so-called "People's House") to represent the people and the Senate to represent the states. In this scheme, every state is equal: each state has two Senators, as provided by Article I Section 3 of the Constitution.

The original Constitution provided that the Senators from each state would be chosen by their respective state legislatures. Only later did states and citizens begin to recognize the value of adopting the more democratic and more representative practice of direct election of Senators by the people. Finally, direct election was mandated by the 17th Amendment to the Constitution, adopted in 1913. (By the way, the fact that we changed the method of Senate elections and removed the power of state legislatures to select Senators proves that we do have the ability to modify the Constitution and to move slowly toward a more representative democracy.) (Also, by the way, I am rather surprised that no one has successfully argued before the Supreme Court that, following adoption of the 17th amendment, the principle of "one man, one vote" should mandate proportional representation in the Senate.)

Perhaps it is time to make another move toward representative democracy in the makeup of the upper chamber of our national legislature.

Did you know that a citizen of Wyoming has 66 times more power in selecting his Senator than a citizen of California has in selecting his Senator? (That is, in the class reunion scenario at the top of this essay, if the 65 folks who voted for Trail A came from California, and the one classmate who voted for Trail B came from Wyoming, then Trail B gets selected fair and square – those are just the rules of our democracy.) Did you know that a citizen of Vermont has 40 times more power in choosing a Senator than a citizen of Texas? The populations of these states are as follows:

State	Census in 2010	Senators	Population per Senator
California	37,253,956	2	18,626,978
Wyoming	563,626	2	281,813
Texas	25,145,561	2	12,572,781

| Vermont | 625,741 | 2 | 312,871 |

Now, if Senator A represents 20 million people, while Senator B represents only a half million people, then each voter in Senator B's state has 40 times as much power to influence the Senate as each voter in Senator A's state. When it comes to the next Senatorial election, voters in Senator A's state who oppose his reelection must convince 40 times as many voters as compared to the voters in Senator B's state. This is inherently unfair. Here is a table of all 50 states, showing the Relative Power Per Person (RP/PP) in each state relative to the power of a person in California, which, with the largest population, has by definition the least power per citizen in choosing his state's Senators:

State	RP/PP	State	RP/PP	State	RP/PP
California	1.0	Missouri	6.2	Nevada	13.8
Texas	1.5	Maryland	6.5	New Mexico	18.1
New York	1.9	Wisconsin	6.6	West Virginia	20.1
Florida	2.0	Minnesota	7.0	Nebraska	20.4
Illinois	2.9	Colorado	7.4	Idaho	23.8
Pennsylvania	2.9	Alabama	7.8	Hawaii	27.4
Ohio	3.2	South Carolina	8.1	Maine	28.0
Michigan	3.8	Louisiana	8.2	New Hampshire	28.3
Georgia	3.8	Kentucky	8.6	Rhode Island	35.4
North Carolina	3.9	Oregon	9.7	Montana	37.7
New Jersey	4.2	Oklahoma	9.9	Delaware	41.5
Virginia	4.7	Connecticut	10.4	South Dakota	45.8

Washington	5.5	Iowa	12.2	Alaska	52.5
Massachusetts	5.7	Mississippi	12.6	North Dakota	55.4
Indiana	5.7	Arkansas	12.8	Vermont	59.5
Arizona	5.8	Kansas	13.1	Wyoming	66.1
Tennessee	5.9	Utah	13.5		

Of course, the relative power of each citizen in the Senate has always been unfair, but two huge facts made it less unfair when the Constitution was written than it is now. First, as pointed out above, the framers of the Constitution were not trying to make a democratic Senate in terms of representing people; rather, they were trying to create a body that would represent states, and in fact they assigned to state legislatures the power to choose that state's Senators. But as time passed, Americans came to value the notions that Senators should represent people and that people should directly elect them. Second, the populations of the thirteen original states were not as dramatically lopsided as the populations of the 50 states are today. Here are the populations of the thirteen original states in the first census after the Constitution was adopted (1790) along with the RP/PP of each citizen relative to the voting power of a citizen of Virginia (since Virginia had the most people):

State	Population in the 1790 census	RP/PP
Virginia	747,610	1.0
Pennsylvania	434,373	1.7
North Carolina	393,751	1.9

Massachusetts	378,787	2.0
New York	340,120	2.2
Maryland	319,728	2.3
South Carolina	249,073	3.0
Connecticut	237,946	3.1
New Jersey	184,139	4.1
New Hampshire	141,885	5.3
Georgia	82,548	9.1
Rhode Island	69,825	10.7
Delaware	59,094	12.7

As you can see, the difference in Senatorial power per person between the least populous state (Delaware) and the most populous (Virginia) was 12.7 to 1 – as compared to today when the largest difference is 66 (Wyoming) to 1 (California), and 19 states have a difference greater than the most lopsided difference in the first Senate under the 1787 Constitution.

Iterative and Perpetual Characteristics of the Senate's Undemocratic Imbalance

Due to the undemocratic imbalance in the Senate, all legislation is held hostage. Because of the Senate's traditional filibuster rules (where 41 Senators can block any legislation by talking it to death), it is possible today for Senators from the 21 least populous states, representing only 10% of the population, to prevent Senate action on any bill. Again, this is hardly a democratic state of affairs.

This imbalance stretches two steps further:

a) The Constitution incorporates the Senate's unfairness into the formula for allocating the number of electors from each state to the electoral college: the number of electors in each state equals the total number of Senators and Representatives, giving a disproportionate number of electors to the states with less population.

b) Article V of the Constitution precludes any constitutional amendment that reduces any state's equal representation in the Senate without its consent. Hence, we cannot fix this problem with a normal constitutional amendment unless the legislatures of all 50 states agree to the fix.

Provenance of Structural Unfairness in our Constitutional System

"In America, everything is about race."

An old adage, oft-quoted by African-American authors

This oft-quoted adage certainly applies to the deliberations of the Constitutional Convention in 1787. James Madison, among others, argued for direct election of the President by nationwide popular vote. However, other delegates from slave-holding states argued against universal suffrage: if the Convention adopted universal suffrage for President and for both Houses of Congress, the Southern states would always lose out. Northern states would let almost everybody vote while the Southern states would refuse to enfranchise slaves, indentured servants, or people without money or property. Hence, given the numbers, Northerners would probably win every Presidential election.

Therefore, the Southern delegates developed a strategy to maintain their political hegemony (note: five of the first six Presidents came from Virginia). This strategy was to apportion seats in the House based on total population including slaves and to count states rather than population for the upper chamber of the legislature. The second half of this proposition was meant to entice convention delegates from states with smaller populations to come on board since this plan gives disproportionate power to small states. The "compromise", such as it was, was to count only 3/5 of the slaves as people for the purpose of allocating seats in the House yet overlook population entirely when allocating seats for the Senate. Furthermore, while voters (white, male, over 21, and with property) would elect members of the House, state legislatures would choose each state's senators. As part of this same compromise, another body, the electoral college, again skewed in favor of states with less population, would choose the President.

In addition to considerations of race, our forebears also had an innate fear of mob rule – entrusting our government to the passing whims of a radical majority. Their fears were not entirely unreasonable. The men who made up the Constitutional Convention of 1787 were products of monarchy and aristocracy, which represented stability if nothing else. They were already taking a huge leap into the unknown, resting the reins of power in the hands of a much wider electorate.

Previous Fixes

Before proposing a solution to the inherent unfairness in the current makeup of the Senate, we will consider what has happened historically when the people decide to change an undemocratic institution. We have instructive examples in the United States and in Great Britain:

- In the US:
    - When the US Constitution was being drafted, the British House of Commons had numerous parliamentary districts based on geography and tradition rather than population. Some districts had close to zero residents. These were derisively referred to as "rotten boroughs". This was such a problem that the American Framers included a constitutional provision for redistributing seats in the House of Representatives every ten years based on a decennial census.
    - When the size of the House threatened to become too large and unwieldy, in 1911 we fixed the size of the House at 435 seats with the number of seats awarded to each state based on the most recent census.
    - As mentioned earlier, we also amended the Constitution to require direct election of the Senate by the people (Amendment 17, ratified 1913)
- In the UK:
    - An 1832 reform fixed the "rotten boroughs" problem by changing the makeup of the House of

Commons, with districts based on population, revised regularly based on the census.
- The Chartists Movement (1836-1848) campaigned for many democratic reforms including One man, One vote.
- The House of Lords was originally comprised of church leaders (Spiritual Lords) and hereditary members of the nobility or "peers" (Temporal Lords). The king and prime minister could appoint additional members to Lords. This system was so unrepresentative of the people that the country demanded institutional changes in both the makeup and the power of the House of Lords. Over time, the House of Lords has become both more representative and less powerful.
- Citizens of the constituent nations that comprise the United Kingdom have even come to view the House of Commons as somewhat unrepresentative. For this reason, Northern Ireland and Scotland now have their own parliaments, with plans afoot for the continuing "devolution" of power from the central government to Scotland, Northern Ireland, England, and Wales.

Conclusion: Institutions do change, and representative democracies do have the power and ability to institute changes intended to make themselves more representative.

It is high time that Americans make their Senate proportionally representative of the people who elect them. Every American should have an equal chance to choose their Senator.

Challenge 3. Gerrymanders

Decennial Reapportionment

In the beginning our Founding Fathers knew that England had a significant problem concerning the boundaries of election districts for the House of Commons. The district boundaries had evolved historically, but by the 18th century, those boundaries no longer reflected (if indeed they ever had reflected) the number of people living within each election district. It became so distorted that some election districts, known derisively as "rotten boroughs", had fewer than 100 electors, and so those few citizens could elect (almost appoint) a Member of Parliament. The Founding Fathers sought a permanent fix.

As a reaction to England's history, our Framers decreed that the election districts for the House of Representatives would be redrawn every 10 years based on a decennial census. Hence each state has a process for redrawing Congressional Districts every 10 years. In most states, the governor and state legislature control this process. If the same political party controls both the governorship and the legislature, then that party controls the process. Therein lies the problem.

The Practice of Gerrymandering

- "Gerrymandering" is the practice of drawing the boundaries of an election district to favor or punish particular candidates or a particular political party. In 1812, Massachusetts Gov. Elbridge Gerry engineered adoption of an obtusely shaped election district to favor his own political party. Cartoonists thought the shape looked like a salamander, and so the term "Gerry-mander" was born – a conflation of the governor's name plus "salamander".[3] Through much litigation over the next two centuries, courts have generally permitted strangely shaped election districts, as long as

- populations of each district are roughly equal,

- every district consists entirely of contiguous land areas, and

---

[3] "Gerry-mander": Cartoonist Elkanah Tisdale, Boston Sentinel, 1812 (Public Domain)

- no protected class of citizens (such as a racial minority) is unfairly marginalized as a result.

However, generally those districts that clearly favor one political party over another have been allowed.

In modern times gerrymandering has become a science in which incumbents draw boundaries that perpetuate the party in power. This is certainly one of the reasons that our current House of Representatives cannot get anything done, why incumbents are almost always re-elected, and why Congressional leaders cannot get Members of Congress to go along with any consistent program – no matter what the people want. It is also a significant factor in explaining why state legislatures are so resistant to change. The fact is that nearly every incumbent resides in a "safe" district, one in which the current Member of Congress has little need to worry about the opposition party. In fact, the only threat that many incumbents fear is a primary challenge from their own party. Gerrymandering is effective for both major parties in almost all districts in almost all states. For example, in the 2014 elections, 416 of the 435 members of the House of Representatives sought reelection, and 393 (or 94%) of them were reelected.

Disenfranchised Voters

Partisan gerrymandering generally comes in two forms, called "cracking" and "packing", both designed to disenfranchise voters in the minority party.

Cracking occurs when the dominant party in a state targets a community with a high concentration of voters from the minority party. To prevent that party from winning the election that that community might normally be expected to win, the dominant party draws congressional district boundaries that break up (or "crack") that community into two or more partitions assigned to different CDs in which the state's dominant party still has a majority.

Packing occurs when the minority party might have a competitive advantage in several adjoining districts. To prevent the minority party from winning multiple elections, the dominant party artificially skews the district boundaries so that the minority party's voters are packed into one district, where the minority party candidate will win by an overwhelming margin, but the dominant party's candidates will win all the other adjoining CDs.

In both cracking and packing, the result of partisan gerrymandering is that the power of the minority party's voters is weakened or extinguished.

CD boundaries are also sometimes artificially rigged to reward a favored candidate or incumbent politician or to punish an unfavored one. The politicians in charge of drawing the boundaries have created unnatural districts so as to include or exclude the residence of a particular person, or to force two incumbents into the same district. Since voters often insist that their Congressperson live within the CD (while the Constitution only requires a Member of Congress to live within the state), a re-districting scheme that places two incumbents in the same district obviously disadvantages one or both of them.

In addition to disenfranchising large groups of voters, we can also point to the negative effect on individual voters. Ongoing research at the University of North Carolina demonstrates that citizen engagement of individual voters lessens significantly when a community is split into two or more congressional districts. Citizens in such split communities are less likely to 1) know who their Congressperson is, 2) contact or meet their Congressperson, or 3) believe that their Congressperson represents their own views or the views of their community.[4]

---

[4] Curiel, J. and T. Steelman, "How to measure the impact of partisan gerrymandering". Presentation at Reason, Reform & Redistricting Conference, Duke University, January 2019.

Worst Cases in Practice

Americans sometimes kid themselves into thinking that this is only a peripheral issue and that most Congressional Districts are drawn pretty fairly with only a few disputable boundaries. So let me give you a few examples of egregious gerrymanders from the 21st century.

Following the 2010 Census, many state legislatures that have a single party controlling both houses of the state legislature as well as the governorship opted for extreme partisan gerrymandering in order to solidify the dominant party's control of seats in the U.S. Congress. Here are three examples from North Carolina (Republican), Maryland (Democratic), and Pennsylvania (Republican). All three of these CD boundaries were used in the Congressional elections of 2012 and 2014.

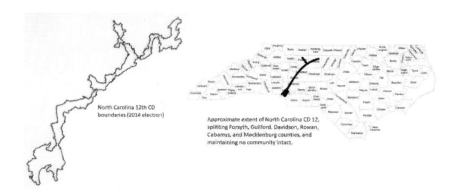

North Carolina 12th CD boundaries (2014 election)

Approximate extent of North Carolina CD 12, splitting Forsyth, Guilford, Davidson, Rowan, Cabarrus, and Mecklenburg counties, and maintaining no community intact.

The U.S. Supreme Court threw out North Carolina's 12th CD before the 2016 elections, stating that this was an unconstitutional racial gerrymander. North Carolina had concentrated black populations across the North Carolina Piedmont into this one district, so that the black community could elect one Congressman, but would not affect elections anywhere else.

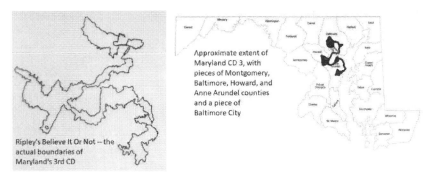

Maryland's 3rd CD, a truly contorted figure, is still in use in 2018. Democrats in the state legislature drew this district to protect John Sarbanes, the incumbent since 2007. One commentator dubbed it a "Marymander".[5]

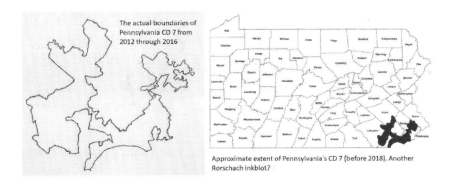

---

[5] "Welcome to America's Most Gerrymandered District", The New Republic (Nov. 8, 2012). Accessed on May 9, 2019, at https://newrepublic.com/article/109938/marylands-3rd-district-americas-most-gerrymandered-congressional-district

Pennsylvania's 7th CD (like all Pennsylvania CDs) was redrawn by order of the Pennsylvania Supreme Court for the 2018 elections.

Compare these three modern examples with Gov. Gerry's original "salamander-gerrymander". We have obviously gotten much more sophisticated at drawing crazy boundaries to suit a particular political purpose.

Worst Case in Theory

Here is a rather dense mathematical analysis of gerrymandering, presenting one simple but extreme hypothetical example of how gerrymandering works and how bad it can get.

- In this fictitious example, a state's 10,000 voters elect a legislative assembly with 100 members from 100 election districts with 100 voters per district. In an election held yesterday, 5500 voters (that is, 55%) voted for Party A, and 4500 voters (45%) voted for Party B. So Party A won the popular vote across the whole state by 10 points. What might the legislative assembly look like after this election?
- Without gerrymandering, Party A can be expected to win 70 seats, give or take. With a 10 point advantage in the popular vote, you might expect it to win every district by 10 points and thus win all 100 seats. Or, since Party A won 55% of the vote, you might expect it to win exactly 55% of the seats. But neither of these scenarios is at all likely for these reasons:
    - In the first scenario Party A wins every seat, which can only happen if Party A's majority is consistent across every district in the state. But such an even distribution rarely occurs because voters in both parties probably reside throughout the state with

pockets of strength in certain areas. Further a party that loses every election will not remain a party for long, while a party that wins every election will soon split into factions and become two or more parties.

- In the second scenario Party A wins exactly 55 seats and wins 55% of the total vote. Party A would need to win those 55 seats by much more than an average of 10 points so that it could lose 45 seats by a small margin. If one party wins 55 seats, it's much more likely that it will have ~51% of the popular vote.
- So the most likely outcome, without gerrymandering, is that Party A will win ~70 seats, give or take. It will win many seats by about 10 points, will win fewer seats by more than 10 or by less than 10 points, and will narrowly lose some number of seats. How many it wins depends on how evenly distributed Party A's voters are across all the districts.

- With gerrymandering, consider what happens. Note that a political party wants to win not only a majority (in this case, at least 51 seats) but also, if possible, a veto-proof majority (in this case, 67 seats). Remember that Party A has a 55% to 45% popular majority, so Party A's objective in drawing district boundaries is to maintain that 10 point spread in its favor in every district. That's probably impossible, but it's not improbable that Party A could concentrate Party B's 4500 voters in 10 districts. Let's say Party B wins those 10 districts 63% to 37%, thereby accounting for 630 of Party B's voters. Then Party B's remaining 3870 voters are distributed across the

remaining 90 districts, giving it 43 votes in each of those districts on average. As a result, Party A wins a solidly veto-proof 90 seats in the legislature.
- But let's say that the minority party, Party B, controls the election districts for whatever reason (perhaps Party B was the majority party the last time the election districts were drawn up). Party B has arranged these districts so that Party B's 4500 voters are concentrated in 80 election districts, and Party B wins each of those contests by a small majority (52 votes to 48). In the other 20 districts, Party A receives 83 votes while Party B gets 17, so Party A elects just 20 representatives. As a result, Party B wins a solidly veto-proof 80 seats in the legislature. What a surprising result!
- The table below shows these results side by side.

	Gerrymandering		
	None	by Party A	by Party B
Districts won by Party A	70	90	20
Party A votes per district	65	57	83
Subtotal Party A votes	4550	5130	1660
Party B votes per district	35	43	17
Subtotal Party B votes	2450	3870	340
Districts won by Party B	30	10	80
Party A votes per district	32	37	48

Subtotal Party A votes	950	370	3840
Party B votes per district	68	63	52
Subtotal Party B votes	2050	630	4160
Total Party A votes	5500	5500	5500
Total Party B votes	4500	4500	4500
Total votes	10000	10000	10000

This might be even more dramatic as a graph. Even though Party A wins 55% of the vote, if Party B controls the district boundaries, Party B could end up with 80% of the seats:

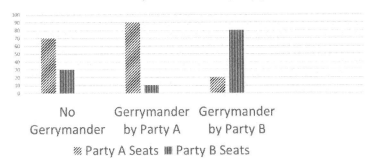

51

Why and How We Need a Fix, and What Clearly Will Not Work

Unfortunately, gerrymandering has become the common practice whenever either party controls the redistricting process in any state. By the way, we should not blame politicians for this state of affairs. For any species, the two most important biological imperatives are reproduction (that is, preservation of the species) and survival (that is, preservation of the individual). Politicians behave like any other species. We may hire them to do the public's business; but, left to their own devices, they will focus first on their party's and their own political survival. We the people are unlikely to change the nature of politicians, nor can we expect them to instigate change themselves, nor can we solve the problem by exchanging current politicians for new ones.

In earlier times, several states had multi-seat Congressional Districts. The reasoning behind multi-seat CDs at that time was this: In some states, the majority party or ideology might hold a significant advantage in many parts of a state (let's say 60% to 40%), but was the minority party in one area, often an urban area. If the state had single-seat CDs, the majority party would win wherever it held the majority but would lose in the one area where it was a minority. But if the state fashioned a multi-seat CD that included that one area where the majority party was in the minority, the majority party could win all the seats in that multi-seat CD.

The multi-seat CDs came to an end with a 1965 reform passed by Congress, which mandated single-seat CDs. The motivation for that reform was the desire to give minority populations the opportunity to elect at least one of their own. As we will see in Part II, we have a better alternative today.

An added thought indirectly related to gerrymandering: While politicians gerrymander districts to favor themselves or their own party, race, or ideology, they also attempt to inhibit voting among the groups they do not like. Voter suppression efforts include Voter ID laws, fewer polling places, limited voting hours, and similar restrictions – just like the poll tax of yesteryear, which we eliminated by the 24th Amendment to the Constitution. But what if we used the number of votes cast in each state in previous elections rather than population figures as a basis for apportioning House seats? Then states which inhibit voting would end up with fewer seats in Congress – probably a reasonable penalty for states that disenfranchise their own citizens.

To get back to the original issue: The systemic problem is that the process of redrawing Congressional Districts after each census is largely in the hands of politicians, who stand the most to gain from gerrymandered districts.

A very good summary of the state of redistricting reform was published in 2015 by US News & World Report (https://www.usnews.com/news/articles/2015/12/01/redistricting-reform-gains-steam).

State Legislative Districts

Gerrymandering may be even more significant when drawing district boundaries for state legislatures. This is true for three reasons: 1) State laws often affect citizens more directly than federal laws. Hence the fair representation of citizens in state legislatures is doubly important. 2) State legislatures usually control the process for drawing the boundaries of federal Congressional Districts. 3) Most members of Congress served first in their state legislature, so the state legislatures serve to a considerable extent as Congress' J.V. Your local state delegate has a reasonable chance of becoming your future Congressman.

Because state legislative districts are so carefully drawn to favor the incumbent politician/party, many would-be candidates choose not to run for elected office at all. They can see that "the fix is in", so there is little point in competing against a rigged system.

Fixing the gerrymander challenge with respect to state legislative district boundaries would go a long way toward repairing our damaged politics.

Challenge 4. Other Election System Deficiencies

First-Past-The-Post (FPTP) Voting

All Congressional elections (both Senate and House) have a single winner. Each voter votes for a single candidate, and the candidate who gets the most votes wins the election even when that candidate earns only a plurality (not a majority) of votes cast. Among political scientists and voting system experts, our system of voting is known as "First Past the Post (FPTP)". (A few states require a runoff election between the top two vote-getters if no one has a majority, or in some cases if no one has more than 40%; and as of 2016, Maine has adopted Ranked Choice Voting – but these are the exceptions.) When the winner has earned a plurality but not a majority, at least four negative consequences ensue:

a) A winner by plurality has less authority, less of a mandate to lead or govern, than a winner by majority.
b) In a three- or four-person contest, candidates tend to focus only on their own base voters, paying little attention to the voters of the other candidates. Rather than appealing to voters with disparate views, each candidate works to split the opposition, get 100% support from their own base, and thus win by a plurality. When elected, winners by plurality often continue to appeal to their base supporters and make only a token effort to represent the majority who voted for their opponents.
c) In a three-candidate race, two candidates with similar majority views may split their combined 60% majority into equal shares of 30%, while a third candidate with minority views earns 40% and is declared the winner.
d) A spoiler candidate, who cannot possibly win, may yet draw enough support away from an "acceptable" candidate so that another candidate, whom most voters do not want, ends up winning with a plurality.

Conclusion: We should adopt a system of voting which ensures that the winner has support from a majority of the electorate.

The Two-Party System

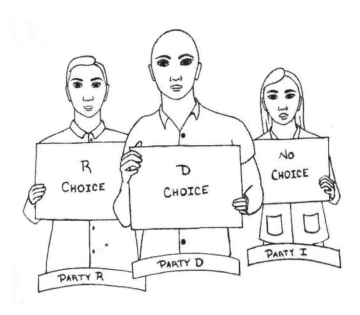

Many of our challenges stem from the dominance of the Republican and Democratic parties. The two-party system has become so entrenched that we cannot envision politics without Republicans and Democrats. We need to remind ourselves of the strong feeling of the Founding Fathers on this subject: George Washington was not alone in warning us about the evils of "factions" (the 18th century word for political parties). Today numerous state and federal laws provide legal status to the two major parties and make it very difficult to implement reforms. Yet we need to confront the dominance of the two-party system if we are ever to return real power to the people of this country.

While decrying the dominance of our two-party system, we must also acknowledge the benefits of political parties. A political party allows people to come together around shared ideas, policies, programs, and priorities. They allow like-minded candidates to support each other. They allow all party members to work together on political campaigns whether those campaigns are geared to electing particular candidates or supporting particular agendas. On the other hand, we must also recognize that powerful political parties can squash reforms within a party, block grassroots political movements, and perpetuate the status quo.

One of the biggest problems of the two-party system is its tendency to produce extremism in both parties. The ideologues of the right and of the left find it much easier to take over the machinery of one political party than to convince a majority of their fellow citizens of the correctness of their views. But with the two major parties dominating the process, often with the support of state and federal laws, a third party, a new movement, or a middle-of-the-road independent usually cannot gain a nomination. A Republican Presidential candidate with moderate views, especially one willing to compromise with Democrats, may be unacceptable to the conservative ideologues who dominate the party apparatus; and so that candidate cannot win the Republican nomination. Similarly, on the Democratic side, a Presidential candidate with moderate views who is willing to work with Republicans may be completely unacceptable to the liberal ideologues who dominate the Democratic party; and so that candidate likewise cannot win his party's nomination. The result is a system that tends to nominate a Republican candidate too conservative for a majority of Americans along with a Democratic candidate too liberal for a majority of Americans. That's why we often end up with candidates with huge unfavourability ratings among all Americans.

Meanwhile, fewer and fewer voters identify with either major party. In the 19 Gallup polls concerning party affiliation taken from January 2018 through April 2019, an average of 27% of voters self-identified as Republican, 30% as Democrat, and 41% as Independent.[6] As a result, few of those unaffiliated voters (41% of the electorate) ever get a chance to be heard in selecting either major party candidate for any office.

Let me rephrase this conclusion in a slightly different way. Over a third of the electorate align themselves with neither major political party, so they do not get to participate in choosing the major party candidate for any office. Among those who do register as Republican or Democrat, the overwhelming majority either live in states without primary elections or they fail to show up for the primary. Hence the percentage of eligible voters who select our general election candidates is quite small. In the race for President in 2016, only 9% of America chose either Trump or Clinton as their candidate![7] Let that sink in: only 9% of us voted for either of the winning candidates in the Presidential primaries!

For two centuries (1789-1976) the Tammany Hall political organization in New York City controlled the city's Democratic Party machinery. Tammany Hall's most notorious and

---

[6] https://news.gallup.com/poll/15370/party-affiliation.aspx (accessed on May 8, 2019).

[7] "Only 9% of America Chose Trump and Clinton as the Nominees". https://www.nytimes.com/interactive/2016/08/01/us/elections/nine-percent-of-america-selected-trump-and-clinton.html?_r=0. Accessed on June 15, 2017.

"entrenched" leader was William "Boss" Tweed, who once famously remarked that voters could elect anybody they want as long as he got to pick the candidates.[8] When people today complain about a "rigged" system and a lack of choice, Boss Tweed comes immediately to mind.

> *"I don't care who does the electing, as long as I get to do the nominating"* – William "Boss" Tweed

As to the "legal entrenchment" of our two-party system, consider how the Presidential primary system works: each of the two major parties nominates a Presidential candidate, and for all practical purposes, those two candidates are our only choices for President. Republicans and Democrats may agree on little else, but they do agree on this one feature of our politics: They all love the two-party system.

---

[8] Top 6 Quotes from Boss Tweed, *AZ Quotes*, http://www.azquotes.com/author/14885-Boss_Tweed [accessed on June 15, 2017].

Caucuses, Conventions, and Closed Primaries

*Independents Need Not Apply

We have evolved a two-stage election system in this country: Stage 1 winnows the field of candidates, ultimately nominating one person from each political party (plus the occasional independent nominee), while Stage 2 (the general election) allows voters to determine the winner of each contest from those nominees who have survived Stage 1. The focus of this discussion is on Stage 1.

Stage 1 consists of primary elections, most of which occur within a political party, as well as caucuses and conventions, all of which occur within a political party. Primaries are either open or closed or mixed: Open primaries are open to all voters; closed primaries are restricted to voters who belong to a particular political party. Caucuses and conventions are gatherings of party activists. In states with caucus systems, caucuses occur simultaneously in districts throughout the state. Each local caucus selects delegates to a state convention, where the party's nominee is selected. The winners of Stage 1 are the party nominees who appear on the general election ballot.[9]

The challenges of the prevailing Stage 1 models are these:

a) Caucuses and state nominating conventions are inherently unrepresentative. These processes attract party activists, a far smaller population than the general public. We need to take some of the parties' power back to the people. There is no good reason that, when it comes to a general election, our only choices are nominees that have been chosen by a relatively small group of activists.

b) The current system produces general election nominees who reflect the views of the party faithful rather than nominees with broad public support. At the end of the nominating process (whether by primary or caucus or party convention or some combination of these), our nominees often reflect the most extreme views of one wing of each political party. As often as not, the public is disenchanted with all the nominees.

---

[9] Only a handful of jurisdictions have an alternative Stage 1 system. Of these, the most popular is a single primary open to candidates of all parties. The two candidates with the most votes survive the primary and compete head-to-head in the general election. Variations on this system exist, but suffice it to say that such systems are the exception.

c) In many instances, two or three of the most popular candidates all belong to the same party. Nevertheless, with only a few exceptions, our state election systems produce only one general election nominee from each party.

d) A majority of Americans reside in a state dominated by one political party. If a voter belongs to the other party or to no party at all, that voter has no opportunity to participate in a meaningful way in the selection of general election candidates for any office.

e) A separate primary ballot exists for each party, and that ballot lists one party's candidates for every office. Except for primaries in a very few states, a voter can vote in only one party's primary. On primary election day, on my party's ballot, I can select my preferred candidate for President, Governor, or senator from among those running for each office from my party. I do not get to participate at all in the primary for local offices, such as county commissioners, county sheriff, mayor, or school board, because my party usually fields zero candidates for those offices. Then in the general election, the person who won the primary from the other party for those local offices runs unopposed. No wonder voters are discouraged!

f) Again, except for primaries in a very few states, if my preferred candidate for President is in one party, and my preferred candidate for senator is in the other party, and my preferred candidate for congressman is in a third party, I cannot vote all three of my preferences in the primary election. That is because the two major parties have rigged the system, forcing me to make all my primary election selections from the same political party.

Single-Member Congressional Districts

If Political Party A holds a 55%-45% majority over Political Party B, and if this split is consistent across the state, then Party A will win every election of single-member districts. But if the state adopted three-member or five-member districts, then Party B would be more likely to capture at least some of those seats. Ideally, the citizens' legislature should represent the views of all the people. When a legislature represents only some of those views or only some of those people, then we have a problem – even if the views represented in the legislature are in the majority.

Consider it this way: If a set of political views are agreed to by a 51%-49% majority, then those views should be reflected by a majority of the legislators – but not 100% of the legislators. Meanwhile, the minority view, held by 49% of the electorate, should be reflected by less than a majority of the legislators – but not zero.

Admittedly, this argument can cut two ways. In some municipalities, when all city council members are elected at large, a minority population concentrated in one district of the city may have little chance of electing even one member of the city council, while single-member districts ensure that the citizens of the minority-populated district at least get to choose one city councilman who represents them. The solution to this conundrum could be multi-seat districts with a voting system that provides for proportional representation.

Electioneering Forever

Imagine you are the owner of an automobile dealership. Just after you hire John as a master mechanic, your Service Manager announces that he plans on retiring in three years. Your new master mechanic John starts out okay, but after only six months fixing cars and satisfying customers, he begins campaigning for the Service Manager position, which is going to become available 2 ½ years from now.

John starts spending more and more of his time cozying up to you, partying with big shots, and getting community leaders to write to you or speak to you on his behalf, recommending John as the next Service Manager. It seems that after only six months on the job, John is no longer functioning as a master mechanic; rather, he is functioning as heir apparent and campaigner-in-chief for his next gig. While you were very keen on John for the first six months, now you are no longer so sure – in fact, his constant pandering has become boring, and meanwhile his real job is not getting done.

If that scenario sounds familiar, it's because it is: That is the behavior of many of our elected representatives. We hired them to govern – as President, Vice President, senator, congressman, or governor. Yet, after doing that job for only a short while, they start spending most of their time glad-handing, pandering, soliciting contributions from the donor class, and campaigning for the next election – be it re-election to their current position or a higher office. American politicians fail to govern and fail to tend to our real and myriad national and state problems at least partly because they are too busy campaigning and raising money.

Don't you wish they'd spend a bit more time doing the job we (the public) hired them to do, before auditioning for their next appointment?

We also have the problem that the incessant campaigning is boring. How many different ways can a politician repeat the same talking points without ever actually doing anything? Congress' job approval rating hovers around 10%, and the public is totally apathetic. It's rare for us to get excited about politics, partly because the politicians are all about scoring political points and very little about accomplishing something on behalf of the people they nominally serve.

We really should consider establishing an abbreviated and fixed election timetable, which might help us become less apathetic and more involved the first couple times we did it.

Voting Rights Restrictions

Just being able to vote is still a challenge in many jurisdictions around the country. This is surely something we should have solved by now – and we can easily solve it if people truly believe in democracy. (Go back to the Preface of this work if you need a primer on this topic ☺.)

Unfortunately, there still seem to be some among us who do not believe in democracy for all, and some of those folks hold positions of power or influence, and they sometimes exercise that power to place roadblocks targeted at people that they would rather not see casting a ballot. Of course, persuading someone to come around to your point of view, while perhaps difficult in the short run, is far more effective in the long run than trying to prevent that person from expressing a point of view different from your own at the ballot box. But I digress.

The challenges include:

a) Making it difficult or inconvenient to register to vote;
b) Limiting vote-by-mail (absentee voting, for any reason);
c) Limiting in-person early voting dates, hours, and locations;
d) Providing inadequate polling locations, inadequate staffing at polling locations, inadequate numbers of voting machines, and too few hours in which to vote;
e) Requiring unreasonable voter identification; requiring cumbersome paperwork for provisional voting when a voter's right to vote is questioned.

Protests against these restrictions have been met consistently with arguments about the need to prevent voter fraud. However, every responsible study of this subject has proven that the incidence of voter fraud in this country is negligible.

If we are true to our democratic ideals, then we need to do everything we can to ensure that all eligible citizens are registered to vote, that we make voting as convenient and accessible for all citizens as we can, and that we then actively encourage them to get out and vote. We might also incentivize states to encourage voter turnout – for example, by apportioning House seats based on the number of people who vote in each state rather than on the number of people who live there.

Congress for Sale

The underlying principle concerning campaign financing reform was stated in the Preface: Every voice deserves to be heard, and no voice should be allowed to drown out all other voices solely because the speaker has more money than most everyone else.

The fight against the undue influence of money in American politics has a long and colorful history. Many Americans may not realize that overt payment for your vote was a common practice until we adopted the secret ballot after the acrimonious Presidential election of 1884. Government jobs were also for sale. Until the Pendleton Act of 1883, which established the federal civil service, many people with government jobs had to contribute a portion of their pay to the political party that had appointed them and whose continuing protection was needed in order to remain employed. Meanwhile, vendors who wanted government contracts contributed Big Money to the party in power. In sum, politicians paid for your vote, government employees paid the politicians for their jobs, and contractors paid politicians for their government contracts. The whole system was essentially for sale.

Though we've come a long way, most observers think we still have a long way to go.

In 2006, the Supreme Court decided the *Citizens United* case, holding that businesses and organizations have a First Amendment right to express their opinion through paid political campaigns essentially without restriction. This decision invalidated limits on campaign expenditures that had been incorporated in several earlier laws.

Financial Disclosures, Transparency, and Nepotism

I was traveling through Southeast Asia while drafting this essay, and I was amazed at the number of countries that give lip-service to democracy while suffering from blatant corruption and venality of public officials. The problems are obvious, systemic, and intractable:

- High public officials have direct financial interests which conflict with their official duties.

- High public officials use close family members to control various government departments and to simultaneously control major corporations and sectors of the economy.

- The public is generally uninformed about these matters. Those few who do know about them are not in any position to do anything about them.

In the USA, we have had our own share of similar scandals. Congress has nibbled at the edges of these problems, but existing legal strictures are rather weak and only marginally effective. We deserve better. We deserve public officials who are completely open and transparent with respect to their personal wealth, who disclose their continuing financial interests, and who avoid using family members to expand their political control or power or to further their own financial interests.

We can try to operationalize these principles through federal laws, but it's unclear whether such rules would withstand challenges on constitutional grounds, especially given the Supreme Court's decision in *Citizens United*. Therefore, it may be necessary to address these matters through one or more constitutional amendments.

Part II. Fixes

Introduction to Part II

Americans can ameliorate or resolve each of the challenges outlined in Part I through new legislation at the state or federal level, through state or federal constitutional amendments, and through social change. The reforms will enhance the power of citizens to control their own lives (that is, freedom) and to control their government (that is, democracy). (A new Constitution II could fix most of these problems all at once; that is the subject of Part III.)

Three of these fixes, "Ranked Choice Voting", "Fix the Two-Party System", and "Empower Voters to Amend the Constitution", relate to more than one challenge. To avoid repetition as we present the fixes to each specific challenge, we start with these three Big Fixes.

All of the Part I challenges relate directly or indirectly to federal elections, and so we address these under "Election System Fixes", namely, "Presidential Selection Fixes", "U.S. Senate Fix", "Gerrymander Fix", and "Other Election System Fixes". For each of the elections-related fixes, we then examine the methods of realization – state or federal laws, constitutional amendments, or cultural shifts. We then present "The Amendment on Federal Elections", a comprehensive constitutional amendment which could fix all of our electoral shortcomings at once.

Three Big Fixes

Big Fix 1. Ranked Choice Voting

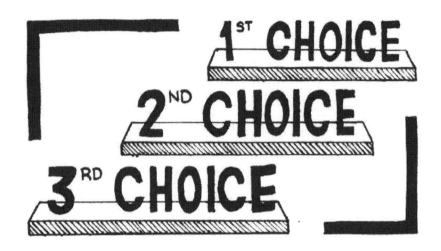

Relevance

This fix relates directly to Challenge 4. "Other election system challenges", especially the two sub-challenges that address the lack of runoff elections and the exclusive use of single-member Congressional Districts. However, this fix also relates to Challenge 1 (regarding how we choose the President and Vice President) and Challenge 3 (the problem of gerrymandering). Therefore, because it has such general applicability to all elections, it deserves to be argued first.

The problem is that the traditional First-Past-The-Post (FPTP) voting scheme leads to undemocratic outcomes, elected officials who often fail to represent the majority of their constituents, and literally millions of voters with no effective representation at all.

Restating the Problem

We have far too many election winners who win with a plurality, that is, with less than majority support from the voters, both in our primary and in our general elections. A person might become Mayor or Congressman or Governor, and only have achieved 40% of the vote, while two or more competitors split the other 60%. It's difficult to claim to have a mandate when you have earned the trust of only 40% of the voters. Governing after such an election, a public official might only look to that 40% base of voters for support.

Ranked Choice Voting solves this problem by ensuring that the winning candidate has at least some level of support from a majority of the voters.

What is Ranked Choice Voting (RCV)?

RCV is an improvement over runoffs between the top two finishers in a traditional, First-Past-The-Post voting scheme. In the traditional runoff, if no candidate wins a majority of the vote (or, in some jurisdictions, if no candidate wins at least 40%), then a subsequent runoff election between the top two finishers decides the contest. Note that, in the runoff election, every voter casts a complete ballot. That is, a voter is not penalized for having chosen a candidate who was eliminated in round 1. Rather, the question voters face in the runoff is, "Which of these two remaining candidates do you prefer?"

An RCV "instant runoff" is a more efficient method of conducting a traditional runoff.

Ranked Choice Voting Procedures
RCV from the voter's perspective

General Election Ballot			
Vote for up to 3 : Mark your 1st, 2nd, and 3rd choices			
CANDIDATE	1ST CHOICE	2ND CHOICE	3RD CHOICE
ADAMS		X	
IVY	X		
BROWN			
ALSORAN			X

From the standpoint of the voter, Ranked Choice Voting is easy and straightforward. After selecting their 1st choice for any office, voters are allowed (but not required) to also select a 2nd choice, 3rd choice, and so on, limited only by the number of names on the ballot.

Since this can become unwieldy – imagine voters trying to rate 36 candidates on a ballot while hundreds of other voters wait in line to vote – I propose limiting the number of selections to three. This will apply to both primary and general elections.

Counting of ballots in all elections with a single-winner

1. Count the 1st choice votes for each candidate, and rank order the results.[10] Repeat steps 2 through 4 until one candidate has a majority of the total vote.

2. Eliminate the candidate with the fewest votes.

3. Reassign each vote for the eliminated candidate to each voter's next highest choice for a candidate not yet eliminated.

4. If a ballot for the eliminated candidate contains no choice for a candidate not yet eliminated, then that ballot is exhausted and is no longer counted as part of the total vote.

Expected RCV Results

RCV produces winners with wider support than a system that declares the person with a plurality as the winner.

Here is a typical example: In a village with 100 voters, 60 voters belong to Party A and 40 voters give their allegiance to Party B. One year, in the election for mayor, Party A and Party B each field one candidate, ADAMS and BROWN, respectively. Then a former Party A mayor, IVY, who does not like ADAMS, decides to run as an Independent, and another local candidate named AlsoRan also runs. Perhaps Party A's 60 voters give 35 votes to the official Party A candidate ADAMS, 23 votes to the Independent former

---

[10] Some elections may have more than one winner, requiring some adaptation of Ranked Choice Voting procedures.

mayor IVY, and 2 votes to AlsoRan. Meanwhile all 40 of Party B's voters support the one Party B candidate BROWN. Here is a table of the results:

Election Results in FPTP Voting Stystem	
Candidate	Votes
Adams	35
Ivy	23
Brown	40 – WINNER
AlsoRan	2

In our current First-Past-the-Post voting scheme, BROWN is elected as the next mayor with only 40 votes.

With RCV, a different outcome is plausible. Let's say that the 23 Party A voters who defected to the Independent IVY as their 1st choice choose the regular Party A candidate ADAMS as their 2nd choice. That is to say, while they may prefer IVY to ADAMS, they clearly prefer their own Party A's candidate ADAMS to Party B's BROWN. The two voters who selected AlsoRan as their first choice also select ADAMS as their second choice. (These results are less complex than a real election in two ways: In a real election, more variability in the 2nd choices could be expected, and in this simplified example, 3rd choices never come into play.) Here is a table showing the 1st and the simplified 2nd choice vote totals:

1st and 2nd Choice Vote Totals in RCV Voting System		
Candidate	1st Choice	2nd Choice
Adams	35	(35 for Ivy)
Ivy	23	(23 for Adams)
Brown	40	(40 for AlsoRan)
AlsoRan	2	(2 for Adams)

When no mayoral candidate has 51 1st choice votes after Round 1, the candidate with the fewest 1st choice votes, AlsoRan, is eliminated, and when still no one has 51, the Independent IVY is also eliminated, causing the reassignment of IVY's 25 1st choice votes to each voter's 2nd choice, namely, the official Party A candidate ADAMS, giving ADAMS a revised 60 votes and the win. In terms of governing, the new mayor can claim to have some measure of support from most of the voters and is also more likely to hear the voices of those who originally had supported the Independent.

RCV Election Results			
Candidate	Round 1	Round 2	Round 3
Adams	35	57	60 - WINNER
Ivy	23	23	(eliminated; votes reassigned to Adams)
Brown	40	40	40
AlsoRan	2	(eliminated; votes reassigned to Adams)	

Because everyone recognized the possibility of this scenario coming true, with RCV the candidates are more likely to try to appeal to the voters who support their opponents. Candidates will use an argument along the lines of, "I understand your support for one of my opponents as your 1st choice, but I would certainly like to earn your vote as your 2nd choice." Then, in a close three-way election, the candidate best able to appeal to his opponents' voters is most likely to win. That outcome is good for democracy.

Additional Rationale

Basically, the credibility of a democratic electoral process derives from the winner's ability to claim the support of a majority or near majority of the voters. Credibility also depends on the public's perception that the process is inclusive, fair, and reflects the views of most of the constituents. In many three-candidate races, the winner cannot claim support from a majority or near majority of voters, nor does the public perceive the process as fair.

First-Past-The-Post (FPTP) vote-counting is a major impediment to new grassroots movements, new political parties, and lesser-known candidates. Voters shy away from voting for a third party or for an attractive but upstart candidate because they are afraid to "throw away their vote" on a candidate or a cause that cannot possibly win. RCV eliminates that barrier.

We have long had exactly two major political parties, and so most of our general elections come down to a choice between the Republican and the Democrat. Occasionally, we have three candidates with significant public support, and these general elections present situations in which RCV works really well.

We also often have primary elections with three or more candidates, and again the RCV system improves the process. All the candidates who survive the primary will have demonstrated significant support among the electorate, and nobody makes it to the general election just because several other candidates split the vote.

Critics and Costs

Critics: The major criticism of RCV is that voters find it confusing; and, say some, many voters simply refuse to vote for any candidate beyond their 1st choice. But experience with RCV does not support this contention.

Costs: The jury is out as to whether RCV would save or cost money. It certainly saves the cost of holding a traditional runoff election, where such a runoff would otherwise be required. But voting machinery may need to be replaced to support RCV, and funding for voter education would also be needed. These are all one-time costs, while RCV's benefits continue indefinitely.

RCV in the US and Around the World

32 of the 50 US states have adopted or have pending legislation to require or to permit Ranked Choice Voting in municipal, state, or federal elections or party caucuses and conventions. Of these 32, Maine has adopted RCV statewide; 9 states (MD, MA, TN, FL, MN, CO, NM, CA, and OR) mandate or allow RCV for municipal elections; 5 states (LA, AR, MS, AL, and SC) use RCV for military and overseas voters (where mailing delays would make it difficult for those voters to participate in runoff elections); 4 states (UT, TX, IA, and VA) use RCV in party elections; and the other 13 states have legislation pending in 2017 to implement or permit RCV in some of their elections.

Australia uses RCV for its national parliamentary elections. In their system, every Australian citizen is required to vote, and every voter must rank order all the candidates on the ballot in order of their preference. In the most recent elections for the Australian Parliament, the candidate receiving the most first place votes won 90% of the seats in parliament; but 10% of the seats were won by a candidate who received fewer first place votes in the initial count, but who captured a majority of the votes only as candidates at the bottom of the tally sheet were successively eliminated.

There are many variations on the Ranked Choice Voting basic scheme, sometimes called Instant Runoff Voting (IRV): see this article on Instant Runoff Voting (IRV) in Wikipedia for the details (https://en.wikipedia.org/wiki/Instant-runoff voting). [11] The article lists the historical and current uses of IRV around the world. For details on American use of RCV and prospects for wider adoption, see the articles at http://www.FairVote.org.

Congress's Power to Act

RCV can probably be implemented by a federal statute, safe from a constitutional challenge, at least with respect to Congressional elections. The Constitution clearly states that Congress has the power to fix the "Times, Places, and Manner of elections for Senators and Representatives", and Ranked Choice Voting deals with the manner of elections.

---

[11] Admittedly, Wikipedia is not the world's most reliable source of information, but this long and well-referenced article seems to be an excellent primer on this topic.

One can argue that this power extends to the election of the electors for President and Vice President (the members of the electoral college) since the Constitution clearly wanted to give Congress the power to control elections for federal offices by the people. At the time of the writing of the Constitution, the people were not constitutionally empowered to vote for the Presidential electors. Now that we are everywhere so empowered, Congress probably has the right to fix the manner of elections for President as well. Constitutional scholars can argue whether Congress has this power.

Big Fix 2. Restrain the Two-Party System

Open Primaries

When the United States began, the Founding Fathers were very concerned about the formation of "factions" (that is, political parties), which could do great damage to the functioning of the Republic. Obviously, we have become wedded to the dominance of political parties in every phase and at every level of our politics. We need to rediscover our Founders' fear of "factions". One such improvement would be the adoption of open primaries, in which all candidates compete (regardless of party affiliation) and in which all voters can vote.

We need to mandate open primaries for all federal offices (President, Vice President, and both chambers of Congress). These are the rules for primaries that we should adopt:

- Any eligible candidate may compete in any primary, subject to state rules for qualifying for the ballot.

- One primary will take place for each elected office. Candidates from every political party and from no party (independents) may participate. The ballot will indicate the party affiliation of each candidate.

- All registered voters are eligible to vote in every primary for every office within the jurisdiction where they legally reside.

For Congressional primaries, these special rules apply:

- The number of successful primary candidates is three.

- The only way to appear on the general election ballot is to earn sufficient support in the primary to qualify for the general election. Therefore, the general election ballot for a seat in the Senate or House will have at most three names.

- With a slight variation, RCV can be applied to primary elections. Naturally, each voter wants the list of successful primary candidates to include the voter's preferred candidate, but, if the voter's preferred candidate does not make the cut, the voter might very well want the list to include the voter's 2nd or 3rd choice. This is the procedure for the primary election for a seat in Congress (either chamber):

Counting of ballots in primary elections for Congress

The number of successful candidates in a primary election for one seat in Congress (House or Senate) is three. This is the procedure for counting votes:[12]

1. Count the 1st choice votes for each candidate, and rank order the results. Repeat steps 2 through 4 until only three candidates remain, or until three candidates each exceed 25% of the total vote. (Note: it is mathematically impossible for four candidates to exceed 25%.)

2. Eliminate the candidate with the fewest votes.

3. Reassign each vote for the eliminated candidate to each voter's next highest choice for a candidate not yet eliminated.

4. If a ballot for the eliminated candidate contains no choice for a candidate not yet eliminated, then that ballot is exhausted and is no longer counted as part of the total vote.

The proposed rules on open primaries will allow all registered voters (Democrat, Republican, any 3rd party, or Independent) to participate in all primaries and will allow voters registered as Republican or Democrat to select a primary candidate from the opposite party. These changes can only be an improvement for our democracy.

---

[12] Appendix 1 summarizes the application of Ranked Choice Voting to various categories of elections.

Party Caucuses and Conventions

A caucus or a convention of Democrats or Republicans is much less likely to select a candidate acceptable to the entire electorate than a primary election open to all voters. Voters should select all general election candidates through primaries rather than caucuses and party conventions. Party activists will not like this change, of course; nonetheless, it would be good for our democracy.

Political parties may continue to hold elections for party offices, and they may hold caucuses and conventions at any level at their own expense. Such activities are completely independent from the public primary elections. Endorsement by a political party helps a candidate raise money and enlist volunteers for a campaign, but that endorsement gains nothing from a legal standpoint. That is, candidates must still qualify to appear on the primary ballot according to the rules of each state, and they must survive the primary to compete in the general election.

All Other Laws, Regulations, and Practices

Statutes and regulations should not favor political parties. Period.

The objective here is not to end political parties. As mentioned earlier, political parties can be quite useful in a democracy. Rather, the objective is to improve ballot access for all candidates, equitable treatment of all candidates, and inclusion of all voters.

Big Fix 3. Empower Voters to Amend the Constitution

The Founding Fathers trusted neither the King nor the people *en masse* – in their view the tyranny of the mob was no better than the tyranny of an autocrat. That is at least a partial explanation for the very limited power of everyday-joe-citizens in the Constitution. This is pointedly true with respect to amending the Constitution.

Article V of the Constitution specifies the two procedures that can be followed to propose amendments to the Constitution: 1) an amendment can be proposed by two-thirds of both Houses of Congress, or 2) two-thirds of the state legislatures can require Congress to call for a convention that will propose constitutional amendments. In either case, Congress then submits the proposed amendments to the states, specifying whether these amendments will be considered by state legislatures or by state conventions. Proposed amendments that are ratified by three-fourths of the states (either legislatures or conventions, as specified by Congress) become part of the Constitution.

Note that regular citizens have little say in any of this. That is most certainly a challenge.

I believe in democracy. When most of the people want to change our constitution, then their collective opinion should carry the day. At the same time, popular opinion should not be just a temporary infatuation with an idea or politician; rather, the collective, considered opinion of the citizenry, taken over time, should determine our collective course.

The reason I have included this fix as one of the three Big Fixes is that a significant number of the fixes proposed in this book either require a Constitutional amendment or would work better with a Constitutional amendment (including, for example, replacement of the electoral college or re-making the US Senate into a representative body). Since the existing procedure for amending the Constitution cuts out all but a few thousand federal and state legislators, it behooves us to come up with a new procedure in which Joe and Jane Citizen cast the deciding vote.

In addition to casting the deciding vote on proposed Constitutional amendments, Joe and Jane Citizen should also have a way of introducing or proposing a Constitutional amendment without waiting for the political class to act. My proposal here is that we use the existing procedures in every state for amending their state constitutions. In about half the states, the citizens can use a petition system to put a state constitutional amendment on the ballot, and in almost all the states, voters must ratify a state constitutional amendment whether proposed by citizen petition or by the legislature. If half of the states, following their own states' procedures for amending their state constitutions, comprising at least half of the US population, propose an amendment to the US Constitution, then that proposed amendment will be submitted to the people. Ratification by the people requires two positive votes in two general elections separated by a new Congress and a new President – preventing adoption of an amendment on the basis of a temporary frenzy or infatuation with a particular personality.

In the revised amendment procedure, I am recommending that Congress may propose a Constitutional amendment by majority vote in both chambers, as opposed to the two-thirds majority currently required. The rationale for this change is that we are consciously shifting power from the professional politicians to the people. We are not making it easier to amend the Constitution, as you will see in the suggested wording of this Article V replacement; rather, we are making it more difficult for a small clique of elected officials to obstruct the will of the people.

Here is suggested wording for the proposed constitutional amendment. This amendment will be referenced as the Amendment on Amendments throughout this document.

Amendment on Amendments

This amendment replaces Article V of the Constitution.

Section 1. Proposing an Amendment

This section prescribes two methods for proposing an amendment to the Constitution.

- **Method 1.** The Congress, whenever a majority of both chambers shall deem it necessary, shall propose an amendment to this Constitution.

- **Method 2.** Each of the several states may propose a Constitutional amendment by approving the amendment according to the procedures of each state for amending their own state constitutions. When at least half of the states comprising at least half of the US population propose such an amendment, then this amendment becomes a proposed amendment.

When an amendment to this Constitution has been proposed according to either method specified in this Section, that amendment shall be valid to all intents and purposes as part of this Constitution, when ratified by the people as specified in Section 3.

Section 2. Constitutional Convention

This section prescribes two methods for proposing a Constitutional Convention charged with the task of drafting a New Constitution.

- **Method 1.** On the application of the legislatures of two thirds of the several states, Congress shall call a Constitutional Convention for the purpose of drafting a new Constitution.

- **Method 2.** Each of the several states may propose a Constitutional Convention charged with drafting a new Constitution by approving the call for a Constitutional Convention according to the procedures of each state for amending their own state constitutions. When at least half of the states comprising at least half of the US population propose a Constitutional Convention, Congress shall call a Constitutional Convention for the purpose of drafting a new Constitution.

When states have called for a Constitutional Convention according to either method specified in this Section, Congress shall convene said convention. The product of said convention shall be the Proposed New Constitution, which shall be valid and will replace this Constitution when ratified by the people as specified in Section 3.

Section 3. Ratification

Two General Elections. Ratification requires the approval of voters in two general elections. Between these two general elections, at least one new Congress must have convened and a new person must hold the office of President.

Ratification Threshold. In both of these two general elections, ratification requires the approval of 1) a majority of all votes cast, and 2) a majority of votes cast in 60% of the states containing 60% of the population.

Election System Fixes (Challenges 1-4)

If we are able to adopt Ranked Choice Voting, eliminate preferences for the two-party system, and empower citizens to enact and repeal laws and amend the constitution, then wholesale improvements to our election system become possible.

The reforms argued here include fixes to the Presidential selection process, the unrepresentative U.S. Senate, Congressional redistricting, and other election reforms.

Challenge 1. Presidential Selection Fixes

We need to improve the process in three ways: 1) shorten, simplify, and democratize the process of choosing Presidential candidates; 2) let voters select Vice Presidential candidates; and 3) provide for direct election of the President and Vice President by the people, that is, do away with the electoral college.

Shorten, Simplify, and Democratize the Process of Choosing Presidential Candidates

Congress needs to pass a law establishing a National Presidential Primary System. Under this proposed scheme, each state holds an open primary election for President in one of three rounds of Presidential primaries. Each primary is held for nine days beginning on the first Saturday in August (Round 1), September (Round 2), and October (Round 3), followed by the general election beginning on the first Saturday in December.

1) Three rounds of Presidential primaries:
   a) The primary system should provide a reasonable opportunity for bootstrap, grassroots campaigns that start out as a small endeavor with only minimal financial and organizational requirements. For this reason, a single national primary day is probably not a good idea even though it seems to be the simplest and most straightforward.

b) The primary system should also encourage every campaign to begin in disparate regions of the country, allowing a candidate to demonstrate appeal beyond a single geographic region. For this reason, the first primary election should be held in perhaps four states spread around the country, avoiding the states with the largest populations and most expensive media markets.

c) The first two rounds provide an essential winnowing process so that only the strongest candidates survive to subsequent contests. If the proposed system is adopted, it's especially important that the first-round voters are thoroughly engaged, so that the country gains confidence in the overall scheme.

d) As it happens, our existing system has evolved with four early primary/caucus states (Iowa, New Hampshire, Nevada, and South Carolina), who have demonstrated that they take their Presidential politics seriously and perform their functions responsibly. One can argue this point, of course, and some might say that the task (and honor) of hosting the first round should be passed around. But at least for the first two cycles, we should depend on these four states to host the first round.

e) The second round should expand to the national stage and involve primaries in ten more states. Again, this is more challenging than the first round but less expensive in staff and money than a nationwide primary would be. This task should fall to ten states that volunteer with a provision for rotating the responsibility if more than ten states wish to do it.

f) The third round includes all other jurisdictions – the remaining states, the District of Columbia, and other territories permitted to participate.

2) Length of campaigns for each round:
   a) One month for each round should do the trick. If the campaigns are thus limited, voters can avoid watching the same ads, hearing the same talking points, and listening to the same stump speeches for 18 seemingly interminable months as at present. Candidates can rest and reflect a bit more. Voters can avoid boredom and exhaustion.
   b) Of course a shortened campaign season should be paired with a shortened fundraising season. One useful suggestion in this regard is to prohibit any fundraising by any candidate or his/her campaign while Congress is in session. This rule would have to apply to all candidates, not just those currently serving in Congress. We'd all welcome relief from incessant fundraising appeals.
   c) Meanwhile, if we curtail the campaign season as suggested here, the candidates (most of whom are currently-serving elected officials) can continue doing their day jobs, that is, serving us, rather than pontificating on the stump and begging for money.
3) Weekend voting:
   a) An 1845 federal law established election day as the first Tuesday after the first Monday in November. This schedule accommodated farmers (that is, most of the voters in 1845). Those rural voters could attend religious services on Sunday, travel to the county seat on Monday (often the sole polling location in a county), vote on Tuesday morning and return home, and then participate in market day (Wednesday). November was chosen, of course, to follow the fall harvest.
   b) This reasoning was great in 1845 but not so much today, when 3% of the voters are farmers. For the convenience of most voters and workers and to encourage greater voter

participation in elections, all our elections should include weekends.

   c) Each election (primary or general) will consist of nine days of in-person voting, beginning on a Saturday. This schedule provides two full weekends of voting when most Americans can get to the polls most conveniently. Including both Saturday and Sunday accommodates those who may not be able to vote for religious reasons on either the Saturday or the Sunday. Including nine days of voting spans a Monday through Friday work week, accommodating those who work on weekends. Votes may also be cast by mail provided they are received by the first date of the election (which allows all mail-in ballots to be counted before the election ends and allows the winners to be announced soon after the polls close). During the nine-day election, a voter may cast an emergency absentee ballot with reasonable cause – such as unexpected travel or an unforeseen medical situation – but such cases should be few, and in all cases the ballot must be received by the last day of the election. A state, as in Oregon, may choose to conduct the entire election by mail, eliminating in-person voting altogether, so that election day is designated only as counting-of-the-ballots day. But the most important change is moving every election to a weekend when most 21st century voters have the time to participate.

4) The Election Season Schedule: The 20th Amendment to the Constitution moved the Presidential inauguration from March to January 20. If we want to shorten and streamline the entire Presidential election season while retaining the current constitutionally-mandated inauguration day, then the Presidential primaries must begin later in the election year.

Further, to minimize the delay between the general election and the beginning of the newly-elected Government, the general election should be held much later in the calendar year. The following election season is proposed:

a) Congress adjourns *sine die,* and the election campaign season begins on or before July 4 in even-numbered years. Congress does not meet again until the new Congress convenes in January following the election. Four huge benefits to the public accrue from this proposal: 1) Congress can keep working until July 4 of every election year. 2) Congress does not need to pretend to keep working during the fall campaign season when every day spent in Washington takes the candidates away from the task they are really invested in – campaigning. By the way, candidates for the House and Senate can also begin campaigning after Congress adjourns. 3) The public only needs to tolerate repetitive campaign ads and stump speeches from July 4 until the general election, in contrast to the 18-month marathon we all must endure at present. 4) We can do away entirely with the lame-duck session of Congress, and we will have a much shorter period between the general election and the start of a new Congress and inauguration of a new President in January.

b) The Round 1 Presidential primaries begin on the first Saturday in August. The Round 1 primaries are held in Iowa, New Hampshire, Nevada, and South Carolina, unless Congress designates different states.

c) The Round 2 Presidential primaries begin on the first Saturday in September. Round 2 primaries are held in the first 10 states offering to hold them unless Congress designates another method for selecting those 10 states.

d) The Round 3 Presidential primary (the National Primary Election) begins on the first Saturday in October. Round 3 primaries are held in the remaining states and in all other jurisdictions authorized by Congress to participate in Presidential primaries.
e) The General Election begins on the first Saturday in December.
f) This schedule of primaries and general election can be adopted by an Act of Congress. The Constitution specifies only that the new Congress will convene on January 3 and the new President will take office on January 20. Therefore, modifying the schedule of primaries and the general election does not require a constitutional amendment.

5) Presidential primary rules:
   a) States and other jurisdictions authorized to hold primary elections conduct these elections as at present.
   b) Presidential primary candidates compete for "Nominating Votes". The total Nominating Votes for President equals the number of seats in the House of Representatives plus the number of Nominating Votes from non-state jurisdictions.
      i) Each CD has the same number of Nominating Votes as it has seats in the House of Representatives. (Since 1965 we have had only single-seat Congressional Districts. However, multi-seat CDs are possible.)
      ii) Congress may authorize certain jurisdictions other than states to participate in Presidential primaries (Washington, DC, Puerto Rico, and other territories and possessions). All such non-state jurisdictions taken together constitute the Non-State Primary District. For each 1 million inhabitants or portion

thereof, this Non-State Primary District is awarded one Nominating Vote.

c) To appear on any Presidential primary ballot, a candidate must sign an affidavit authorizing the IRS to release the tax returns of the candidate and his/her spouse for the preceding five years, if that candidate should qualify for the general election. (Knowing this requirement and the public's expectation of transparency, most Presidential candidates are likely to release their tax returns early in the primary season, as most candidates have done in the past.)

d) Any candidate who meets a state's requirements to appear on the primary ballot for President will appear on the primary ballot in that state. In addition, any candidate who earns at least one Nominating Vote in a Round 1 or a Round 2 primary automatically qualifies to appear on the ballot in all subsequent primaries. There will be one primary ballot containing the names of all candidates regardless of party. The party affiliation (if any) of each candidate will be indicated on the ballot.

e) State primary rules in most states will need to be modified so that only one primary is held (rather than a primary for each party and rather than caucuses and state-level party conventions).

f) Votes will be tabulated and winners determined by Congressional District (CD) using RCV procedures for elections with a single winner. The winner in each CD receives the "Nominating Votes" for that CD. The winner of the Non-State Primary District receives the Nominating Votes from that district.

g) General Election Ballot: At the conclusion of the Presidential primaries, any candidate who has received at least 15% of the total Nominating Votes qualifies for the general election ballot in all states. If fewer than three candidates achieve the 15% threshold, then the three candidates with the most Nominating Votes qualify for the general election ballot in all states. Further, any candidate who has won any Nominating Vote in any state qualifies for the general election ballot in that state. No other candidates will appear on the general election ballot for President in any state.

Let Voters Select Vice Presidential Candidates

The United States should adopt a nationwide primary election for Vice President, which will take place as part of the National Primary Election. This solution has the advantage of being achievable without the necessity of a constitutional amendment.

Any candidate who meets a state's requirements to appear on the primary ballot for Vice President will appear on the primary ballot in that state.

Anyone who was a candidate for President in Rounds 1 and/or 2, who won at least one Nominating Vote, and who then withdrew from the Presidential contest, automatically qualifies as a candidate for Vice President in all jurisdictions unless that candidate officially withdraws from consideration.

At the conclusion of the primary election for Vice President, any candidate who has received at least 15% of the total Nominating Votes for Vice President qualifies for the general election ballot for Vice President in all states. If fewer than three candidates achieve the 15% threshold, then the three candidates with the most Nominating Votes qualify for the general election ballot in all states. Further, any candidate who has won at least one

Nominating Vote in any state qualifies for the general election ballot in all CDs in that state. No other candidates will appear on the general election ballot for Vice President in any state.

Better Solution to the Vice-Presidential Selection Challenge: Replace the Vice President with an Elected Chancellor of the Senate

Some have argued that the Presidential candidate should be able to choose his running mate because after the election this pair is more likely to function as a team if they are united throughout the campaign.

Here are my responses to that argument:

- As to the Vice President's role as a member of the President's team, the President can appoint as many advisors as he likes and does not need a Vice President for that role. In fact, through most of our history, the President has largely ignored his Vice President. For example, FDR chose Missouri Senator Harry Truman as his new Vice-Presidential candidate in 1944 without knowing him at all, and when Roosevelt died in April 1945, Roosevelt and Truman had met each other no more than eight times, usually with a group of legislators. When Truman became President, he had not yet been briefed on the Manhattan Project (the development of the atomic bomb).

- We also have the inarguable truth that many modern Vice-Presidential candidates were far from the cream of the crop: Truman selected the quite elderly Kentucky Senator Alben Barkley in 1948 (ever hear of him?); Nixon chose the inexperienced and rather sketchy Maryland Governor Spiro Agnew in 1968, who resigned in disgrace the year before Nixon himself did the same; George H.W. Bush selected the intellectual lightweight and disinterested Indiana Senator Dan Quayle in 1988; and, in the most unqualified selection of all, Senator John McCain in 2008 picked first-term Alaska Governor Sarah Palin. Certainly the voters could find better candidates.

What are the duties of the Vice President? Essentially, there are two duties: 1) succeed the President if that position becomes vacant and 2) preside over the Senate. We could solve the issue most directly through a constitutional amendment to

- Replace the position of Vice President of the United States with the position of Chancellor of the Senate (the presiding officer of the Senate);

- Hold a direct national election for Chancellor. Like the presidency, this position could have a four-year term of office; but to keep it distinct from the Presidential election, the Chancellor election could be held at the time of the general election in non-Presidential election years, that is, even-numbered years not evenly divisible by 4. In this way, the Chancellor could very well develop a national following and gain meaningful experience in preparation for a run for the presidency two years later;

- Make the Chancellor first in the line of succession to the presidency; and

- Give the Chancellor meaningful responsibilities. The Chancellor should take over the responsibility for making all judicial appointments. The Chancellor should also truly preside over the Senate, controlling the agenda and the debate, and appointing the other Senate officers, such as the Chancellor Pro-Tempore and committee assignments – in the same fashion that the Speaker runs the House of Representatives.

The Vice President has become President multiple times in our history, either through the death or resignation of the President or through a subsequent election in which a sitting Vice President is seen as having a considerable built-in advantage over any other Presidential aspirant. Therefore, in a democracy, it is reasonable that the people should choose the second-most important job under our Constitution, rather than leaving that selection to a single person, who, at the time the decision is made, has not yet been elected as President. This is the main argument for making the election of Chancellor distinct from the election of the President.

Reassigning the responsibility for judicial appointments to someone other than the President could be part of the constitutional effort to regain balance among the three branches of government and strip away some of the inordinate power of the presidency. Although we have three distinct branches of government, there are points at which one branch is intimately involved in another branch. While the President obviously should make all executive branch appointments, the appointment of judges is a point at which he is involved in the judiciary. It might make more sense to let the Chancellor of the Senate perform that function. And if we made that change, then one of the major issues in the national election for Chancellor would be the candidates' potential selections for the federal judiciary.

Part III of this book, containing a proposed new constitution, includes the replacement of the Vice President with the new position of Chancellor. This change makes much more sense were it adopted in conjunction with a series of other related changes.

Provide for Direct Election of the President and Vice President

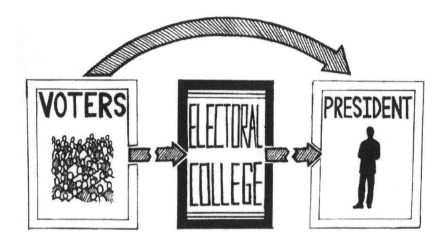

In 1823 the former President James Madison returned to his earlier view in favor of universal suffrage and against the electoral college as it had evolved. By that time, almost all states had adopted the winner-take-all practice still used by 48 of the 50 states today: the winner of the statewide popular vote receives all of that state's electoral votes. Madison also opposed the provision that gives the election to the House of Representatives with one vote per state when no candidate has a majority of the electoral votes. Madison proposed a constitutional amendment[13] (which obviously never passed) (see sidebar).

---

[13] http://www.fairvote.org/why-james-madison-wanted-to-change-the-way-we-vote-for-President. [Accessed on June 16, 2017.]

> # Interesting sidebar: James Madison's Constitutional Amendment
>
> Proposed in 1823. Never passed. Key elements:
>
> a) Voters in Presidential election districts in each state choose Presidential electors, with no more than two electors per district.
>
> b) Each elector chooses two persons for President, a 1st choice and a 2nd choice.
>
> c) If one person receives a majority of the 1st choice votes, then that person becomes President.
>
> d) If no one receives a majority of 1st choice votes, then the 2nd choice votes are added, and if one person receives a majority, he becomes President.
>
> e) If still no one has a majority, then Congress in a joint session of both chambers selects the President from the two names with the most 1st plus 2nd choice votes.
>
> When we consider improvements to the manner of choosing the President, James Madison's proposed constitutional amendment might be a good place to open the discussion.

As Madison's proposal demonstrates, Americans have long debated the elimination of the electoral college. Here are three alternatives for fixing the electoral college along with the pros and cons of each.

Each alternative still works within the framework of the electoral college as provided in the Constitution. We currently have 538 electoral votes, made up of 435 electoral votes equal to the number of seats in the House of Representatives, 100 electoral votes equal to the number of seats in the Senate, and 3 electoral votes for Washington, DC. (The 3 votes for DC are based on the electoral votes that DC would have if it were a state – one seat in the House and 2 in the Senate.) If one candidate receives a majority of the electoral votes (270), that candidate is elected President. If no candidate receives a majority, the House of Representatives determines the winner, and each state delegation has one vote.

Because the Constitution specifically empowers states to choose their electors however they see fit, any scheme that garners 270 electoral votes will work. As an extreme example, we could adopt simple random selection: People who want to be President throw their names into a hat, and one name is randomly drawn as the winner. If states with 270 electoral votes agree to give all their electoral votes to that randomly-selected candidate, then that person becomes President.

The following three alternatives are feasible.

Alternative 1: The National Popular Vote Interstate Compact (NPVIC)

NPVIC could bring about the direct election of the President by popular vote without needing to amend the Constitution. Under this initiative, identical laws have been introduced in 47 states, which provide that that state will cast all its electoral votes for the candidate who wins the national popular vote. These state laws only become effective when states having at least 270 electoral votes in aggregate have adopted NPVIC.

Pros and cons of Alternative 1

The pros of the NPVIC proposal are easy to see. Every vote counts equally. This feature eliminates the preference given to voters in less-populous states. NPVIC also eliminates the state-by-state winner-take-all system, which currently causes most states and most voters to be ignored. As a result, the notion of "swing states" would disappear. It would no longer matter whether a candidate "won" a particular state or not. 70% of American voters believe that the candidate with the most votes should become President. NPVIC gives us that result without amending the Constitution.

The Con of this proposal is that the need for candidates to appeal to every geographic region of the nation would be reduced. (Of course, one can argue rather persuasively that the current system also does not require candidates to appeal across many regions since the entire Presidential election campaign focuses only on eight or nine "swing" states.) Another Con is that, by not amending the Constitution, NPVIC could be undone by states that change their mind and drop out or fail to follow the compact. Hence, the failure to amend the Constitution is a two-edged sword: what a state legislature can do, that state legislature can undo a week later.

Can NPVIC succeed?

As of this writing, 15 states plus Washington, DC have passed the National Popular Vote Interstate Compact. These states control 196 electoral votes, 72% of the number needed to reach 270. However, the states that have adopted NPVIC (MD, NJ, IL, HI, WA, MA, VT, CA, RI, NY, CT, CO, DE, NM, OR, and DC) are primarily the more progressive states; gaining the requisite 74 additional electoral votes will be difficult. NPVIC may well be the current effort closest to a successful conclusion, but success is still very far away. Some folks prefer to retain the current electoral college with its built-in protections for less populous states and its requirement that a successful candidate demonstrate support across all regions of the country.

Alternative 2: Voting by Congressional District, as in Maine and Nebraska

In Maine and Nebraska, the winner of the Presidential election in each congressional district (CD) is awarded one electoral vote (representing the electoral votes allocated to that state based on its seats in the House), and the winner statewide is awarded two electoral votes (representing the electoral votes allocated to that state based on it seats in the Senate).

Pros and cons of Alternative 2

This system is much fairer than the winner-take-all approach followed in the other 48 states although it does not eliminate the built-in preference for states with small populations. Another Pro is that it does not require a constitutional amendment; but a Con is that it would not be really effective unless it were implemented in all 50 states, a tough nut to crack. Probably the biggest Con is that it gives no credit at all to the candidate who wins the national popular vote, which makes Alternative 2 much less popular among reformers than NPVIC.

Can Alternative 2 succeed?

Maine and Nebraska adopted this system for reasons unique to the internal politics of those states. Its chances of wider adoption in its present form are slim. Most states perceive only a loss of power and influence by dividing their electoral votes among multiple candidates.

Alternative 2 might have greater appeal if its implementation followed the NPVIC model. Specifically, states would agree to cast all their electoral votes for the candidate who wins according to this system, but implementation would only take place after states with at least 270 electoral votes adopted it.

Alternative 3: Local-State-National (LSN) Voting – A Hybrid Solution

This system represents a hybrid, giving weight to each vote at the local, state, and national levels. Basically, each vote contributes to the preferred candidate winning within a congressional district (CD), within a state, and across the whole nation. Like the NPVIC, this solution can be implemented as soon as states with at least 270 electoral votes adopt it.

Here is how LSN Voting works:

Under the LSN voting scheme, the number of LSN votes equals the number of electoral votes (538). LSN votes are tabulated as follows:

- One LSN vote is awarded to the winner of each CD. This is the "Local" component of LSN voting. This accounts for 436 LSN votes.

- One LSN vote is awarded to the winner of each state. This is the "State" component of LSN voting. This accounts for 51 LSN votes.

- One LSN vote is awarded to the winner of the national popular vote for each state in the Union. This is the "National" component of LSN voting. This accounts for 51 LSN votes.

- If one candidate has at least 270 LSN votes, that candidate is the winner. If no candidate has at least 270 LSN votes, then the winner of the national popular vote is the winner of the election.

The Local-State-National Interstate Compact (LSNIC): States adopting the LSN voting scheme agree to cast all their electoral votes for the candidate who wins the election according to the LSN voting scheme. These state laws only become effective when states with 270 electoral votes have adopted it.

Pros and cons of Alternative 3

LSN Voting accomplishes all the major objectives of reform:

1. Values every voter in every congressional district, every state, and the nation as a whole;
2. Retains a role for the states, while also recognizing both a smaller (local CD) and larger (national) component of each voter's choice;
3. Requires the winning candidate to have broad appeal at all three levels (local, state, and national) and across all regions of the country;
4. Bypasses the electoral college, removing any possibility that "faithless electors" could alter the outcome of the contest; and
5. Eliminates the possibility that the Presidential election will ever be thrown into the House of Representatives.

Can the LSN solution succeed?

In terms of effectiveness and possibility of adoption, this compromise proposal might satisfy sufficiently those who want every vote to count and want the winner of the popular vote to win the election. It might also satisfy those who want the winner to have broad appeal across the nation and want the states to still matter.

The major parties will likely rail against this proposal (since it reduces their clout), and they are very likely to resuscitate the old debate during the 1787 Constitutional Convention about large states overpowering small states. But as pointed out earlier, that is a bogus argument: A strong difference of opinion between large and small states has never been a decisive factor in any US Presidential election. We have had differences between regions, between parties, between personalities, and between ideologies; but we have never had differences because all the large states gathered in one corner and all the small states gathered in the opposite corner – it just never happened.

This author endorses the LSN Solution. Adoption of LSN through the LSN Interstate Compact would be a huge step forward for our democracy. Adoption of LSN through a constitutional amendment would be even better.

Challenge 2. U.S. Senate Fix

Article V Provision

If Americans decided to change the Senate from a body that represents states (two Senators per state) to a representative body (on the principle of "one citizen one vote", while also representing states), it's not as simple as adopting a constitutional amendment to modify Article I Section 3, which specifies that the Senate will be composed of two Senators per state. This is because Article V, which delineates the procedures and rules for amending the Constitution, specifies that no state will be denied equal suffrage in the Senate without its consent. Faced with this intentional roadblock to changing the makeup of the Senate, we are left with the following possibilities:

1. We could propose an amendment to change the makeup of the Senate, and get every one of the 50 states to adopt it – probably an impossible hurdle, since at least one state with a small population would almost certainly object, and an objection from any single state would nullify this approach.
2. We could amend the Constitution to reduce the powers of the Senate, so that, even as the Senate remained unrepresentative, this wouldn't matter so much. For example, rather than requiring the Senate to pass all legislation before it becomes law, we could give the Senate only the power to block a law passed by the House, provided that the Senate rejects that law by a 2/3 majority within 30 days after it is passed by the House. Many other similar measures could be used to reduce the Senate's role. (This was the type of change the British used to reduce the power of the very unrepresentative House of Lords.) While this approach has merit, we might end up with a unicameral legislature, with none of the checks and balances which a bicameral legislature provides.
3. We could eliminate the Senate altogether. This is cleaner than method 2 but still leaves us with a unicameral legislature, subject to the whims of the voters every two years, and without the benefits of a bicameral legislature. Having two chambers, one designed to change laws quickly in response to public opinion, the other designed to operate more slowly and carefully, is probably a good feature of the American system.
4. We could accomplish our objective in two steps, which is the process I recommend:

    Step 1. Replace Article V, rewriting the procedures for amending the Constitution (see Big Fix 3 above).

Step 2. After that amendment is adopted, we could then proceed to adopt another amendment to change the makeup of the Senate. In this new configuration, each Senator will represent BOTH the people of the state and the state itself. The reconfiguration of the Senate could be combined with the replacement of the position of Vice President of the United States with the new position of Chancellor of the Senate.

Proposed Makeup of the New Senate

To clarify the discussion in this section, I use the term "Original Senate" to refer to the existing Senate as prescribed by the 1787 Constitution, and the term "New Senate" to describe the reconstituted Senate suggested here.

The New Senate will be a representative body, made up of Senators elected for six-year terms. The number of Senators for each state equals the number of that state's Representatives divided by five, with fractions always rounded up. Thus states with one to five Representatives in the House get one Senator; states with six to ten Representatives get two Senators; those with 11 to 15 Representatives get three Senators; and so on. The following table shows the allocation of Senators to the 50 states, based on the apportionment of Representatives following the 2010 Census. It also shows the number of people represented by each Senator, and the final column shows the ratio of power between the citizens of this state and the citizens of the state with the least power – the Ratio of Power Per Person, or RP/PP. The least powerful citizens reside in the state with the highest number of people per Senator, so their relative power is defined as 1.0. Finally, the table shows that the New Senate would have

110 Senators, not much different from the Original Senate, which has 100 Senators:

State	Reps in House	Senators	2010 Census	Population per Senator	RP/PP
Alabama	7	2	4,802,982	2,401,491	1.6
Alaska	1	1	721,523	721,523	5.3
Arizona	9	2	6,412,700	3,206,350	1.2
Arkansas	4	1	2,926,229	2,926,229	1.3
California	53	11	37,341,989	3,394,726	1.1
Colorado	7	2	5,044,930	2,522,465	1.5
Connecticut	5	1	3,581,628	3,581,628	1.1
Delaware	1	1	900,877	900,877	4.3
Florida*	27	6	18,900,773	3,150,129	1.2
Georgia	14	3	9,727,566	3,242,522	1.2
Hawaii	2	1	1,366,862	1,366,862	2.8
Idaho	2	1	1,573,499	1,573,499	2.4
Illinois	18	4	12,864,380	3,216,095	1.2
Indiana	9	2	6,501,582	3,250,791	1.2
Iowa	4	1	3,053,787	3,053,787	1.3
Kansas	4	1	2,863,813	2,863,813	1.3

Table title: Apportioning Seats in the New Senate

Kentucky	6	2	4,350,606	2,175,303	1.8
Louisiana	6	2	4,553,962	2,276,981	1.7
Maine	2	1	1,333,074	1,333,074	2.9
Maryland	8	2	5,789,929	2,894,965	1.3
Massachusetts	9	2	6,559,644	3,279,822	1.2
Michigan	14	3	9,911,626	3,303,875	1.2
Minnesota	8	2	5,314,879	2,657,440	1.4
Mississippi	4	1	2,978,240	2,978,240	1.3
Missouri	8	2	6,011,478	3,005,739	1.3
Montana	1	1	994,416	994,416	3.9
Nebraska	3	1	1,831,825	1,831,825	2.1
Nevada	4	1	2,709,432	2,709,432	1.4
New Hampshire	2	1	1,321,445	1,321,445	2.9
New Jersey	12	3	8,807,501	2,935,834	1.3
New Mexico	3	1	2,067,273	2,067,273	1.9
New York	27	6	19,421,055	3,236,843	1.2
North Carolina	13	3	9,565,781	3,188,594	1.2
North Dakota	1	1	675,905	675,905	5.7
Ohio	16	4	11,568,495	2,892,124	1.3
Oklahoma	5	1	3,764,882	3,764,882	1.0

Oregon	5	1	3,848,606	3,848,606	1.0
Pennsylvania	18	4	12,734,905	3,183,726	1.2
Rhode Island	2	1	1,055,247	1,055,247	3.6
South Carolina	7	2	4,645,975	2,322,988	1.7
South Dakota	1	1	819,761	819,761	4.7
Tennessee	9	2	6,375,431	3,187,716	1.2
Texas*	36	8	25,268,418	3,158,552	1.2
Utah	4	1	2,770,765	2,770,765	1.4
Vermont	1	1	630,337	630,337	6.1
Virginia	11	3	8,037,736	2,679,245	1.4
Washington	10	2	6,753,369	3,376,685	1.1
West Virginia	3	1	1,859,815	1,859,815	2.1
Wisconsin	8	2	5,698,230	2,849,115	1.4
Wyoming	1	1	568,300	568,300	6.8
Totals	435	110	309,183,463	2,810,759	1.3

The power inequalities of the Original Senate have been largely corrected in this suggested makeup of the New Senate. Rather than a worst case of 66 to 1 (the exorbitant relative power of voters in Wyoming to voters in California in the Original Senate), the worst case in the New Senate would be 7 to 1 (Wyoming to Oklahoma or Oregon).

Terms of Office for the New Senate

One of the purposes of the Original Senate, as established by the Founding Fathers, was to be a more deliberative body, as a counterweight to the House, which was expected to be elected directly by the people every two years and thus to be more responsive to the changing views of the citizenry. For this reason, Original Senate terms were fixed at six years, with a third of the Senate elected every two years. Change would therefore come to the Senate more slowly than to the House.

The New Senate should follow exactly the same scheme, with a third of the Senators elected every two years, and with staggered elections for Senators from the same state. The only issue occurs when a state gains or loses a Senator as a result of the decennial census. This can be easily handled as follows:

- When a state loses a Senator as a result of reapportionment, the Senator whose term of office next expires simply is not replaced.
- When a state gains a Senator, the additional seat is filled at the next biennial election, and the term of office for the new Senator is either two, four, or six years, depending on how it fits into the scheme of staggered terms for the Senators within a state.

It should be noted that few changes in the number of Senators apportioned to a state can be expected. For example, if this system had been in place beginning in 2000, then only Florida and Texas (asterisked in the table above) would have seen an increase of one Senator as a result of the 2010 reapportionment, and no state would have experienced a decrease. Therefore, this system is rather stable.

Senate Elections

In the New Senate, as in the Original Senate, all Senators are elected at large, so that each Senator represents not only the citizens of a state but also the state itself. This means that voters will select from one to three Senators at a time in 49 of the 50 states, and four Senators at a time in California.

When one Senate seat is at stake, the primary election shall be conducted as specified in the earlier discussion of Open Primaries, specifically in the section entitled "Counting of ballots in primary elections for Congress". The regular Ranked Choice Voting (RCV) procedure for elections with a single winner shall govern the general election.

When more than one Senate seat is at stake, we need a different procedure. We should adopt RCV for all elections, both those with a single winner and those with multiple winners. RCV produces fairer representation of the entire electorate than the First-Past-The-Post scheme. However, the scheme proposed for elections with a single winner will not work as intended when an election will fill multiple positions. This is because the voters need to have their say with respect not only to their one preferred candidate but also with respect to all the positions being filled.

A variety of voting schemes for elections with multiple winners exist.[14] The scheme proposed here is based on a scheme that has been used for determining the top-ranked teams in college sports: To rank the top 25 football or basketball teams, the voters

---

[14] FairVote.org advocates a different procedure for handling multi-winner elections. See Appendix 1.

(sportswriters or coaches) rank 25 teams. To count the ballots, the 1st choice gets 25 votes, the 2nd choice gets 24, the 3rd choice gets 23, and on down to 1 vote for the 25th choice. The same principle applies here. To fill two or three Senate seats, the voter makes three choices in order: the 1st choice is the voter's top candidate, the 2nd and 3rd choices follow. In counting ballots, the first choice counts as three votes, the 2nd choice counts as two votes, and the 3rd choice counts as one.

An election to fill four Senate seats requires a variation in voting: Voters will select a 1st choice, a 2nd choice, and two "3rd choices".

I have proposed open primaries for every elected position. If that proposal is adopted, I propose further that the number of successful candidates in the primary election for multiple Senate seats be two more than the number of seats being contested, that is, four candidates qualify for the general election when two seats are at stake, five candidates advance to the general election when three seats are at stake, and six candidates compete in the general election when four seats must be filled. The procedure below applies to open primaries for a two-seat, three-seat, or four-seat Senate contest.

VOTING in two-seat or three-seat Senate elections (both primary and general), voters select a 1st, a 2nd, and a 3rd choice. In a four-seat Senate election (both primary and general), voters select a 1st choice, a 2nd choice, and two 3rd choices. (In this way, in a four-seat race, voters can express their preferences for all four positions.)

COUNTING of ballots: Calculate the weighted vote for each candidate, which equals 3 X the candidate's 1st choice votes + 2 X the 2nd choice votes + the 3rd choice votes. Rank order the results.

This is the table of successful primary and general election candidates for all Senate contests:

Number of Senate seats	Voters select	Counting process	Primary winners	General winners
1	1st, 2nd, and 3rd choices	RCV for one seat	Last 3, or 3 > 25%	1 > 50%
2	1st, 2nd, and 3rd choices	Weighted voting	Top 4	Top 2
3	1st, 2nd, and 3rd choices	Weighted voting	Top 5	Top 3
4	1st, 2nd, and two 3rd choices	Weighted voting	Top 6	Top 4

Let me stipulate again that this is only one possible "proportional representation" scheme that could be applied. FairVote.org has proposed a scheme that appears fairer than this one, but its implementation is far more complex, and even understanding the mathematics behind it is a challenge. Hence, I have opted for a scheme that is simpler and easier to understand but admittedly not ideal. Nevertheless I've included an explanation of FairVote's multi-winner vote-counting procedure in Appendix 1.

Conclusion

The makeup of the Original Senate, as prescribed in Article I of the Constitution, is far from representative. In a representative democracy we should not forever retain a construct in which half of the national legislature fails to properly represent the

American population. Many solutions to this problem present themselves, but only a structural solution such as replacing Article V concerning the procedure for amending the Constitution combined with the New Senate proposed here solves the challenge of the Article V provision concerning the Senate as well as the challenge of the non-representative makeup of the Original Senate. The advantage of this proposal is that it builds on and largely retains many features of the Original Senate, including its continued dependence on state elections, six-year terms of office, and the election of Senators at large (so that they represent the state as well as its citizens), while also accommodating future population shifts as reflected in the census. We should carefully consider potential solutions and move forward on one of them.

Challenge 3. Gerrymander Fix

My gerrymander fix consists of two completely independent components. That is, either component stands alone and represents a considerable improvement over where we are today. But both components taken together really slay this monster once and for all.

The first component is a rule-based scheme for drawing congressional districts without human decision-making. The second component is multi-seat congressional districts combined with Ranked Choice Voting.

Redistricting without Gerrymanders

An old saying is most relevant here: "Perfection is the enemy of the good." I do not claim that this solution is perfect, that it meets every conceivable objective of redistricting reform, or that it is the very best way to draw congressional districts. I do claim that it is far preferable to the system we have now. Further, it is achievable on a state-by-state basis or, preferably, through national legislation.

Redistricting Principles

We need a completely mechanical, replicable, transparent, uniform-across-all-states, and (especially) non-partisan process for redistricting.

Seven states have only one seat in the House, so this discussion pertains to the 43 states that have more than one House seat. However, the problem of gerrymandering may be even more pronounced with respect to drawing election districts for state legislatures. The solution recommended here for Congress can be applied to legislative districts in all 50 states.

Most observers would agree that the optimal solution to this problem is to 1) remove redistricting from the control of politicians and 2) adopt a rule-based process to make redistricting easy and automatic. The solution proposed in this paper satisfies both of those criteria. This section explains the proposed redistricting solution as a manual process, which lends itself to automation.

PRELIMINARILY we should all agree on the basic objectives for any non-partisan redistricting scheme:

- Equalize the population per House seat within a state;

- Keep neighbors together in the same congressional district;
- Ignore all other considerations.

Equalize population per House seat: The first of these objectives, equalizing the population per House seat, reflects basic fairness, the time-honored notion of "one person – one vote".

Keep neighbors together: The second objective is intuitively obvious to Americans, but geography is not necessarily the only criterion that could be used. In Florence in the Middle Ages, representatives to the city Senate were chosen by occupation: construction trades elected one rep, farmers another, merchants another, and so on. We could use religion: Catholics elect their representatives and all other denominations theirs. We could use age: everyone 18 to 30 elects their reps, those 30 to 55 elect theirs, and so on. We could divide ourselves by social class, as France did before the French Revolution: churchmen in the First Estate, noblemen and aristocrats in the Second Estate, and the bourgeoisie in the Third Estate.[15] We could do it by income or net worth: Starting at the top, the wealthiest 710,000 residents of a state elect one congressperson, then the next wealthiest 710,000 elect the second congressperson, on down to the poorest who elect the last. We could also just let a computer randomly assign each voter to a congressional district. But having said all that, we in this country still have some affinity for geographic proximity as a basis for deciding which folks belong in the same election

---

[15] When we describe journalists as "members of the Fourth Estate", that is actually a reference to the Three Estates in pre-revolutionary France.

district. Hence a rule-based solution to redistricting must consider neighborhoods. As a first rule, people residing in the same county should vote in the same election district if possible – that is, we should minimize the number of counties partitioned into two or more congressional districts. With rare exceptions, each congressional district should also (1) keep together everyone who lives in the same zip code and (2) occupy a contiguous and compact land mass.

We should also admit that both natural and man-made barriers affect the formation of communities. Buda and Pest were separate towns on opposite sides of the Danube River until bridges appeared, allowing Budapest to form. Boundaries between Swiss cantons often consist of a high Alpine ridge, impassable for half the year. These and countless other examples demonstrate the importance of geography. But we also observe that the resulting communities – on either side of a river or mountain pass or lake or ravine – are often in separate political jurisdictions, that is, separate counties or at least separate zip codes, so that keeping counties and zip codes together largely addresses the issue of natural geographic boundaries.

I would like also to posit that the notion of keeping neighbors in the same CD is sufficiently important that fidelity to this standard affords some relaxation in the rule to equalize populations. I do not know the magic number or percentage here, but in this proposal I am using 5% as the norm: I allow a CD to have up to 5% more or 5% less than the requisite population of a CD if doing so allows an entire county to stay in the same CD. When a county needs to be partitioned, I use the same 5% rule with respect to splitting zip code tabulation areas into census tracts (explained later).

Ignore all other considerations: Many state statutes, some federal statues, and countless court cases have addressed the allowable criteria in drawing election districts. Laws and courts have mandated equal populations in each district as well as geographic compactness. Some redistricting plans consider race or other demographic factors to ensure that the redistricting scheme does not unfairly disadvantage any protected class. Those responsible for drawing district boundaries have also considered (whether openly or secretly) party registrations, previous voting patterns, city and county boundaries, and wealth, among other criteria. Since the 1960s, the major debates have centered on race, socio-economic status, political affiliation, and previous voting history. It appears that every redistricting plan from every state has been subject to litigation; and courts have had a devil of a time trying to sort out these competing interests in order to decide what is legal, fair, and reasonable. After the last round of redistricting based on the 2010 Census, 38 of the 43 state redistricting plans faced legal challenges.

The multiple criteria for setting election district boundaries all seem to relate to the perceived misuse of redistricting as a method to achieve partisan political objectives rather than the need to ensure fair and free elections. Yet if we remove politicians from the process and focus only on the twin objectives of equalizing population and geographic proximity, we will eliminate the need for all other criteria. This proposed plan does exactly that.

NEXT, we should agree that a non-partisan redistricting solution should satisfy these guidelines:

- Avoid human decisions concerning any particular election district boundary;

- Adopt a completely rule-governed process;
- Follow the same process in every state;
- Make the process transparent to and replicable by anyone so interested

Avoid human decisions: Most published proposals for redistricting have included some kind of state-level commission to oversee the process in each state. Some plans specify a completely non-partisan body. Other plans specify a commission balanced between the major political parties, perhaps with a third group of independents or non-partisan participants. The problem with all of these proposals is that politicians, lobbyists, or other influence peddlers can manipulate or control any such commission. Then the task of guarding against such corruptions becomes a permanent feature of the political landscape. Furthermore, in all of these schemes the state commissions, legislatures, and courts still spend a considerable amount of time and effort drawing election district boundaries. A better system would make the redistricting process automatic, so we could spend our time discussing substantive issues rather than focusing on process.

In a democracy, people get to choose their representatives; the representatives do not get to choose their constituents. Anytime politicians draw the election districts, we tend toward a system where the representatives choose the voters rather than the reverse. Therefore, a truly non-partisan redistricting system should remove humans from making any election district boundary decisions. Full Stop.

Rule-Governed Process: Any proposed process should be governed by specific rules that spell out precisely how to draw the election districts. The process must work for any jurisdiction in the country subdivided into any number of election districts, again maintaining allegiance only to the two principles of equalization of population and geographic proximity. Such a mechanical process could be automated. The Federal Elections Commission should publish the resulting computer program and make it freely available.

Uniform in Every State: The **U.S. Constitution, Article I, Section 4 Elections, Meetings** grants Congress power to regulate elections for members of Congress should Congress choose to do so:

> *The Times, Places and Manner of holding Elections for Senators and Representatives, shall be prescribed in each State by the Legislature thereof; but the Congress may at any time by Law make or alter such Regulations, except as to the Place of Chusing [sic] Senators.*

Based on that paragraph, in 1845 Congress established a uniform day for holding the national elections. Before that law was passed, each state chose when to conduct its election. Today we take it for granted that all our national elections take place on the same day, but it was not always so. Based on the same Constitutional authority, in 1965 Congress mandated single-seat election districts. Similarly, Congress has the authority to determine how congressional districts are drawn since this is very much a part of the "Manner" of holding elections.

The reason for Congressional action with regard to gerrymandering is obvious. If Party A dominates one state and has gerrymandered its congressional districts while Party B dominates another state and has likewise gerrymandered its districts, why would either state unilaterally disarm? The only viable and long-lasting solution is one that applies equally to every state.

Transparent and Replicable: Drawing election districts should not be rocket science – one should not need an engineering or math degree to do it. The process only becomes complicated when we introduce objectives and criteria which ought to be irrelevant such as race, wealth, or political affiliation. Therefore, a process that eliminates those irrelevant factors should be something any citizen can comprehend and any citizen with the desire to do so can replicate.

The actual physical process of drawing boundaries for congressional districts should be straight-forward, uncomplicated, easy to understand, completely non-political, and fully automated. Since the computer software to do this has not yet been created, I will explain the process in narrative form. Once we have come to agreement on the process, computer programmers will then be able to write the computer software to do this automatically.

Redistricting Process Summary

I propose to end all the debate and all the litigation. This solution is not perfect, but it's far better than any other I've encountered to date. I'm not wedded to this particular solution just because I came up with it. Any solution that satisfies the aforementioned principles should be considered. But let me put this one on the table, and then we can all discuss this proposal and any others that may also fit the bill. What follows here is a broad summary of the process and maps of several sample states.

We will draw congressional districts by scanning a state according to a prescribed set of scanning rules, adding counties to a congressional district one by one. When the addition of one more county would make the district's population too large, we partition that county into its Zip Code Tabulation Areas (ZCTA's), adding ZCTA's to the district until the district contains the requisite population.

Since the notion of "counties" ("parishes" in Louisiana and "boroughs" in Alaska and in New York City) is familiar to everyone, I need only explain ZCTA's. The U.S. Census Bureau developed Zip Code Tabulation Areas (ZCTA's) from the US Postal Service's 5-digit zip codes. Think of a ZCTA as a zip code with geographic boundaries. Everyone resides within a ZCTA, even if your mailing address is a P.O. Box and even if your house is not on any mail delivery route. Further, since some zip codes include addresses in two counties or two states, the Census Bureau draws a ZCTA in each jurisdiction and tabulates the population in each. Therefore, we begin with a map of a given state's counties and the ZCTA's within each county, along with the population of each county and each ZCTA.

What remains is to determine how to establish the scan lines.

One method that can work well is to draw a Reference Line between the two most widely separated points in the state and then add a Scan Line perpendicular to the Reference Line. Scanning will take place by dragging the Scan Line along the Reference Line. Redrawing the Reference Line and Scan Line after completing each CD changes the slope of the Scan Line, and avoids excessively long and narrow CDs, which would otherwise ensue in large states. Without this rule, Texas, for example, might end up with a number of narrow CDs 600 to 800 miles long.

The following images show the placement of the Reference Lines, Scan Lines, and election district boundaries for an imaginary state with four CDs. In this imaginary state, the four CDs will consist of whole counties, so we will not partition any county into ZCTA's. Here is the imaginary state before we begin drawing CDs:

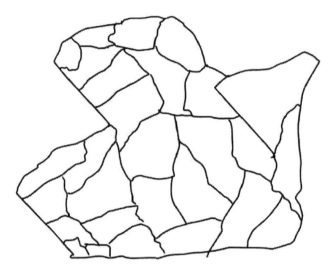

To begin building Congressional District 1, start by drawing a **Reference Line** between the two most distant points:

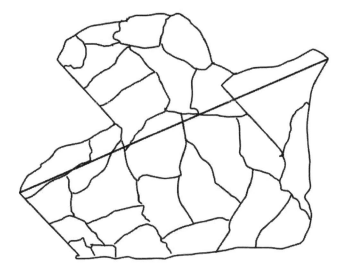

Select one end of the Reference Line as the **Starting Point** – the westernmost point on the Reference Line:

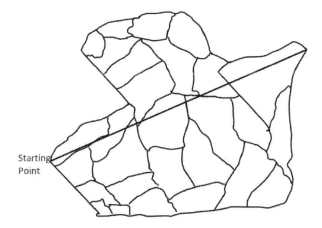

Next, draw the **Scan Line** perpendicular to the Reference Line and through the Starting Point.

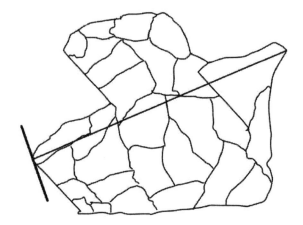

Next, drag the Scan Line along the Reference Line, touching counties as you go. Add each touched county to CD 1. Stop adding counties when the addition of one more county (LAST County) would cause the CD 1 population to be too large:

This is the completed CD 1:

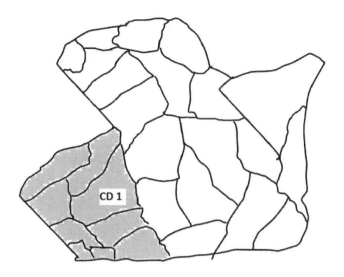

For CD 2, draw a new Reference Line and Scan Line. (The Starting Point is always at the western end of the Reference Line, and the Scan Line passes through the Starting Point.):

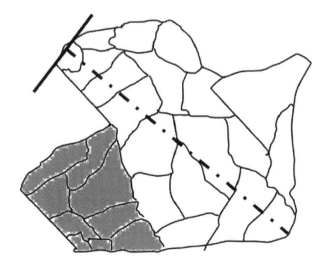

Voila! CD 2 complete:

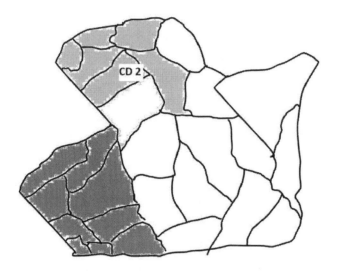

For CD 3, again redraw the Reference Line and Scan Line:

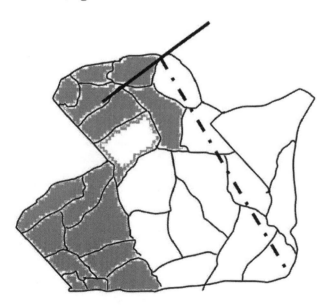

CD 3 Complete:

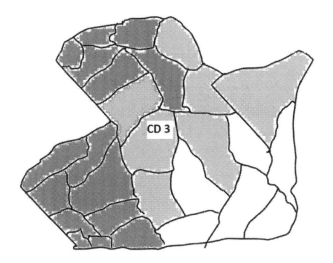

CD 4 complete: By definition, after all CDs save one have been drawn, the last CD perforce contains everything left over:

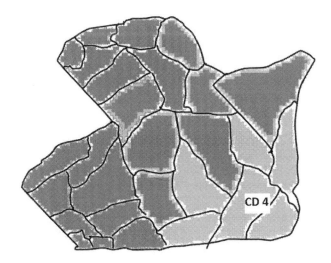

Here is a summary of the proposed process for drawing congressional districts in every state:

1. Create a Reference Line, connecting the two most distant points in the area of the state not yet assigned to a CD.

2. Determine the Starting Point at the westernmost point of the Reference Line.

3. Create a Scan Line, perpendicular to the Reference Line and through the Starting Point.

4. Keeping the Scan Line perpendicular to the Reference Line, drag the Scan Line along the Reference Line, touching counties.

5. Add each touched county (land and population) to the current district.

6. Stop when adding one more county ("LAST County") would put too many people in the CD.

7. Add or skip LAST County in its entirety, if doing so would result in a total CD population within 5% of target (target = the average population per House seat in that state). Otherwise, partition LAST County: using the same Scan Line, scan LAST County, adding ZCTA's until the CD population target is reached.

8. Repeat these steps until all CDs for the state are created

Proposed Scheme in Maryland, North Carolina, and Pennsylvania

Here are a few examples based on this proposed scheme, showing the congressional districts which would have resulted from the 2010 Census in Maryland, Pennsylvania, and North Carolina. (As sample states, I used the same states that served as examples of the worst gerrymanders in Part 1 of this book.)

All 8 Congressional Districts in Maryland

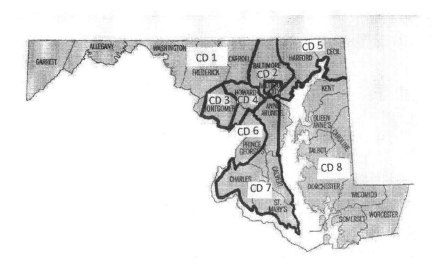

All 13 CDs in North Carolina

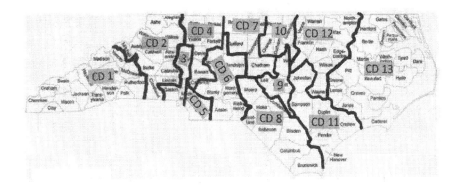

All 18 Pennsylvania Congressional Districts

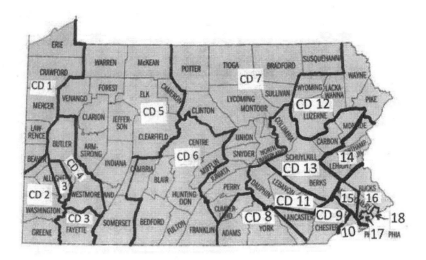

Political Results in Maryland and North Carolina

Republicans versus Democrats in Maryland

Of course, everyone reading this wants to know how this might affect ME. Let's examine the political implications of the proposed scheme on Maryland. While no one can predict how people will vote in future elections, we can get a hint of expected results by examining the voting patterns of the areas that make up each of the proposed CDs.

As a starting point, Maryland Democrats outnumber Republicans about two to one. In this heavily gerrymandered state, Maryland elected seven Dems and one Repub to the House in each of the last two elections. None of the third party, independent, or write-in candidates moved the needle in any of these 16 elections, so I decided to tabulate only the votes for Republicans and for Democrats.

To get a hint at expected political results using the CD boundaries proposed herein, I added up the votes cast in the general elections for the House of Representatives in 2016 and 2018. If a county is wholly within one CD, I added all the votes from that county to the totals for that CD. If only a percentage of a county lies within a CD, I multiplied the total county votes by the percentage of the county population that lies within that CD. Here are the results:

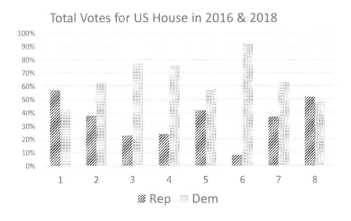

Maryland Votes for House in 2016 & 2018

Total Votes Cast in MD in 2016 & 2018					
CD	W	Rep		Dem	
1	R	348840	57%	267680	43%
2	D	230308	38%	381271	62%
3	D	142097	23%	483578	77%
4	D	149235	24%	466924	76%
5	D	238439	42%	325244	58%

6	D	47104	8%	522075	92%
7	D	229021	37%	389790	63%
8	R	315036	52%	292769	48%
All		1700080	35%	3129331	65%

As expected, Democrats in Maryland got 65% of the vote for major party candidates, and Republicans got 35%. Democrats would have won six of Maryland's eight seats in the House. Only one CD is fairly competitive: CD 8 would have been a Republican win by 4 points. The other Republican victory (CD 1) would have been by 17% (57 to 43). All six Democratic wins would have been by wider margins.

Racial Profile of Proposed CDs in Maryland

The chart below, based on census data, shows the percentage of residents in each proposed CD who identify with each race.

Ever since a Boston cartoonist in 1812 introduced the term "gerrymander" to the American political lexicon, Americans have argued about unfair influences on drawing election district boundaries. Editorials and lawsuits abound concerning the influence of race, religion, party registrations, age, income, education, and rural-versus-urban demographic characteristics of the population.

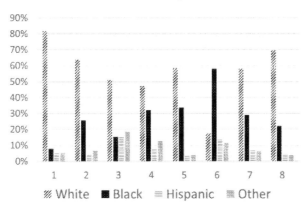

Racial Profile of Proposed CDs in Maryland

Of all the characteristics that have been the subject of discussion and debate, the one factor that always seems to dominate such discussions is race. Hence this chart might be instructive. But also consider this:

- Half the population is female, but 0 of 8 House Members are female.

- 31% of the population is African-American; currently 2 of 8 House Members are African-American.

- 30% of voters are registered as Republican, but only 1 of 8 House Members is a Republican.

- The mostly white, mostly Democratic voters of Maryland elected a black Republican Lieutenant Governor in 2002 and voted twice for an African-American for President. So race and party affiliation are important and instructive but not determinative.

Considering only race as a predictor of election results, the chart shows that a black candidate would be expected to win CD 6, and black candidates would at least be competitive in CD 4 and CD 5.

Republicans versus Democrats in North Carolina

Again, though we cannot predict how people will vote in future elections, we can gain some limited insight by examining how they have voted in the past. This chart shows the number of votes for Democrats and for Republicans in the last two general elections for the House of representatives in each of the proposed CDs. In the national vote for Congress, 2016 favored Republicans, and 2018 was a Democratic wave. So putting the two together might be a fair representation.

In constructing this chart, I used a list of voting results by county. If only a portion of a county is included in a CD, I used the percent of the county that is in the proposed CD.

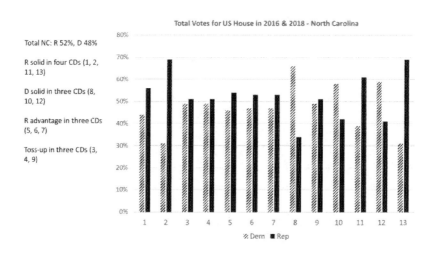

North Carolina Votes for House in 2016 & 2018

52% of NC votes cast in these two elections were for R candidates, while 48% were for D's. With these proposed CDs, R's would have a solid majority in four CDs (CDs 1, 2, 11, and 13), Dems in three (CDs 8, 10, and 12), advantage to R's in three more (CDs 5, 6, and 7), and three would be toss-ups (CDs 3, 4, and 9).

Reference and Scan Lines for drawing CD 1 in Several Other States

Here are a few more sample states, showing the initial Reference Line and Scan Line, used for drawing CD 1 in each state:

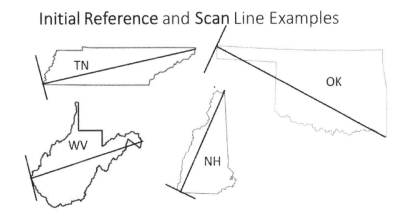

Redistricting Process Details

I recognize that cartography (map-making) is not everyone's cup of tea. Many readers may find this subject confusing or tedious or both. For that reason, I have placed the detailed explanations of the process in appendices:

- Appendix 2. Maryland Redistricting
- Appendix 3. Pennsylvania Redistricting

- Appendix 4. North Carolina Redistricting
- Appendix 5. The Rules in Excruciating Detail

Conclusion and next steps

When it comes to re-drawing legislative boundaries, gerrymandering is a significant impediment to our "Forming a More Perfect Union". Until now, the technical challenge is that the process itself has been tedious and complicated. The political challenge is that those who stand to benefit from the results of the process have overseen the process.

Gerrymandering can be solved if we simply decide to do it, and it's not all that hard to accomplish. It only becomes hard when we take into consideration factors other than population and geographic proximity. If we implement redistricting based solely on these two factors, we can pretty well lick the gerrymandering problem in one reapportionment cycle. Furthermore, if we adopt this rule-based solution, we can automate it.

Finally, let me again stipulate that this solution is less than perfect. But it's much better than the disparate systems now in place in every state, much better than manipulating CD boundaries for any political purpose, and easier to implement nationally than the other solutions currently on the table.

Multi-Seat CDs Combined with Ranked Choice Voting

This solution by itself does not eliminate gerrymandering. Rather, this solution makes gerrymandering less important.

Multi-Seat Congressional Districts

In Part I, we mentioned that from time to time some states have had multi-seat CDs. States sometimes created multi-seat CDs as a tool in partisan redistricting and as a method for disenfranchising black voters. This worked as follows: A single-seat CD has a majority black population, let's say 2/3 black. Two adjacent CDs have majority white populations, let's say 2/3 white. All three CDs together have a majority white population, about 56%. Therefore, in the traditional voting scheme, where voters select three candidates to fill three seats, three whites are likely to win.

A 1965 civil rights era law ended multi-seat CDs, but that occurred before Ranked Choice Voting was on the table. Let's apply RCV and multi-seat CDs to the question of CD boundaries and the problem of gerrymandering.

In this paper, we first describe how to construct the House of Representatives with as many three-seat CDs as possible. Second, we describe an adaptation of Ranked Choice Voting that will give the minority party in each three-seat CD a clear opportunity to win one seat and even a shot at winning two.

We should require states with fewer than four seats in the House to elect all their representatives at-large. At present seven states have only one House seat, so these seven are already elected at-large. Eight states currently have two or three House seats. Hence, with this new rule, fifteen states are removed from the Congressional gerrymandering challenge. And eleven additional states have 4, 5, or 6 seats, so these states would have two CDs and would only need to draw one congressional district boundary between them.

With the mandated three seats per CD, the number of 3-seat CDs in any state is given by the formula N = INT(Seats/3), where N is the number of 3-seat CDs and Seats is the number of seats apportioned to a state. If Seats is not evenly divisible by 3, then that state will have one CD with either one or two seats. This will always be the highest numbered seat. So, for example, Maryland's eight seats will be distributed as follows: CD 1 and CD 2 will each contain 3 seats, and CD 3 will contain 2 seats. Here is a table of the CDs in all 50 states, based on the apportionment of House seats following the 2010 Census.

In this table, note these column definitions:

- Sts: # of house seats apportioned to each state following the 2010 census.
- 3-St CD's: # of CD's that elect 3 members, viz., INT(Seats/3).
- 2-St CD: x indicates this state has a 2-Seat CD, to wit: If Seats modulo 3 = 2, then this state has a 2-Seat CD.
- 1-St CD: x indicates this state has a 1-Seat CD, to wit: If Seats modulo 3 = 1, then this state has a 1-Seat CD.
- All At-Large: x indicates this state has 3 or fewer seats, so all seats are in one CD.

Apportionment Populations 2010 and number of CDs with 3 seats per CD							
State	Pop	Pop per Seat	Sts	3-St CDs	2-St CD	1-St CD	All At-Large
Alabama	4,802,982	686,140	7	2		x	
Alaska	721,523	721,523	1	0		x	x
Arizona	6,412,700	712,522	9	3			
Arkansas	2,926,229	731,557	4	1		x	
California	37,341,989	704,566	53	17	x		

State						
Colorado	5,044,930	720,704	7	2		x
Connecticut	3,581,628	716,326	5	1	x	
Delaware	900,877	900,877	1	0		x	x
Florida	18,900,773	700,029	27	9		
Georgia	9,727,566	694,826	14	4	x	
Hawaii	1,366,862	683,431	2	0	x	x
Idaho	1,573,499	786,750	2	0	x	x
Illinois	12,864,380	714,688	18	6		
Indiana	6,501,582	722,398	9	3		
Iowa	3,053,787	763,447	4	1	x	
Kansas	2,863,813	715,953	4	1	x	
Kentucky	4,350,606	725,101	6	2		
Louisiana	4,553,962	758,994	6	2		
Maine	1,333,074	666,537	2	0	x	x
Maryland	5,789,929	723,741	8	2	x	
Massachusetts	6,559,644	728,849	9	3		
Michigan	9,911,626	707,973	14	4	x	
Minnesota	5,314,879	664,360	8	2	x	
Mississippi	2,978,240	744,560	4	1	x	
Missouri	6,011,478	751,435	8	2	x	
Montana	994,416	994,416	1	0		x	x
Nebraska	1,831,825	610,608	3	1		x
Nevada	2,709,432	677,358	4	1	x	
New Hampshire	1,321,445	660,723	2	0	x	x
New Jersey	8,807,501	733,958	12	4		
New Mexico	2,067,273	689,091	3	1		x
New York	19,421,055	719,298	27	9		
North Carolina	9,565,781	735,829	13	4	x	
North Dakota	675,905	675,905	1	0		x	x
Ohio	11,568,495	723,031	16	5	x	
Oklahoma	3,764,882	752,976	5	1	x	
Oregon	3,848,606	769,721	5	1	x	
Pennsylvania	12,734,905	707,495	18	6		
Rhode Island	1,055,247	527,624	2	0	x	x
South Carolina	4,645,975	663,711	7	2	x	
South Dakota	819,761	819,761	1	0		x	x
Tennessee	6,375,431	708,381	9	3		
Texas	25,268,418	701,901	36	12		
Utah	2,770,765	692,691	4	1	x	
Vermont	630,337	630,337	1	0		x	x

Virginia	8,037,736	730,703	11	3	x		
Washington	6,753,369	675,337	10	3		x	
West Virginia	1,859,815	619,938	3	1			x
Wisconsin	5,698,230	712,279	8	2	x		
Wyoming	568,300	568,300	1	0		x	x
TOTAL[1]	309,183,463	710,767	435	145	16	19	15

Sample CDs

Applying this redistricting solution to two sample states, Louisiana and Minnesota, here are the resulting CDs. In each case, the CD boundaries are drawn by using the "Redistricting without Gerrymanders" solution recommended herein.

Louisiana (6 seats, hence 2 CDs of 3 seats each)

Louisiana's completed CDs, based on 3-seat CDs. For the details, see Appendix 6:

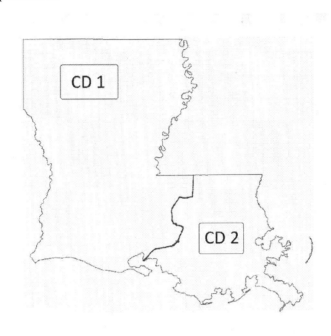

Minnesota (8 seats, hence 2 CDs of 3 seats each plus one CD with 2 seats)

Minnesota's completed CDs, based on 3-seat CDs. For the details, see Appendix 7:

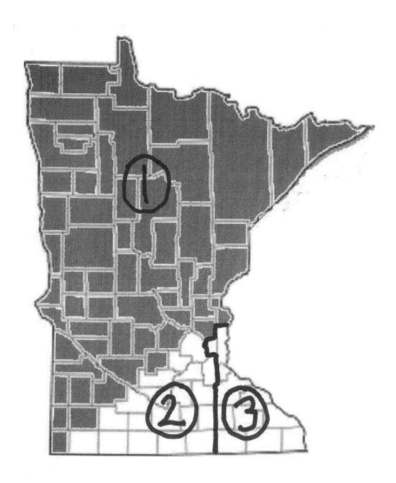

Ranked Choice Voting in Multi-Seat Congressional Districts

The basic idea here is two-fold:[16]

1. Ranked Choice Voting (RCV) increases the probability that, in any election with multiple winners, opinions held by a significant portion of the electorate will be represented by at least some of the winners.
2. With RCV, we can expect that multi-seat Congressional Districts will result in a majority of winners who represent the majority view of a CD, but some winners will also represent a widely-held minority view.

The voting and counting procedure proposed for multi-seat Congressional Districts is the same as the procedure for multi-seat Senate races. To wit:

VOTING in all primary and general elections: Voters select a 1st, a 2nd, and a 3rd choice.

COUNTING of ballots:

- Elections in single-seat CDs: Follow the rules for open primaries described above in the section "Counting of ballots in primary elections for Congress". For the general election, follow the normal RCV rules for an election with one winner.

---

[16] Appendix 1 summarizes all the RCV procedures and variations recommended in this book.

- Elections in two-seat and three-seat CDs: Calculate the weighted vote for each candidate, which equals 3 X the candidate's 1st choice votes + 2 X the 2nd choice votes + the 3rd choice votes. Rank order the results.

This is the table of successful primary and general election candidates for all House contests:

Number of House seats	Voters select	Counting process	Primary winners	General winners
1	1st, 2nd, and 3rd choices	RCV for one seat	Last 3, or 3 > 25%	1 > 50%
2	1st, 2nd, and 3rd choices	Weighted voting	Top 4	Top 2
3	1st, 2nd, and 3rd choices	Weighted voting	Top 5	Top 3

Political Impact

To see how multi-seat CDs with Ranked Choice Voting might affect the political makeup of Congress, let's examine the expected results in three-seat and in two-seat CDs dominated by one political party.

Three-Seat Congressional Districts

The scheme outlined here, based on the 2010 census and apportionment, would result in 145 three-seat Congressional Districts. Based on county voting patterns of the recent past, we can expect that many of these three-seat CDs would be dominated by either Republicans or Democrats. So what would be the result? Given that RCV systems tend to favor candidates who appeal to all sides and also give an opportunity for independents and third parties, the results surmised here may not obtain for even one election cycle much less for a decade. Nevertheless, we might try to guesstimate the result.

Given two major parties, Party A and Party B, if Party A has 55% of the voters and Party B has 45%, in most elections we can expect Party A to end up with two seats, and Party B to win one seat. Here is the logic, using plausible suppositions. To keep this simple, let's assume that there are exactly 100 voters.

Each party fields three (or more) candidates for the three available seats. Each party has one very strong candidate, along with two less strong candidates. So the candidates are designated as A1, A2, and A3 from Party A, and B1, B2, and B3 from Party B. Let's also assume that Party A's voters select A1 as their 1st choice, A2 as their 2nd choice, and A3 as their 3rd choice. Similarly, Party B's voters select B1, B2, and B3, in that order.

Applying the RCV procedure for tabulating votes in a three-winner election, we can expect the winners to be candidates A1 (165 weighted total vote), B1 (135), and A2 (110). Here is the table of voting results:

Candidate	Three-seat CD			Weighted Total
	Votes			
	1st	2nd	3rd	
A1	55			165
A2		55		110
A3			55	55

B1	45			135
B2		45		90
B3			45	45

Two-Seat Congressional Districts

Given the same 55% to 45% advantage for Party A over Party B, in a two-seat contest we can expect each party to win one seat. The voting for two positions proceeds exactly the same as the voting for three positions, and the winners are candidates A1 and B1.

Conclusions

We can derive several conclusions from this analysis: 1) We are likely to end up with better representation of voters' views using RCV and multi-seat CDs, and 2) candidates of both Party A and Party B will increase their chances of winning if they appeal to voters of both parties. This tendency will be even more pronounced if we also adopt single, open primaries for all offices. The result will almost inevitably be a Congress that is less partisan, less extreme at both ends of the political spectrum, and more interested in catering to the needs of all voters in their districts.

The advantages of RCV combined with multi-seat districts also accrue to states that adopt these reforms for their state legislatures.

Challenge 4. Other Election System Fixes

Fixes Previously Addressed

Several of the challenges and fixes in this volume overlap, and several fixes have already been discussed, so we will not belabor those details again. These include

- Manner of choosing the President,
- Ranked Choice Voting (RCV),
- Three rounds of Presidential primaries,
- A Vice Presidential primary and general election separate from the election for President,
- Replacement of the position of Vice President of the United States with Chancellor of the Senate,
- Reconstitution of the US Senate as a representative body,
- Redistricting through a rule-based process with no human decision-making, and
- Multi-seat Congressional Districts along with RCV.

Some items remain to be discussed in this chapter, including

- A compressed election season schedule
- Voting rights, voting registration, and election procedures
- Campaign finance reform
- Candidates and elected officials: Financial disclosures, transparency, and nepotism

2 Compressed Election Season Schedule

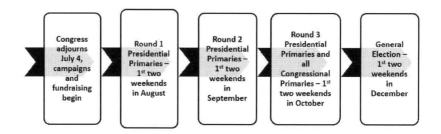

We observed earlier that the Presidential election season is too long. The same can be said for the hundreds of House and Senate campaigns.

So let's do something about this. Let's force politicians to restrict their campaigning to a limited and designated time period before each election, which might accomplish two things: 1) We will not need to endure incessant TV ads (with the same repetitive sound bites and talking points *ad nauseam*) and campaign signs and literature and robocalls and solicitations for money 24/7 as we are today, leaving us perchance the opportunity to become excited about politics and a particular campaign when the designated time for campaigning rolls around; and 2) Maybe, just maybe, if politicians do not need to spend all of their time raising money and campaigning, perhaps they will find time to actually tend to the people's business, and if they did that, then maybe, just maybe, their collective job approval rating would move somewhere north of abysmal.

But how, I hear you ask, can we make this happen?

First, consider how our British cousins do it. They do not tolerate incessant political campaigns. In 2015, the election season began with the dissolution of Parliament on March 30, and elections took place six weeks later, on May 7. Our British cousins crammed all of the campaigning into those six weeks. Every day, a spokesperson for each major party held a press conference to discuss their party's platform, while all the Members of Parliament and candidates were out on the hustings, and every party and political organization ran a zillion ads. Meanwhile, no one was failing to do their day job, because Parliament had been dissolved and was not in session. When the election was over, the leader of the winning party asked Her Majesty for leave to form a new Government. The Queen accepted the new Prime Minister, who moved into #10 Downing Street the same day, and the new Parliament convened before the end of May. I probably got a few of the details wrong here, but you pretty much get the picture. The campaign was brief but intense, and when it was over, it was over.

So how can we accomplish a similar result, but based on our American political system?

Here is a simple consolidated proposal for conducting all national elections. Each election takes place over a nine-day period including two weekends:

- July 4 of even-numbered years: Congress adjourns *sine die*; candidate campaign fundraising may begin; candidate campaigning for all federal offices begins
- First Saturday through second Sunday in August: Round 1 Presidential primaries
- First Saturday through second Sunday in September: Round 2 Presidential primaries

- First Saturday through second Sunday in October: National Primary, consisting of Round 3 Presidential primaries, Vice Presidential or Chancellor primary, and all Congressional primaries
- First Saturday through second Sunday in December: General Election

Implementing this abbreviated election season requires some national legislation, but even more importantly, it requires a cultural shift. People must recognize the value in overhauling our current perpetual campaigning practices, and citizens will have to demand a shortened campaign season.

Some currently elected officials will oppose this change because change is always fraught with uncertainty. The current officials know how the current system works, and even if they do not like perpetual campaigning and fundraising, they have mastered the art and they know that it keeps them in office. However, one can hope that enough of them will see the advantage to the public in adopting these changes and perhaps also political advantage to themselves in becoming reform advocates.

Because of the free speech clause of the First Amendment, we cannot stop politicians from campaigning outside the "official" campaign season, which will begin on Independence Day. However, news media can refuse to cover campaign events and can also point out that those conducting such events are violating the spirit of the rule that the public insisted on. Finally, the voters can punish such violators at the polls. The shortened campaign season may take some time to really sink in, but voters are bound to prefer it over the existing interminable cacophony.

We really should consider giving an abbreviated and fixed election timetable a chance. If nothing else, it would at least help all of us become less apathetic and more involved the first couple times we did it.

Voting Rights

Let Everyone Vote!

From South Africa to Nigeria to Egypt, universal suffrage swept across the African continent in the latter half of the 20th century and became a hallmark of the post-Colonial landscape. Americans watched their televisions with fascination as urbanites and villagers alike waited in long lines to be able to vote for the first time.

Yet in our own country, many citizens still struggle to secure their right to vote. Many citizens, discouraged at their perceived lack of political power, fail to try to vote at all.

The preface to this work laid out what needs to be our underlying principle: Democracy works best if all participate. If we wish to build and maintain a vibrant democracy, we must work diligently to make universal suffrage in America a reality rather than merely an idealistic but unachievable dream, or, what's worse, a principle to which we give lip service but do not really wish to achieve.

Some of the improvements that voting rights proponents need to champion include:

- The Constitution should guarantee that all citizens have the right to vote as soon as they reach their 18th birthday. This is a fundamental right that should not be left to the discretion of each state.
- We should consider the notion of compulsory voting. After all, this is the practice in Australia, a country known for its uncompromising protection of individual rights.
- Automatic registration of all citizens upon their 18th birthday should become our normal practice. What plausible argument can be offered in opposition to this idea? Potential voter fraud is not credible: few 18-year-olds are credible fraudsters.
- Automatic voter registration when a citizen interacts with government for any reason should also become normal practice: filing taxes, filing for Medicaid or welfare, recording a real estate transaction, enrolling at a public school or college, as well as showing up to vote. Again, why not?
- Weekend voting: polls should open on Saturday and Sunday rather than a weekday. The argument for voting only on the first Tuesday in November was based on an agricultural society, in which farmers needed to buy and

sell at the farmers' markets on Saturday, attend church on Sunday, then perhaps travel by horse and buggy on Monday to reach the polling place (usually the county seat) on Tuesday, and return home later Tuesday to again participate in the markets on Wednesday. That argument no longer obtains. Today, most Americans work Monday through Friday, so the time to vote ought to be on Saturday and Sunday when relatively fewer citizens must be at work. In fact, the preferred option is to combine early voting and weekend voting, so that in-person voting in all elections occurs over a nine-day period, including two weekends, and ending on a Sunday.

- Voters need convenient polling places and extended hours of operation. Again, why not?
- Absentee ballots must be available to all voters without giving a reason. Vote counters must accept and count all absentee ballots received before the beginning of in-person voting. Again, we should make voter participation as convenient as possible.

Various organizations are involved in efforts to bring about these reforms, including the League of Women Voters (http://lwv.org/issues/protecting-voters), Common Cause (http://www.commoncause.org/issues/voting-and-elections/), and Fair Vote (http://www.fairvote.org/).

One recommendation deserves special consideration, namely, universal automatic voter registration along with a national, permanent Voter-ID, issued through a National Voter Registration Authority. Americans have long resisted any form of national identification card, and this idea smacks of a national ID card. You might recall the vigorous debate concerning the growing use of the Social Security Number as an ID number by various entities, both public and private. That debate ended with federal legislation forbidding the use of SSNs for anything other than paying taxes and tax-related transactions. States, for example, could no longer use the SSN on drivers licenses, and the Feds quit using the SSN as a Medicare ID. Congress was responding to the public's perception that the ever-expanding use of a person's SSN reflected Big Government intruding on our personal privacy.

Fast forward 20 years, and the problem today is that the public does not yet recognize that personal privacy in any sphere is largely a thing of the past. When a terrorist bomb explodes in an urban area, police have video surveillance of nearly every person and nearly every square foot of the impacted area for the hours before the attack, and law enforcement has this information very quickly after the attack occurs. When you pass through a toll booth on the highway, a camera captures your license plate and a snapshot of the driver. Google knows of your travels through the GPS in your vehicle, Apple knows where you've been and who you've been talking to through your use of your iPhone, Bank of America knows your every use of an ATM, Amazon knows what you like to buy and when and to whom you ship it, and every retailer who accepts a credit/debit card knows what you purchased and when you were in the store, Websites track your visits, and your Internet Service Provider knows all the places you go on the Web. This is only the beginning of the list of large data collection agents who have built and continue to amass an amazingly extensive record of your life. Furthermore, these data can be subpoenaed by a court, and the private entities who have collected the data can be required to reveal it. All this is occurring even before we consider what the federal government is collecting directly or inadvertently, from NSA or FBI captures of telephone or Internet traffic to background checks for getting a government job or obtaining a security clearance or qualifying for a government-insured loan. It really is high time that the public realize that having a national Voter ID does not compromise your privacy – you've lost that a long time ago through disparate aspects of modern life. Please believe me about this – I have been involved in the cybersecurity world for many years, and I can testify that this list is only the beginning of the information about you that is readily available to the government in cyberspace. The very last thing you need to worry about with respect to your privacy is the potential loss of that privacy through a national voter database.

So what are the Pros and Cons of having a national Voter-ID? First, we should mention that Congress could and should restrict its use only for voting. Just like the SSN, we should not start using your Voter ID as your universal identification every time you want to borrow a book from the library. So, the Pros are as follows:1) we can expand the voter rolls to include every single American citizen upon reaching age 18 or upon interacting with government at any level at any time or when proactively registering to vote; 2) we can eliminate duplicate registrations for the same person in multiple jurisdictions, because as soon as your eligibility in a new location is recorded, your eligibility in the former location will be automatically canceled; 3) the same system which automatically registers new voters will also purge voters who have died; 4) as a result, voter fraud, already a minuscule problem as every serious study of this subject has demonstrated, will practically cease to exist; and 5) states can save all the money currently spent on voter fraud investigations and on maintaining and purging voter rolls. The Cons of the national voter database are that, like any database, it could be hacked and/or abused. In the grand scheme of things, this risk is minimal. The Pros vastly outweigh the Cons.

Campaign Finance Reform

Congress outlawed campaign contributions from corporations and passed restrictions on unlimited contributions to political parties, political campaigns, and individual candidates, as well as rules requiring public disclosure of people and organizations making such contributions. The core legislation is called the McCain-Feingold law, after its principal sponsors, Senators Russ Feingold (D-Wisconsin) and John McCain (R-Arizona). In the *Citizens United v. Federal Elections Commission* case, the Supreme Court threw out many of the significant provisions of the McCain-Feingold law, especially the provisions dealing with corporate contributions and with disclosure.

While Americans hold their First Amendment rights very dear, we need also to protect our democracy from domination by Big Money. For this reason, we must overturn *Citizens United* -- either by legislation that passes constitutional muster or by new justices on the Supreme Court or by a constitutional amendment. Public financing of all federal election campaigns could also do the trick and, whatever the cost, would be a small price to pay for a Congress that could not be bought and sold.

So, in sum, campaign finance reform has these components:

- Limits on who can contribute to political campaigns,
- Limits on when campaign contributions can be made,
- Limits on the amounts that can be contributed to one campaign, to one party, or in one election cycle,
- Limits on candidates soliciting campaign contributions,
- Disclosure of all campaign contributions, and
- Public financing of political campaigns.

Several grassroots organizations are working on this problem, including Wolf-PAC (http://www.wolf-pac.com/), EveryVoice.org (http://everyvoice.org/), End Citizens United (http://endcitizensunited.org/), Common Cause (http://www.commoncause.org/issues/money-in-politics/), League of Women Voters (https://www.lwv.org/voting-rights/money-politics), MoveToAmend.org (https://movetoamend.org/), and MAYDAY.US (https://mayday.us/). Follow the links to these organizations and their campaigns to find out more, join, volunteer, and contribute.

Advocates for campaign finance reform have already written a ton about the need to reduce the influence of money on politics and on political campaigns, and I have nothing new to contribute to this debate. I'll only say that I believe strongly in this cause, and I contribute to each of these grassroots organizations.

Candidates and Elected Officials: Financial Disclosures, Transparency, and Nepotism

We must demand that all candidates for federal office from President on down, as a condition for appearing on a general election ballot, release their personal tax forms and disclose their personal finances, including assets, income, transactions, and liabilities as well as details concerning creditors, investors, and customers. We must require all federal elected officials to continue to do this annually. We must also forbid elected officials from nominating or appointing members of their immediate family to any post in the Government.

Summary of Electoral Fixes by Method of Realization

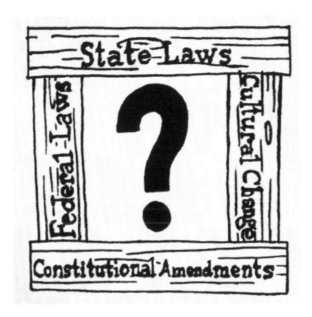

This paper has presented quite a few fixes to the way we choose our federal office-holders. We can achieve some of these fixes through new or amended state or federal statutes, while others require a constitutional amendment. For many of these fixes to really take hold, we need a cultural shift. Here is a summary of the suggested improvements broken down into these four categories: state law, federal law, constitutional amendment, and cultural change. This discussion does not repeat the thrust of the arguments in favor of each reform but rather presents the possibility of achieving the reform through each method of realization.

Fixes Through State Laws

We can implement some fixes through state laws, but such laws would be effective only if all or most of the states passed those laws. Gerrymandering is a good example. In some states a grassroots citizens' movement has fought to remove politics from Congressional redistricting. But the politicians in each state's majority party ask,

> Why should we unilaterally disarm? If we get rid of gerrymandering in our state, the minority party in our state will gain more members in Congress. But I do not see their party getting rid of gerrymandering in the states their party controls – so the result would be that our party loses. Sure, we favor reforming the system but only if everyone does it together.

This then becomes an argument for the status quo.

One solution to this conundrum could be a compact among states, all agreeing to adopt the same reform when other states agree to do likewise. Of course, this type of solution only works if the argument about "unilateral disarmament" is the real objection to reform and not just an obstructionist tactic. To improve its chances of success, groups of states could adopt it. For example, Maryland State Senator Jamie Raskin introduced legislation to eliminate gerrymandering simultaneously in Maryland and

Virginia.[17] The two states are good candidates for this type of deal because they are mirror images of each other politically. Maryland, with a Republican governor but Democratic legislature, is heavily gerrymandered to favor Democrats, resulting in 7 Democrats and only 1 Republican in Congress. Virginia is the opposite: With a Democratic governor but Republican state legislature, the state is heavily gerrymandered to favor Republicans, who hold an 8-3 majority in Congress. If both states drew district boundaries without partisan considerations, the expected results in each state would more fairly represent their electorates, but the total number of Congresspersons from each party would probably remain about the same. Repubs might pick up 2 seats in Maryland; Dems would do likewise in Virginia.

Reformers might be able to identify similar groupings of states all across the country.

Like all solutions implemented by state statute, what lawmakers enact today they can repeal tomorrow. So one approach, that of amending state constitutions, is a considerable improvement over a simple state statute.

Manner of choosing the President

Local-State-National Interstate Compact (LSNIC): States could pass laws binding themselves to cast all their electoral votes for the winner of the election according to the LSN vote counting

---

[17] http://www.baltimoresun.com/news/maryland/politics/blog/bal-senator-proposes-twostate-solution-on-redistricting-reform-20160209-story.html. [Accessed July 25, 2017.]

scheme. These state laws would become effective as soon as enough states pass it so as to constitute a majority of all electoral votes.

Ranked Choice Voting:

In the 2016 election, Maine became the first state to adopt Ranked Choice Voting for most of its elections. The good folks at FairVote.org believe that this Maine victory may be a harbinger of the future and that more states and other jurisdictions around the country will also begin to adopt RCV.

Although Congress can and should mandate RCV for elections to federal offices, states are responsible for elections for their own Governors, other state-wide offices, and state legislatures. Therefore, every state should adopt Ranked Choice Voting for all the elections it controls. This should include the state's elections for federal offices if Congress fails to act.

Solutions to gerrymandering for state legislatures as well as Congress

While the best solution to the gerrymander challenge is a Federal law mandating a uniform rule-based process without human decision making for all states, individual states can adopt that same process until Congress acts.

The same redistricting plan proposed for Congress might offer the best option for solving the gerrymandering challenge for state legislatures. In some states, certain ZCTA's might be home to too many people for state legislative districts, representing much smaller populations than Congressional Districts. In such cases, the same Scan Line used for the counties and for ZCTA's within

LAST County can also be used to partition LAST ZCTA into the Census Bureau's census tracts, which contain ~4000 people each.

If a state finds the fully mechanical solution infeasible for some reason, it could still adopt a non-partisan redistricting commission, assisted by appropriate technology, and charged only with drawing election districts based on geographic proximity, roughly equal populations, and no other considerations.

Automatic voter registration

While the best solution in this matter might be a federal statute or constitutional amendment, individual states can achieve this for their own citizens. States could automatically register voters when they reach their 18th birthday (most of them are in school and therefore a captive audience, making this easy enough to implement). States can also verify a citizen's voter registration status and then automatically register them if necessary whenever the citizen interacts with state or local government in any way – getting a driver's license, purchasing and registering a vehicle or a boat, engaging in any real estate transaction, paying taxes, registering for a public college, applying for welfare or unemployment compensation or Medicaid, perhaps even paying for a parking ticket.

Just as an aside, high schools should require every high school student to "vote" in a mock election, using the same ballot that their parents are using in the real election and at the same time. This will help our young people get into the habit of voting.

Convenient voting procedures

Every state can adopt welcoming rather than restrictive voting rules: absentee ballots available to all citizens without needing to give a reason; absentee ballots accepted if received before in-person voting starts (with no excuse needed) and up through the last election day (with an excuse for voting late); early in-person voting to include at least one weekend; adequate polling stations, voting machines, and voting hours. For reasons of election security, a paper ballot should be required in all elections everywhere.

Fixes Through Federal Laws

For our national fixes to be most effective, we must adopt them nationally – which means either a federal statute or an amendment to the US Constitution. However, federal statutes sometimes run afoul of the Constitution itself. The Constitution contains two provisions which often appear in conflict with each other:

- Article I Section 8 lists the powers of Congress, and then contains this final power: "To make all Laws which shall be necessary and proper for carrying into Execution the foregoing Powers, and all other Powers vested by this Constitution in the Government of the United States, or in any Department or Officer thereof."
- Amendment 10 states, "The powers not delegated to the United States by the Constitution, nor prohibited by it to the states, are reserved to the states respectively, or to the people."

In practice, when Congress proposes a law concerning an issue not expressly within Congress's authority, proponents argue that

Congress's power to act on this issue is implied by its express powers. Those who oppose the law disagree, contending that the 10th Amendment supersedes, so the issue must be left to the states or the people. In some cases Congress goes ahead and passes the proposed law. Then someone files suit against it, claiming that the law violates the 10th Amendment. Sometimes the Supreme Court agrees with the opponents and determines that the law is unconstitutional, while in other instances the Court allows the law to stand.

Thus the question of constitutional limits on Congress's power is clearly an issue concerning many of the fixes suggested in this volume. For example, concerning the time when elections take place, Article I Section 4 states, "The Times, Places and Manner of holding Elections for Senators and Representatives, shall be prescribed in each state by the Legislature thereof; but the Congress may at any time by Law make or alter such Regulations". Originally, every state selected the date of the general election as it saw fit, but in 1845 a federal statute fixed the date of the general election as the first Tuesday after the first Monday in November. So Congress clearly has the authority to fix the date of the general election for Congress. But what about the general election for the electoral college? And what about primaries? When the Constitution was written, primary elections did not exist. Some might argue that Congress's authority to set the date of the general election for Congress implies that it has the authority to also set the dates of primaries. Actually, the Constitution does not distinguish between primary and general elections – it just refers to "elections".

One solution to the question of federal versus state authority has had some success over the years and could be used as a model for wider application. This solution is the use of block grants in which

Congress allocates sums of money to individual states, based on the varying needs of each state. Each state then has the authority to spend the block grant funds as it sees fit within the broad parameters of the purposes of the block grant. Congress has used block grants for education assistance programs (clearly a state matter), healthcare (Medicaid, administered by the states), emergency relief from natural disasters, and infrastructure projects. The federal government can sometimes smooth out differences between the states based on the relative wealth of each state, while in other cases state needs differ widely. Landlocked states do not need money for ports, for example, while other states never suffer earthquakes. In all these cases, governmental assistance may be necessary to give each citizen the right to "life, liberty, and the pursuit of happiness", but the Feds are not always the best source for that assistance.

Ranked Choice Voting

The Constitution explicitly gives Congress the power to fix the "manner of elections" for Senators and Representatives; and implicitly, Congress probably also has the power to fix the "manner of elections" for President and Vice President. While state laws can implement RCV on a state-by-state basis, it would be far preferable, quicker, and more effective for Congress to mandate RCV in all federal elections.

Three rounds of Presidential primaries

Because Congress can fix the "manner of elections" for Senators and Representatives, Congress can certainly fix both primary and general election dates for members of Congress. We can debate whether or not Congress has the constitutional authority to mandate primary election dates for President. If Congress adopts a national Presidential primary system, the Supreme Court might rule it unconstitutional. Were that to happen, then we would need a constitutional amendment to get to a national Presidential primary – but we're not there yet, so a federal law instituting a national Presidential primary system is certainly worth a try.

Vice Presidential primary and general election separate from the election for President

The original Constitution says very little about the election for Vice President, and nothing at all about primary elections for any office. (The only mention of primary elections in the Amendments is in Amendment 24, which barred the poll tax.) Therefore, as in the case of three rounds of Presidential primaries, the question is whether Congress has authority to legislate on the topic of the Vice Presidential primary and general election. Again, it's worth a try – and if Congress were to establish a primary election for Vice President and separate voting in the general election for President and for Vice President, and if the courts then ruled that this law is unconstitutional, then we would need to pass a constitutional amendment to make it happen. But again, we could give it a go, and see whether such a law will be upheld.

Multi-seat Congressional Districts

Congress should not just repeal the 1965 law that prevented multi-seat CDs; rather, Congress should mandate multi-seat CDs combined with Ranked Choice Voting. As in many electoral reforms, a constitutional amendment might be an even better approach. But also like many suggested electoral reforms, we might learn from the experience of having multi-seat CDs, and then conclude that that solution produces results as unsatisfactory as the system we have now. In that event, having a federal statute that Congress can modify might be preferable to having a constitutional amendment that is far more difficult to modify.

Congressional Redistricting Solution

The comments about multi-seat CDs also apply here. Congress can mandate this; a constitutional amendment can solve it more permanently; but if the fix does not work well or leads to other challenges, a federal statute is easier to replace than a constitutional amendment. Perhaps the best approach would be to adopt a federal statute first, try it out for a few election cycles, and then initiate a constitutional amendment when we have determined that this is a good permanent solution.

A compressed election season schedule

Congress can fix the dates of primary and general elections for members of Congress, and probably also for President and Vice President – after all, in 1845 Congress mandated the date of the general election for all federal offices as the first Tuesday after the first Monday in November. Congress can choose to adjourn whenever it pleases. Hence, Congress could eliminate the lame duck session of Congress and greatly shorten the transition period for the office of President.

Convenient voting procedures

The argument that Congress has the power to effectuate these reforms is based on the same constitutional provision as other congressional election reforms, namely, the first clause of Article I Section 4, giving Congress the power to determine the manner of holding elections for the Congress. If a federal law in this area is determined not to be constitutional, then a constitutional amendment giving Congress the power to establish such regulations might be in order.

Automatic, universal voter registration

Congress already has the authority to implement laws ensuring the voting rights of all citizens (Amendment 14), regardless of race (Amendment 15), religion (Amendment 1), sex (Amendment 19), or age (for anyone at least 18 years old) (Amendment 26). A federal law providing universal, automatic voter registration for all adult citizens would be a fine way to exercise that authority and would likely pass constitutional muster. Again, if not, then a constitutional amendment is the alternative.

Campaign finance reform

There are several parts to campaign finance reform, each amenable to different solutions:

- Concerning campaign contributions, Congress could try to pass new campaign finance reform laws, avoiding the elements that the Supreme Court found unconstitutional.
- The President, with the advice and consent of the Senate, could appoint new Supreme Court justices, who could overturn the *Citizens United* decision.
- Congress could legislate public financing of all federal political campaigns.

Candidates and elected officials: Financial disclosures, transparency, and nepotism

Congress could pass federal laws that require candidates and elected officials to disclose their tax returns and their assets and other financial interests. We already have laws preventing nepotism, but the President is exempt from that law; we should fix that; the President and Vice President should be subject to the same law as our legislators. However, it's unclear whether courts would consider such laws constitutional.

Fixes Through Constitutional Amendments

Some fixes require a constitutional amendment, an exceedingly high bar to pass.

Article V of the Constitution provides two methods for proposing amendments to the Constitution:

- Congress, by a two-thirds vote in both chambers, can propose an amendment. This is the only method that has been used so far.

- Two-thirds of the state legislatures can also request Congress to call for a constitutional convention for the purpose of proposing constitutional amendments. This method has not yet been used.

To become part of the Constitution, a proposed amendment must be ratified by three-fourths of the state legislatures or three-fourths of state conventions, whichever mode of ratification is specified by Congress.

Amending the Constitution is difficult. In the 230 years since the Constitutional Convention of 1787, we have only managed to adopt 27 amendments.

A constitutional amendment is a most desirable fix, precisely because it is so difficult to undo; but for exactly the same reason, it is also the most difficult to achieve.

Amending the Constitution

We need to replace the amendment process itself. Though this is not an election system fix *per se*, its adoption will greatly facilitate the other proposed constitutional changes, including an entirely rewritten constitution.

Manner of choosing the President

A constitutional amendment to adopt the Local-State-National Presidential voting scheme is much better than the Local-State-National Interstate Compact precisely because no state can undo it. An amendment would also eliminate the electoral college and the possibility of sending the Presidential election to the House of Representatives.

New Senate to replace the Original Senate

Even one or more constitutional amendments may not bring about this fix, but clearly the constitutional amendment route or a brand new Constitution are the only fixes available.

Replace the Vice President with the Chancellor of the Senate

The only way to effect this change is through a constitutional amendment. Of course this change could be combined with an amendment to reconstitute the Senate.

Apportion House seats based on voting rather than population

In counting the population of each state in order to apportion seats in the House of Representatives, Article I Section 2 of the 1787 Constitution counted 3/5 of all slaves, and did not count

Indians at all. The 1787 Constitution also specified the number of seats apportioned to each of the thirteen original states. A law passed in 1913 (when the US population stood at 92 million) set the total number of seats at the current 435. With a population of 330 million today, it might be advisable to revisit the total number of seats. Obviously, we should remove the enumeration of particular states from the Constitution. We should have an odd number of seats, which becomes apparent when reading the proposed scheme for electing the President.

Following each decennial census, we should apportion House seats among the several states based on the average number of votes cast in each state in the two most recent Presidential elections (rather than the population of each state, as at present). However, for drawing the boundaries between Congressional Districts within a state, we must still use population figures.

The idea of basing reapportionment, not on population, but rather on the number of people who voted, serves several purposes: 1) this provision encourages citizens to vote, because more voters means more Representatives in the House; 2) similarly, this provision encourages states to design election procedures that will maximize voter turnout, rather than intentionally discouraging certain kinds of voters from exercising their franchise; and 3) the numbers cannot be easily fudged, since the number of votes cast in every election are publicly announced and readily available. Also, the notion that the number of qualified voters (called "electors" in the 1787 Constitution) is a relevant factor in composing the House is adapted from the 1787 Constitution, Article I, Section 2, which states: "The House of Representatives shall be composed of Members chosen every second Year by the people of the several states, and the Electors in each state shall have the Qualifications requisite for Electors of the most numerous Branch of the state Legislature."

Candidates and elected officials: Financial disclosures, transparency, and nepotism

This amendment would require all federal general election nominees and all federal elected officials to disclose their tax returns, their income, assets, transactions, creditors, investors, customers, and liabilities. It would also prohibit federal elected officials from hiring, nominating, or appointing any immediate family member to any federal position.

Comprehensive constitutional amendment on electoral reform

For all the electoral reforms proposed in Part II, a single constitutional amendment might be best. The proposed amendment would cover both the principles and the procedures of all federal elections. For safety's sake, it should also give Congress the power to modify procedures that turned out not to work as intended.

Chances for adoption of this single constitutional amendment concerning elections will be greatly enhanced if we are able to first adopt the Amendment on Amendments.

The single amendment on elections (The Amendment on Elections below) will
- change the basis for reapportioning seats in the House;
- reconstitute the Senate as a representative body;
- replace the position of Vice President with the new position of Chancellor;
- require Ranked Choice Voting;

- require multi-seat Congressional Districts;
- institute a uniform and rule-based process for drawing Congressional District boundaries in every state based only on population and geography;
- establish the election schedule for all federal primary and general elections, including three rounds of Presidential and Chancellor primaries and one National Primary Day;
- require open primaries, with all candidates for a given office competing against each other in a single primary, without regard to political party;
- establish uniform, convenient voting procedures throughout the country;
- establish the rules by which candidates qualify for primary and general elections;
- establish the LSN voting scheme for determining the winners of the Presidential and Chancellor elections, while eliminating the electoral college;
- establish a National Voter Registration Authority to provide universal, automatic voter registration and a permanent Voter Identifier for every eligible citizen;
- remove political parties from all election laws and regulations;
- allow Congress to modify any election procedure which turns out to have been ill-advised.

Fixes Through Cultural Change

Many of the fixes proposed in this paper will only become useful improvements to our democracy when people believe in them and act accordingly. That will require a cultural change. Let me recite a few examples:

- Ranked Choice Voting only really works if voters mark their ballots with more than one choice for each office. Even if RCV is the legal voting procedure, if few voters vote for more than their 1st choice, then the candidate with a plurality after round 1 will always end up the winner as other candidates are progressively eliminated. So we will need a significant public education effort to encourage voters to understand their enhanced voting power. And then we will need the voters to actually use that power.
- We can establish an official season for electioneering that begins on July 4, but because of our First Amendment freedoms, candidates can say anything they want at any time. Therefore the public's recourse is to discourage media outlets from giving free coverage to political campaigning outside the approved season and to punish at the polls those candidates who violate the agreed-upon conventions.
- Many Americans have become apathetic about politics, disengaged from political discourse altogether. Compared to other Western democracies, America's voter participation is abysmal. A significant percentage of our fellow citizens have become completely disenchanted with Congress (which garners an 11% approval rating from the public), and we have turned away from the two major political parties: for twenty years, new voters are opting more and more to register as independents, if they even register to vote at all. The various fixes proposed in this paper could motivate uninvolved citizens to re-engage in the political process. When we empower people more than parties, when independents can participate in primaries, when every vote counts, when people see that

they can have more opportunities to contribute and more leverage to affect the outcome, then and only then can we entertain the hope that the new cultural norm will favor engagement over apathy.
- To encourage greater voter participation, every student in grades 9 through 12 in the country should vote in every election, using a sample or specimen ballot. The ballot itself can be the actual ballot for the precinct where the school is located. We should give awards to schools with the highest participation rates. In this way, every high school graduate will have participated in one Presidential and one mid-term election while in school.

Portrait of Future Congressional Elections

Putting this all together, here is a snapshot of future Congressional elections if all these proposals are adopted by the year 2021:

- We will have adopted Ranked Choice Voting (RCV) for Congressional elections along with multi-seat Congressional districts, specifying 3-seat CDs.

- After the 2020 Census is complete, apportionment of House seats will occur, based on the number of ballots cast in the two most recent Presidential elections.

- States with 3 or fewer seats will elect all House members at large. States with 4 or more House seats will create new CDs, using these rules:

- Each state will create as many 3-seat CDs as mathematically possible. When this is done, the number of seats left over will be 0, 1, or 2.

- If the number of seats left over is > 0, then the state will have either a 1-seat CD or a 2-seat CD. This CD will be the highest-numbered CD in the state.

- Next, redistricting will occur in every state that has more than 3 House seats. Each state will implement redistricting according to the rules for redistricting without human intervention described in this document, based only on the twin criteria of equalizing the population per House seat in each district and keeping neighbors together. States will publish their CD boundaries, which will remain in effect until the next decennial census.

- Primary Rules:

  - Any citizen can become a candidate for the House, according to the rules of that state.

  - All candidates will appear on the singular primary ballot. The ballot will indicate the party affiliation of each candidate.

  - All registered voters may vote in the primary.

  - RCV procedures apply to voting (that is, voters will rank order their selected candidates) and to the counting of ballots.

  - The number of successful candidates in the primary depends on the number of House seats in the CD: For one House seat, 3 candidates are successful; for two House seats, 4 candidates are successful; and for three House seats, 5 candidates are successful.

- General Election Rules:
    - The general election ballot will contain the names of only those candidates who were successful in the primary.
    - All registered voters may vote in the general election.
    - RCV procedures apply to voting (that is, voters will rank order their selected candidates by preference) and to the counting of ballots.

- Election Season Rules:
    - In even-numbered years, Congress adjourns *sine die* before Independence Day, and campaigning begins.
    - National Primary Election lasts for nine days, ending on the second Sunday in October.
    - General Election lasts for nine days, ending on the second Sunday in December.
    - New Congress convenes in January. (Note: No lame-duck session occurs.) (Note also: In a national emergency, the President may convene a special session of Congress.)

- Political Parties:
    - Political parties, like any benevolent association, at their own expense, may hold caucuses, conventions, polls, and elections. They may

endorse candidates, raise funds, articulate positions, advertise, and lobby.
- None of these activities have any legal standing or bearing on elections.

Single Constitutional Amendment Concerning Federal Elections

Here is a draft of a single constitutional amendment that addresses all the federal electoral reforms recommended in this volume.

Note that this amendment reconstitutes the U.S. Senate. Therefore we need to replace Article V with the Amendment on Amendments before considering the following Amendment on Elections. This amendment replaces the Vice President of the United States with the Chancellor of the Senate.

Amendment on Federal Elections

Section 1. Composition of the Legislature.

Article I Sections 1, 2, and 3 are repealed and replaced as specified in 1.1, 1.2, and 1.3 of this section of this amendment.

1.1 The Legislature

All legislative Powers herein granted shall be vested in a Congress of the United States, which shall consist of a lower chamber called the House of Representatives and an upper chamber called the Senate.

1.2 The House of Representatives

The House of Representatives shall be composed of 501 Members chosen every second year. Congress may modify the number of members by law.

Seats in the House of Representatives shall be apportioned among the states during the first year of each new decade, based on the average number of voters who voted in each state in the two most recent Presidential general elections: but each state shall have at least one Representative, and each Representative shall have one vote. If a new state is admitted to the Union, it shall have 1 seat in the House for every one million inhabitants, until the next reapportionment after it has voted in two Presidential elections.

When he/she takes office, a Member of the House of Representative must be

- At least 25 years old;

- At least 7 years a citizen of the United States;
- Less than 20 years a Member of the House of Representatives;[18] and
- A resident of the state from which he/she shall have been chosen.

When vacancies happen in the Representation from any State, the Executive Authority thereof shall issue Writs of Election to fill such Vacancies.

The House of Representatives shall choose their Speaker and other Officers; and shall have the sole Power of Impeachment. The Speaker, who may or may not be a Member, shall have no vote unless the House be equally divided.

1.3 The Senate

The Senate of the United States shall be composed of Senators from each state, chosen at large by the voters for a six-year term of office; and each Senator shall have one vote. The number of Senators from each state is one-fifth of the number of Representatives from that state, with fractions always rounded up, so that each state will have at least one Senator.[19]

---

[18] This provision implements term limits for the House. Ten 2-year terms is specified as the maximum amount of time a member may remain in the House.

[19] That is, a state with 1 to 5 House seats will have one Senator; a state with 6 to 10 House seats will have two Senators; a state with 11 to 15 House seats will have three Senators; and so on. This provision

Seats in the Senate shall be divided as equally as they may be into three classes (Class I, Class II, and Class III). For any state, the number of seats assigned to each Class shall be the same, as nearly as possible. One Class shall be elected every two years. Thus one-third of the total Senate, and one-third of the seats in the Senate from each state, shall be elected every two years.

When, due to the decennial Congressional reapportionment, the number of Senators for any state is decreased, the next Senator from that state whose term of office is expiring shall not be replaced after his term expires. When the number of Senators from any state is increased, a new Senator from that state shall be elected at the next election, and that seat will be assigned to Class 1, 2, or 3, so that, as far as possible, one third of the Senate remains elected every two years, and one third of the Senators from each state remains elected every two years.[20]

The first election cycle following reapportionment will include separate primary and general elections for all three Senate classes. This will include elections for 6-year terms for all the seats in the class normally scheduled for elections that year, as

---

mandates that every state shall have at least one Senator. This scheme still gives more power to states with small populations than is strictly justified based on population alone, but it is vastly fairer than the current scheme of two Senators per state regardless of population, and it is much easier to implement than a scheme based only on population, which would require election districts that cross state boundaries.

[20] This provision could result in the election of a Senator to a newly-created seat for a term of only two years or four years, that is, until such time as that seat's class next comes up for election.

well as elections for 4-year terms and for 2-year terms for those seats in the other two classes which do not have an incumbent.

When he/she takes office, a Senator must be

- At least 30 years old;
- At least 9 years a citizen of the United States;
- Less than 18 years a Senator;[21] and
- A resident of the state from which he/she shall have been chosen.

In accordance with Section 3 of this amendment, voters shall elect a Chancellor to a four-year term of office in even-numbered years not evenly divisible by four. The Chancellor shall preside over the Senate. The Chancellor shall have no vote unless the Senate be equally divided. The Chancellor shall appoint a Chancellor Pro Tempore, with the concurrence of a majority of Senators present and voting. The Chancellor Pro Tempore shall preside over the Senate in the absence of the Chancellor, or when the Chancellor shall exercise the office of President of the United States.

The Chancellor (but not the Chancellor Pro Tempore) shall have power to nominate, and by and with the advice and consent of the Senate, shall appoint Associate Justices of the Supreme Court, provided two thirds of the Senators present and voting concur; and he shall nominate, and by and with the advice and consent of

---

[21] This provision implements term limits for the Senate. Three 6-year terms is specified as the maximum amount of time a member may remain as a Senator.

a majority of Senators present and voting, shall appoint federal judges of inferior courts.

Any current or former federal judge is eligible to be nominated to serve as an Associate Justice of the Supreme Court. When the position of Chief Justice of the United States becomes vacant, the sitting Associate Justices shall select one of their own number as the next Chief Justice.[22] No one shall serve as a Supreme Court Justice for longer than 15 years; however, after 15 years on the Supreme Court, a Justice is entitled to continue serving as a federal judge on an inferior court.[23]

In all cases of Chancellor judicial nominations, if the Senate fails to approve or disapprove a nomination within 60 calendar days after the Chancellor has made the nomination, the Chancellor may appoint the nominee, and the nominee may temporarily assume the position to which he was nominated, pending Senate action on that nomination. However, the Chancellor may not make such a temporary appointment to the Supreme Court unless the Court at the time of the appointment has fewer than 9 Justices. All temporary appointments expire when the Senate acts, or when a new Congress convenes, whichever comes first.

---

[22] The purpose of this provision is to encourage comity among the Justices. They will be more likely to work well together if their leader is chosen by them.

[23] The 15-year term of office provides a new check on the unfettered power of Supreme Court Justices.

The Senate shall have the sole power to try all impeachments. When sitting for that purpose, they shall be on oath or affirmation. When the President of the United States or the Chancellor of the Senate[24] is tried, the Chief Justice shall preside: And no person shall be convicted without the concurrence of two-thirds of the members present.

Judgment in cases of impeachment shall not extend further than to removal from office, and disqualification to hold and enjoy any office of honor, trust or profit under the United States: but the party convicted shall nevertheless be liable and subject to indictment, trial, judgment, and punishment, according to law.

Section 2. General Provisions on Federal Elections

2.1 Voter Eligibility

All citizens who have attained the age of 18 are eligible to vote in all federal and state elections and in the state in which they reside, provided that a state may temporarily disenfranchise a citizen, on a case by case basis, for reasons of mental deficiency or because the citizen, at the time of an election, is incarcerated due to a felony conviction.

---

[24] The Chancellor, as the presiding officer of the Senate, were he/she impeached by the House, should not preside over his/her own trial. Therefore, the Chief Justice should carry that responsibility.

2.2 Automatic Voter Registration

Congress shall establish a National Voter Registration Authority, which will

- create a national database of registered voters, to be shared with all jurisdictions that conduct elections,
- prevent the national database of registered voters from unauthorized disclosure or access from unauthorized entities,
- ensure that the national database of registered voters is used for no other purpose than voter registration, authentication, and authorization,
- assign to each voter a unique Voter Identifier which remains with that voter for life,
- maintain for each voter both their legal (voting) address and current contact information,
- accept and process voter registration applications from all eligible citizens,
- automatically register each citizen to vote upon their 18th birthday,
- automatically register each citizen to vote, or verify his/her earlier registration, whenever a citizen interacts with a state or federal government entity,
- remove a voter who has deceased, and
- establish appropriate means of voter authentication and authorization to vote.

2.3 Voting Procedures and Ranked Choice Voting (RCV)

All elections are conducted by the several states and by any other United States territories or possessions so authorized by Congress.[25] A secret ballot is guaranteed. Every vote must be recorded on a paper ballot, retained for subsequent audit for 10 years. Votes may be cast by mail provided such votes are received by the first weekday of the election; votes may also be cast in person for nine days, beginning on a Saturday, except that a state may choose to conduct its entire election by mail.[26] A state may authorize a citizen, with reasonable cause, to cast an emergency absentee ballot during the nine-day voting period. By law, Congress may authorize other methods of voting.

Election officials shall count, tabulate, and announce the first-choice results of every election by midnight after polls close each day during the in-person voting period. Such totals will include votes cast by absentee ballot. After applying RCV procedures, election officials shall announce and certify election results within one week after the end of the in-person voting period.

---

[25] The current, well-established system gives the responsibility for conducting elections to the states. There is no compelling reason to change this.

[26] This provision establishes mail-in voting, early voting, and in-person voting for all federal elections.

Ranked Choice Voting (RCV) is mandatory for all federal elections.

VOTING: For each office being contested, voters will be able to rank their choices, selecting a 1st choice, a 2nd choice, and a 3rd choice. For elections for more than three positions, voters may select additional 3rd choices, so that the total candidates selected does not exceed the number of positions to be filled.

COUNTING BALLOTS:

- For an election with a single winner:[27]
    1. Count the 1st choice votes for each candidate, and rank order the results. Repeat steps 2 through 4 until one candidate has a majority of 1st choice votes.
    2. Eliminate the candidate with the fewest votes.
    3. Reassign each vote for the eliminated candidate to each voter's next highest choice for a candidate not yet eliminated.
    4. If a ballot for the eliminated candidate contains no choice for a candidate not yet eliminated, then that ballot is exhausted and is no longer counted as part of the 1st choice votes.

---

[27] Single-winner elections include the primary and general elections for President and for Chancellor (which elections are conducted within each Congressional District) and general elections for a single seat in Congress (which elections are conducted within a CD or at-large within a state).

- For a primary election for a single seat in Congress, three primary winners qualify for the general election:

    1. Count the 1st choice votes for each candidate, and rank order the results. Repeat steps 2 through 4 until only three candidates remain, or until three candidates each exceed 25% of the 1st choice votes.

    2. Eliminate the candidate with the fewest votes.

    3. Reassign each vote for the eliminated candidate to each voter's next highest choice for a candidate not yet eliminated.

    4. If a ballot for the eliminated candidate contains no choice for a candidate not yet eliminated, then that ballot is exhausted and is no longer counted as part of the 1st choice votes.

- For elections for two or more seats in Congress.

    1. For both the primary and the general election, calculate the weighted vote for each candidate, which equals 3 X the voter's 1st choice votes + 2 X the 2nd choice votes + the 3rd choice votes. Rank order the results. Winners are at the top of this list.

    2. In the primary, the number of candidates who qualify for the general election equals two more than the number of positions to be filled.

    3. In the general election, the number of winners equals the number of positions to be filled.

Congress shall have the power to refine the above RCV procedures.

2.4 Primary Elections

Open primaries are mandatory for all federal elections (for President, Chancellor, and both chambers of Congress). Open primaries are non-partisan; the party affiliation of a candidate, if any, will be indicated on the ballot. All registered voters are eligible to vote in every primary and general election within the jurisdiction where they legally reside.

Any eligible candidate may compete in any open primary, subject to state rules for qualifying for the ballot. The results of the primaries determine the candidates whose names will appear on the general election ballot. Those eligible to compete in the general election may withdraw within one week after they have been certified to appear on the general election ballot.

To appear on a primary ballot, a candidate must authorize the US Treasury to release, two weeks after the National Primary election, the five most recent tax returns of that candidate and his or her spouse, if that candidate qualifies for the general election, and if that candidate does not withdraw as a candidate before such tax returns are released. Each general election candidate must also release, on the same schedule, a statement of net worth, showing his/her complete assets and liabilities and those of his/her spouse.[28]

By the Sunday after the National Primary, any candidate who has qualified to appear on any general election ballot may withdraw as a candidate.

---

[28] This provision requires all general election candidates to be completely transparent with respect to their personal finances.

Section 3. Elections for President and for Chancellor

3.1 Elections and Terms of Office.

The President of the United States and the Chancellor of the Senate shall be elected directly by the voters for four-year terms. The President shall be elected in years evenly divisible by 4. The Chancellor shall be elected in even-numbered years not evenly divisible by 4.[29] Votes for President and for Chancellor in both the primary and general elections shall be cast and counted by Congressional District (CD).[30] In counting ballots, RCV procedures are used to determine the single winner in each CD.

Congress shall establish a National Vote Tabulation Authority, whose responsibility is to collect from the states the results of the primary and general elections for President and for Chancellor, to tabulate and summarize the results, and announce the winners.

The President's term of office shall commence at noon on the second Sunday in January following the Presidential election. The Chancellor's term of office shall commence at noon on the first Sunday in January following the Chancellor's election.

---

[29] One of the most important democratic improvements of this Amendment on Elections is the direct election of the President and the Chancellor by the voters.

[30] Article II Section 2 specifies 501 seats in the House. Hence, there will be 501 electoral votes, and 251 is needed for a majority.

3.2 Primary Elections for President and for Chancellor

The total Nominating Votes for President and for Chancellor equals the number of seats in the House of Representatives, plus the number of Nominating Votes from non-state jurisdictions.

- Each CD has the same number of Nominating Votes as it has seats in the House of Representatives.
- Congress may authorize certain jurisdictions other than states to participate in Presidential and Chancellor primaries (Washington, DC, Puerto Rico, and other territories and possessions). All such jurisdictions taken together constitute the Non-State Primary District. For each 1 million inhabitants or portion thereof, this Non-State Primary District is awarded one Nominating Vote.
- A primary election shall be held at large in each CD and in the one Non-State Primary District. The winner of each primary election shall be awarded all of that jurisdiction's Nominating Votes.

The candidates for President and for Chancellor who qualify for the general election ballot are determined through three rounds of primary elections, including four states in Round 1, ten states in Round 2, and all other states and non-state jurisdictions in Round 3.

Unless Congress adopts a different scheme for selecting the states for Rounds 1 and 2, Round 1 primaries will occur in New Hampshire, Iowa, South Carolina, and New Mexico; and Round 2 primaries will occur in 10 states who volunteer for that duty. If more than 10 states apply, random selection will be used to select

10 of them; if fewer than 10 apply, random selection from the remaining states will be used to round out the 10.

Any candidate who meets a state's requirements to appear on the primary ballot for President or for Chancellor will appear on the primary ballot in that state. In addition, any candidate who earns at least one Nominating Vote in a Round 1 or a Round 2 primary automatically qualifies to appear on the ballot in all subsequent primaries.

At the conclusion of the three rounds of Presidential or Chancellor primaries, any candidate who has received at least 15% of the total Nominating Votes qualifies for the general election ballot for President or for Chancellor in all states. If fewer than three candidates achieve the 15% threshold, then the three candidates with the most Nominating Votes qualify for the general election ballot in all states. Any candidate who has won any Nominating Vote in any state qualifies for the general election ballot in all CDs in that state. No other candidate will appear on the general election ballot for President or Chancellor in any state.

Any candidate who withdraws as a Presidential or Chancellor candidate within one week after Round 2 of the primaries may become a candidate for the Senate or for the House. A person can be a candidate for only one federal office at a time.

3.3. General Elections for President and for Chancellor

The general elections for President and for Chancellor take place on the date specified for the General Election for all federal offices. The winner of each election is determined by Electoral Votes. The total Electoral Votes for President and for Chancellor equals the number of seats in the House of Representatives, plus twice the number of states. The number of Electoral Votes in each CD equals the number of house seats in that CD.

Using the RCV procedure for an election with one winner, the winner within each CD will be awarded all the Electoral Votes for that CD; the state-wide winner will be awarded one additional Electoral Vote; and the winner of the national popular vote will be awarded one additional Electoral Vote for each state in the Union.

If one candidate has earned a majority of the Electoral Votes nationally, that candidate will be declared the winner and will become the President-elect or Chancellor-elect.

If no candidate has a majority of the Electoral Votes, then all but the top two candidates will be eliminated, and a final round of ballot counting using the RCV procedure for a single winner will take place, in order to determine the voters' preference among the two remaining candidates. When the Electoral Votes are reassigned to the two remaining candidates, the one with a majority of all Electoral Votes will be the winner. If these last two candidates are tied, then the winner of the national popular vote will be the winner.

Section 4. Elections for Members of Congress

Elections for Congress shall occur in even-numbered years. In each such election cycle, all Members of the House shall be elected for two-year terms, and one Class of the three Senate Classes shall be elected for six-year terms.

If a state has fewer than four House seats, then all House members will be elected at-large, that is, in one Congressional District (CD). For states with four or more House seats, the state shall be divided into 3-seat CDs as far as possible, leaving one 1-seat or 2-seat CD if necessary.

Congress shall establish a rule-based procedure for drawing CD boundaries without human decision-making, based solely on the two principles of equalizing populations per House seat and keeping communities together in the same CD.

For the Senate, all Senators will be elected at large.[31]

Section 5. Dates of Primary and General Elections, Convening of Congress, and Inauguration

Federal elections for Congress occur in even-numbered years. Congress must adjourn *sine die* by July 4 of every election year. Except when called into emergency special session by the President, Congress will not meet again until a new Congress convenes the following January.

Presidential elections occur in years evenly divisible by four; Chancellor elections occur in even-numbered years not evenly divisible by four. For each primary and general election, the nine-day period of in-person voting begins on the following days:

---

[31] Electing all Senators at large ensures that every Senator considers the entire state to be his constituency. Hence both people and states are represented in the Senate.

Presidential or Chancellor Primary Round 1: First Saturday in August

Presidential or Chancellor Primary Round 2: First Saturday in September

National Primary (which includes Presidential or Chancellor Primary Round 3, plus Congressional Primary for House and Senate): First Saturday in October

General Election: First Saturday in December

Convening the new Congress and Inauguration of the Chancellor: Noon on the first Sunday in January following their election

Inauguration of the President: Noon on the second Sunday in January following the election

Section 6. Continuance in Office

To continue in office, all federal elected officials, by October 1 of each year, must authorize the US Treasury to release the five most recent tax returns of that official and his or her spouse. Each official must also release, on the same schedule, a statement of net worth, showing his/her complete assets and liabilities and those of his/her spouse.

Every federal elected official is prohibited from hiring, nominating, or appointing any member of his/her immediate family to any position within the federal government.

Section 7. Transition to the Reconstituted Congress

After this Amendment is adopted, and before the beginning of the year when the first elections under this Amendment will be held, the Vice President, acting as President of the Senate, will arrange for an orderly transition from the Congress under the 1787 Constitution to the Congress under this Amendment.

The 501 seats in the House of Representatives shall be apportioned to the several states based on the average number of votes cast in the two most recent Presidential general elections. After the apportionment of seats in the House, apportionment of seats in the Senate is automatic.

In the first election cycle, all members of the House of Representatives and the Senate will be elected.

After the completion of two Presidential election cycles under this Amendment, Congress may modify any of the provisions of this Amendment, provided two-thirds of both chambers concur.

Part III. A Revised Constitution

Introduction to Part III

"It must be considered that there is nothing more difficult to carry out nor more doubtful of success nor more dangerous to handle than to initiate a new order of things; for the reformer has enemies in all those who profit by the old order, and only lukewarm defenders in all those who would profit by the new order; this lukewarmness arising partly from the incredulity of mankind who does not truly believe in anything new until they actually have experience of it."

<u>Nicolo Machiavelli</u> (1469 - 1527)
<u>The Prince</u>

Authority and Necessity

Why Do We Think We Have the Authority to Do This?

So you are telling me that we should keep a system that gives each voter in Wyoming 66 times more electoral power in the Senate than each voter in California? and the reason we should keep this system is because some Virginia plantation owners in 1787 wanted to ensure that their stranglehold on political power would not be diluted by the radicals in Massachusetts and New York who allowed nearly everybody to vote? Really? and this despite the fact that neither Wyoming nor California was party to this "deal"? and you still want to call this a democracy?

Please.

Let me review the considered opinion of the "Father of the Constitution"[32]:

> *If there be a principle that ought not to be questioned within the United States, it is that every man has a right to abolish an old government and establish a new one. This principle is not only recorded in every public archive, written in every American heart, and sealed with the blood of American martyrs, but is the only lawful tenure by which the United States hold their existence as a nation.*
>
> *James Madison*

The Articles of Confederation of 1781 permitted amendments to those articles, but only if the amendment was agreed to by Congress and then ratified by the legislatures of all 13 states. There were lots of shortcomings to the Articles of Confederation, not the least of which was this requirement for unanimous agreement by all the state legislatures to any changes.

Therefore, when the Constitutional Convention was held in 1787, the Framers of the Constitution quite simply ignored the method for amending the Articles of Confederation spelled out therein. In fact, if they had followed the Articles of Confederation's rules for making amendments, the whole effort would have been scuttled from the get-go, since the state of Rhode Island declined to even send a delegation. Rather, the Framers created a completely new form of government, and they announced that this new

---

[32] James Madison, Helvidius No. 3, September 7, 1793.

government would come into force in all the states that adopted it, as soon as 9 states had adopted it. (In the long run, all 13 states, even including Rhode Island, did ratify the 1787 Constitution.) Note that 9 is more than two-thirds but less than three-fourths of the 13 states.

I feel now like the Framers did in 1787: There is no way that the existing system will be dramatically changed by all those who benefit from it. Therefore, it becomes necessary to go beyond the bounds of the existing constitution and create something very new.

Perhaps the Framers were on to something valuable as a precedent: We may not need to amend the 1787 Constitution by following the rules for amending the Constitution prescribed in Article V thereof. Rather, we can simply create an entirely new Constitution II, an entirely new Government, and adopt it with the consent of the governed. Who gives us the authority to do this? James Madison, of course – the guy who wrote the 1787 Constitution.

Why Do We <u>Need</u> to Do This?

Just look at the process for amending the Constitution, as spelled out in Article V: Congress can propose an amendment by a two-thirds majority in both Houses, or alternatively two-thirds of the state legislatures can call for a convention to propose an amendment; and the proposed amendment becomes part of the Constitution when ratified by three-fourths of the state legislatures. Note, first of all, that the people have no say whatsoever – it is entirely dependent on politicians in the Congress and in state legislatures. Maybe that was okay when the country was just starting out, at a time when even giving power to elected representatives was looked upon as somewhat radical. (In their previous model, the Framers had only England to look at, where power generally derived from the King.) In addition to the amendment process which shuts out the citizenry, look also at the protections built into the 1787 Constitution to ensure that the people would not really be able to affect any outcome: state legislatures chose US Senators; electors in the electoral college, beholden to nobody, selected the President; and even though the voters did elect members of the House, the role of the people was to play second fiddle at best.

Today, our modern American society is far more tolerant of the active participation of all citizens in our politics. Therefore, our new Constitution II should codify the empowerment of the people over the power of politicians.

Since we cannot depend on the existing Powers-That-Be to cede power to the people, it behooves us to assert that power ourselves. The premise of the "Constitution II Convention" – or whatever we choose to call it – is that we the people have the power to create our own democratic government, and we the people have the power to put a new/revised form of government into practice.

Guidelines for the Contents of Constitution II

The new thing we create must be far more democratic, far more subject to the will of the people. It must empower all Americans to play a role, to have a stake, and to have the ability to affect the outcome.

At the same time, we need not, indeed we should not, start over from scratch. As noted in Part I, what the Founding Fathers created was enormously creative, visionary, brave against all odds, and long-lasting. Most of their work retains these qualities. But many details remain incomplete, some provisions are outdated and no longer work as smoothly as intended, some are intentionally anti-democratic and continue to deny us a real democracy, and quite a few significant issues of our time could not have been foreseen when the Framers created the 1787

Constitution. Therefore, for those of us who would like our Constitution and basic form of government to keep working but also want to reform the parts that are broken and fill in the parts that are missing, we are left with two possible courses of action: 1) We could choose to introduce and fight for dozens of Individual constitutional amendments to fix every broken or missing part, including some which we know from the get-go have just about zero chance of ever gaining acceptance from the current power structure; or 2) we could opt for a substantial rewrite of the whole document.

In fact, that is essentially what Constitution II is all about: Keep the original wherever possible, incorporate all previously ratified Amendments, and also incorporate the fixes contained in Part II of this work. The structural changes in Constitution II include the replacement of the Original Senate by the New Senate as well as the replacement of the Vice President by a new Chancellor of the Senate.

Also consider the rather mundane question of language:

- The original 1787 Constitution contained 4490 words. Since ratification, we have adopted 27 Amendments containing a total of 3300 words, or 73% of the original length. The two dozen or so amendments suggested in Part II of this work would add about 3000 words, making the amendments longer than the original document.
- The previously adopted and newly proposed amendments modify or supersede numerous original provisions of the 1787 Constitution, scattered throughout the document, so that even just reading it straight through and understanding how it all fits together is something of a challenge.

- The English language has also changed since 1787. Americans ought to be able to read their foundational document and understand what it means. We ought to be able to teach this in middle school, and pupils should be able to internalize its core concepts.
- The Model-T Ford was a fine machine in its day. If you still owned one in 2017 and wanted to modernize it, you could retrofit it to have an automatic transmission, a powerful engine, air conditioning, visible taillights, modern bumpers, and maybe even seatbelts and airbags; the result would be a patchwork quilt of alterations and make-do fixes and hardly recognizable as a derivative of the original. But inevitably there comes a point at which it's time for a new car, incorporating all the wonderful Model-T features that were novel at the time but also all the advances that have been invented since. That's where we are with our Constitution.

On the basis of language alone, it's time to replace the 1787 Constitution as written and amended with a new version, incorporating all the existing amendments into the body of the basic document and also incorporating our new provisions.

Therefore, Constitution II updates the document's English language usage, punctuation, and spelling. By incorporating all previous amendments into the constitution itself, the whole document becomes much more readable and understandable.

Additional Challenges and Fixes Addressed in Constitution II

The challenges and fixes discussed in Parts I and II of this discourse relate specifically to elections, representation, and voting. If we are going to replace the 1787 Constitution with Constitution II, then we probably ought to fix a number of other challenges which bear fixing at the same time. This section addresses challenges and fixes in two categories: those dealing with Congressional rules and those dealing with the Bill of rights.

Congressional Rules Challenge and Fixes

Arcane rules in both the Senate and the House combine with partisan intransigence to make our Congress woefully ineffective. (See Dems-Repubs, Yin-Yang[33])

Our Government was purposely designed to provide for competing interests, checks and balances, and representation of minority views. At its most basic level, this includes the federal system itself, in which governmental powers are divided between states and the federal government. Within the federal government, powers are divided among three co-equal branches

---

[33] https://all-free-download.com/free-vector/yin-yang.html (adapted from original)

– legislative, executive, and judicial, and each of these branches has a distinct role to play with respect to federal laws. The sole responsibility for making law is vested in a bicameral legislature, both chambers of which need to agree on a proposed law. The President also has a legislative role, in that he can either sign or veto a bill passed by both houses of Congress; but if he vetoes a law passed by Congress, the Congress can override that veto by a 2/3 vote in both chambers. Finally, the Supreme Court is the final review authority, as the Court can reject a law that it deems in violation of the Constitution.

Given the many intentional, constitutional obstacles to passing a law, our Congress has nevertheless opted to adopt several additional obstacles, which are unnecessary from a constitutional standpoint and which serve to only further slowdown or block Congressional action. Inadvertently, these rules have also contributed significantly to the rise of the "imperial presidency". Proponents argue that these extra limits are necessary to protect minority rights (in the case of the Senate's filibuster and other procedural roadblocks) or a minority of the majority party (in the case of certain House rules). However, the simple fact is that our Congress has become muscle-bound and incapable of acting on even the most basic functions of governance.

When we hear that Americans are fed up with Congress, one of the principal complaints is that Congress cannot act, cannot actually do anything. Congress seems to spend all its time in endless arguing while legislating little of substance.

At the same time, often because Congress is unable or unwilling to act, Presidents of both parties have issued Executive Orders to accomplish things that Congress won't. Presidents will always claim that they are acting within their constitutional authority or they are merely providing the necessary administrative details to implement laws that Congress has already passed. Be that as it may, we have witnessed the gradual accumulation of Presidential power and authority at the expense of Congress, with loud complaints by whichever political party does not currently hold the White House.

So the challenge for us is twofold: 1) change the rules of the House and Senate to force Congress to function or at least to reduce their many excuses for failing to function; and 2) restore some balance between the President and Congress by giving Congress a role in the issuance of Executive Orders and restraining the President's power to act unilaterally by declaring a national emergency.

Even though Americans are disgusted by the performance of our Congress, we seem to have little stomach for doing anything about it. Many seem to think that Congress will ultimately work it out for themselves, or they seem to think that we the people are powerless.

We are misguided if we think that we can leave it to Congress to figure it out and fix it. Legislatures sometimes die of self-inflicted wounds. A most famous example occurred in the Sejm (Parliament) of Poland in the 17th and 18th centuries. The Sejm at that time had a rule called the *liberum veto* which allowed any single senator to veto and thus kill all the legislation passed by the Sejm in its current session, thereby causing its dissolution. Poland's kings needed to raise armies to fight invaders, but a single senator, sometimes bribed by foreign officials, nullified every Sejm session that attempted to pass the needed laws. As a result, Poland had no army to defend itself, the country was invaded and partitioned by its neighbors (Russia, Austria, and Prussia), and Poland ceased to exist as a separate nation from

1795 until the end of World War I. Throughout Europe, the term *Polish parliament* came to be a synonym for inept government. With no major legislation and very little legislation of any kind, our last Congress was about as inept as that 18th-century Polish parliament; and like the Sejm of that time, Congress better get its act together soon, before it just withers away into total irrelevance.

It's time that Americans demand that the Congress find the means to break through its own gridlock before we become an American version of the Polish Sejm, that is, before we too have a legislature known only for its inability to act. Find some *cajones*, you guys, and ACT to save your own institution before it crumbles into carping, name-calling, gotcha-moments, political theatre, and total incompetence. You have the power to fix this. Here are several specific proposals to accomplish just that.

Reform the Filibuster

Senate rules permit any senator to talk forever on any legislation under consideration. These rules also allow the senator who is speaking to pass the baton to any other senator, who can continue speaking without interruption until again passing the baton to someone else. In this way, a small group of senators can prevent any legislation from coming to a vote – they just keep speaking until the Senate leaders agree to withdraw the bill the minority doesn't like. It does not matter how important that legislation is – defending our country, paying our bills, whatever.

During the nineteenth century, Senate minorities perfected the rarely-used practice of talking a bill to death, which came to be known as filibustering. Unlimited debate continued in the Senate until 1917, when the Senate adopted a rule that permitted a two-thirds majority of senators present and voting to end debate on a bill, thus allowing the bill to come to the floor for an up-or-down vote. This device is called "invoking cloture" – that is, choking off further debate. With 100 senators, this meant that 67 votes were needed to invoke cloture. In 1975, the number of votes needed to invoke cloture was reduced to three-fifths, or 60 senators. So at present, 41 senators can kill any bill, even if 59 senators want to vote on it. In practice, it's often not even necessary to mount the filibuster – just threatening to filibuster is enough to kill the proposed law: Senators do not need to actually filibuster; they can just declare their intention to do so, and the 60-vote majority is in effect.

Many Americans might be surprised to learn that the Constitution does not prescribe rules of debate for the Senate. The filibuster rules are only traditional practices adopted as Senate Rules of Order, which the Senate adopts anew as its first order of business whenever a new Congress convenes. The Senate has the authority to amend those rules by a two-thirds vote whenever it so chooses or by a simple majority vote at the beginning of a new Congress. Without any question, we should demand that the Senate change these rules. (You might be interested to learn that the original House of Representatives also had unlimited debate, but the increasing number of House members made the practice unwieldy, and so the House changed its rules – just like the Senate should do now.)

The Original Senate could eliminate the filibuster today by amending its own rules. Just in case that doesn't happen, Article II Section 5 of Constitution II eliminates the filibuster by mandating that decisions in both chambers will be taken by majority vote, and by providing further that any member may call a bill or nomination to the floor. Article II Section 7 provides further that the effective date of any law is July 1 of the year following the next general election, giving a new Congress the opportunity to change or repeal it. (The same section allows an earlier effective date of legislation, provided 3/5 of both chambers agree.)

Blocking Presidential Appointments

At present any senator may block any Presidential executive or judicial appointment. Recent modifications to Senate rules have curtailed this practice to some extent, but the practice or tradition of blocking appointments through the actions of a single senator should be abandoned altogether. The new provision in Article II Section 5 of Constitution II allowing any Senator to call a nomination to the floor eliminates the ability of any one Senator to block a nomination indefinitely.

The President should also have the power to make temporary appointments when the Senate fails to act on a nomination. Article III Section 2 of Constitution II contains new wording concerning Presidential appointments, which would allow the President to appoint someone temporarily if the Senate fails to act on a Presidential nomination for 60 days. The temporary appointment would end when the Senate acts or when the next Congress convenes, whichever occurs first.

Rules for Bringing Legislation to the Floor of the House of Representatives

Both major political parties, at various times, have used their majority status in the House to prevent House consideration of legislation which might pass the whole House with bipartisan support but which does not have enough support to pass the whole House within the majority party itself. From 2010 to 2018 this problem manifested itself as Republican obstructionism, but that is only because the Republicans were the majority party in the House of Representatives. Democrats are equally capable of these shenanigans.

Here is how this works: We have 435 members of the House, so 218 constitute a majority. In the Congress from 2016 to 2018, Republicans had 240 representatives, and 195 representatives were Democrats. Before any legislation came to the floor for a vote, it had to be passed by the House Republican Conference – that is, all the Republican representatives. But if a bill had the support of fewer than 218 Republicans within the Republican Conference, the leadership did not allow the bill to come to the floor of the whole House.

The purpose of this rule or practice was to block any legislation that would need votes from the minority party in order to become law. Thus it prevented the minority party from taking any credit. The real effect of this practice was to give any group of 23+ Republican representatives veto power over all legislation. It ruined the Speakership of Representative John Boehner and damaged that of Paul Ryan. It made governing extremely difficult if not impossible. It brought the US House of Representatives that much closer to becoming the Polish Sejm of the 18th century.

Fixing this could involve the following new House rules:

1. Any bill that has the support of a majority of the majority party in its conference will advance to the floor of the House.
2. Any representative may introduce a motion to bring any matter to the floor, including any pending legislation. If a majority of House members agree, that matter will

become the first order of business on the next day that the House is in session.

3. As a most extreme solution, the Speaker of the House could become a non-partisan position, perhaps not even an elected politician or member of the House; or it could become a bipartisan position, in which the Speaker of the House must be approved by a majority of the members of both political parties. In either case, the job of Speaker should be to ensure the smooth functioning of the House and to bring to the floor any measure recommended by the leadership of the majority party or by a majority of all House members.

The same Article II Section 5 provision of Constitution II referenced earlier that allows any Member to call a bill to the floor with the approval of a majority of the House will solve this problem. If Members can cobble together a bipartisan majority of House Members, they can ensure that a bill will be brought to the floor for a vote by the full House.

Executive Orders

Congress should pass a law that requires the President to give Congress a 30-day warning before the effective date of any Executive Order. In addition, during that 30-day waiting period, either House by a majority vote can prevent that Executive Order from going into effect. (Of course, in the event of a national emergency, Congress could simply pass a law equal to the Executive Order, allowing it to go into effect immediately.)

The courts may find such a law to be an unconstitutional infringement on the authority of the executive under the 1787 Constitution. To circumvent any such finding, Article III Section 3 of Constitution II contains a new paragraph concerning Executive

Orders. This provision gives Congress 30 days to block an E.O. that it finds objectionable. Hence, if Congress allows an E.O. to go into effect, it must accept at least partial ownership of the result.

Congress also needs to amend the Emergency Powers Act, under which any President can declare a national emergency for any reason and thereby amass a plethora of additional power. At present, overriding the President's declaration of a national emergency requires a resolution passed by both chambers which the President can veto. A new version should make a Presidential declaration of a national emergency null and void if either chamber objects to it within 30 days – that is, the same Congressional power as we prescribe for an Executive Order.

Conclusion

In sum, we need an overhaul of the procedures that govern the way Congress operates. Americans deserve a Congress that serves the interests of the people. We do have the power to insist upon a functioning democracy. To achieve this fundamental goal, we will need to elect senators and representatives who actually want to govern and who want to work with all sides to arrive at solutions that work for all. We should also include specific provisions in Constitution II that will facilitate a functioning Congress.

Bill of Rights Challenge and Associated Fixes in Constitution II

Often bitter debates took place between the federalist and anti-federalist forces before the 1787 Constitution was ratified. Anti-federalists held that the Constitution as written failed in two major respects: it lacked sufficient protections for individual liberties, and it did not impose strong enough limitations on the power of the federal government. The anti-federalists finally gained assurances from those in favor of the new Constitution that, as soon as the new federal government became operative, the anti-federalists would be able to recommend the kinds of changes that they insisted on.

Accordingly, during the very first Congress elected under the newly-ratified Constitution, James Madison (who had been elected a member of the House of Representatives from Virginia) introduced a series of Amendments; the House approved 17 of these Amendments and sent them over to the Senate, who approved 12 of them and sent them to the states in August 1789. The states ratified 10 of these 12, which became effective in December 1791.

These first ten Amendments to the Constitution, which became known as the Bill of Rights, layout fundamental rights that the Constitution guarantees. Subsequent constitutional amendments guaranteed voting rights to former slaves, to women, and to all citizens over age 18.

Several Supreme Court decisions and federal laws have expanded on some of our basic rights. A few examples:

- A Supreme Court decision interpreted the 2nd Amendment as guaranteeing gun rights to individual citizens.

- Another Supreme Court decision interpreted the 1st, 3rd, 4th, 5th, and 9th Amendments as implicitly recognizing the right to privacy.

- A federal law, the Voting Rights Act, expanded voting rights for all citizens but especially for racial minorities.

However, Congress can alter laws. and court decisions can be overturned. Therefore, to secure these and other individual rights for present and future generations, we need to enshrine these fixes in the Constitution. The challenge lies in the fact that, without such constitutional guarantees, our Bill of Rights remains somewhat incomplete.

Several citizen rights exist in various states but not at the federal level, including Initiative, Referendum, and the right to amend the constitution. States do not have the right to supersede a federal statute or to secede from the Union.

Again, we must remember that in 1787 the authors of the Constitution had limited experience with the rights of individual persons or citizens, so we should not criticize them for not including some of these rights in the original document. They feared the tyranny of the mob almost as much as they feared the tyranny of a king, and with good reason. The Jacobite Rebellions in England (ending in 1746) were still fresh in their consciousness. Hence our Founding Fathers trusted Congress more than they trusted a President, and they trusted state legislatures more than they would ever trust the people to protect the freedom of all citizens and freedom from either form of tyranny.

We have come a long way since the 18th century. Today we have relatively more faith in the people though we retain a somewhat jaundiced view of government and especially of professional politicians. The trick is to devise a system of government that protects both individual and collective rights while limiting the ability of government to trample over those rights.

One principal piece of a solution is to divide governmental functions into three parts: make laws, enforce laws, and interpret laws; and then to assign these three basic functions to three co-equal branches of government – Congress, the President, and the Courts. A second piece is to divide power between the federal government and the state governments. The Framers implemented both of these pieces fairly well. But the third piece is to carve out a special role for the people, which the Framers did only in part.

We the people have been clamoring for more power ever since. For example, we campaigned for and obtained direct election of senators, and we insisted that voters select Presidential electors. We gained voting rights for women, for former slaves, and for all racial and ethnic minorities.

Though we have made significant progress, the task of "people empowerment" is not complete. All the items presented in the Bill of Rights Challenge relate in some way to the empowerment of people and of the states and/or to limiting the power of the federal government. These are all stated as "challenges" because none of them are fully realized in our Constitution. In this section, the discussion of each challenge ends by citing the provision of Constitution II that addresses that challenge.

Equality of Persons; Freedom from Discrimination; Freedom from Torture; Right to Privacy

- The Declaration of Independence states unequivocally:
   We hold these truths to be self-evident, that all men are created equal, that they are endowed by their Creator with certain unalienable Rights, that among these are Life, Liberty and the pursuit of Happiness.
   However, this fundamental assertion did not find its way into the Constitution.
- Congress has passed laws prohibiting discrimination on the basis of sex and sexual orientation, and it has outlawed age discrimination in employment after age 40. But these prohibitions are not in the Constitution. Other forms of discrimination are partially prohibited, such as

discrimination based on race, ethnicity, religion, and national origin.
- While the 8th Amendment to the Constitution outlaws "cruel and unusual punishments", the Constitution does not forbid the use of torture for purposes other than punishment. Some have argued that torture used for the purpose of gaining information from a known or suspected traitor or spy or terrorist is not a punishment but rather an effective interrogation device justified by military necessity during war or by the need for public safety during periods of civil unrest or threatened terrorist activity. Others have argued that torture is always inhumane, reduces the government that practices torture to the same level as the terrorist, and furthermore is ineffective at gaining actionable intelligence. Social science research, testimony from victims of torture, and the historical record largely support the latter argument. Most modern societies have abjured the use of torture for any purpose whatsoever.
- In a landmark 1965 decision (Griswold v. Connecticut), the Supreme Court found a right to privacy implicit in the 1st, 3rd, 4th, 5th, and 9th Amendments. Subsequently the Court based several significant decisions at least in part on that 1965 decision including the right to an abortion (Roe v. Wade, 1973) and the ban on sodomy laws (Lawrence v. Texas, 2003).

The related fixes in Constitution II appear in:
- Article I, Section 2, ¶ 2.1 Equality of All Natural Persons
- Article I, Section 2, ¶ 2.3 Freedom from Discrimination
- Article I, Section 2, ¶ 2.5 Prohibition on Cruel and Unusual Punishment and on Torture

- Article I, Section 3, ¶ 3.4 Search and Seizure

Rights to Healthcare, Education, and the Necessities of Life

If we can argue that all of us have the right to "life, liberty, and the pursuit of happiness", then it follows that we as American citizens have the right to those basic necessities that sustain life and that allow us to pursue happiness. This includes at least the provision of healthcare, education, food, clothing, and shelter:

- Healthcare is needed to sustain life itself; without it, citizens die of disease prematurely and unnecessarily.
- Education is needed to prepare citizens for the pursuit of happiness; without it, a citizen's prospects are severely limited.
- Without food, citizens starve.
- Without clothing and shelter, citizens freeze, suffocate, or die from exposure.

There are limits to what governments can and should provide or guarantee. We do have a free-market economy, a capitalist economic system, which encourages entrepreneurship, investment, invention, creativity, risk-taking, and hard work. Those things deserve to be rewarded. However, the cards should not be so stacked against an individual, especially when the circumstances are beyond that individual's control, that "life, liberty, and the pursuit of happiness" are impossible.

Interestingly, the original Constitution does not mention capitalism, private property, or free markets. The term "private property" does appear in the 5th Amendment to the Constitution in the clause "nor shall private property be taken for public use, without just compensation." Article I Section 8 of the Constitution gives Congress the power to protect the rights of authors and inventors to benefit from their writings and discoveries, so this clause suggests a right to private property. Nevertheless, I find it most interesting that the foundational document of the greatest capitalist nation on earth does not discuss the role of free enterprise at all.

We need to also mention that our system of federalism allows us to construct a system of national, state, and mixed national-state programs that address these challenges. No one should assume, for example, that if a citizen has a constitutional right to something, the federal government must perforce provide it to everyone for free.

The related fixes in Constitution II appear in Article I, Section 3, ¶ 3.8 Healthcare, Education, and Necessities of Life

Clarification of 2nd Amendment

Here is the Second Amendment to the Constitution in its entirety: "A well-regulated Militia, being necessary to the security of a free State, the right of the people to keep and bear Arms, shall not be infringed." This Amendment became part of the original Bill of Rights when it was ratified in 1791.

The provenance of the 2nd Amendment is the English Bill of Rights of 1689, which explicitly forbade the Catholic monarch from forcibly disarming Protestants. The English Bill of Rights stated that the English king had no right to take away his subjects' means of defending themselves. In the US, the debate centered on the ability of states and citizens to protect themselves from forcible takeover by the federal government. The Framers argued that no federal standing army would be able to overcome resistance from a well-organized state militia. However, some also made the personal self-defense argument, harking back to the English Bill of Rights of 1689.

For 217 years, the Second Amendment was interpreted by federal courts as guaranteeing the right of each state to maintain its own militia (or national guard, as we now call it). But in 2008, in Heller v. District of Columbia, the Supreme Court held that the Second Amendment guaranteed each citizen the right to possess a firearm for traditionally lawful purposes, such as self-defense within the home. This decision invalidated a District of Columbia law that had outlawed handguns altogether. And interestingly, the Supreme Court based its decision at least in part on English Common Law and specifically on the English Bill of Rights of 1689.

People still argue vehemently over the Heller decision – from gun-rights advocates who argue that the Second Amendment prevents the government from imposing any limits whatsoever on personal weapons, to gun-control advocates who believe that Heller was wrongly decided and should be overturned, or that the Heller decision still allows regulation of firearms, just not their outright prohibition. The challenge here is to come up with a scheme that protects the right of each state to maintain a militia, the right of every individual to protect himself with a firearm, and the right of all citizens to protect themselves from totally unregulated firearms.

The related clarifications in Constitution II appear in:

- Article I, Section 3, ¶ 3.2 Right to Bear Arms and Article I, Section 4, ¶ 4.6 State Militia

Distinguish Between the Rights of Persons, of Citizens, and of States

We have entertained many arguments over constitutionally-guaranteed rights, not the least of which has been the argument over whether a particular constitutionally-guaranteed right pertains to all persons within the jurisdiction of the United States or only to citizens of the United States. For instance, do visitors to the US or permanent residents of the US have a right to free speech, free exercise of religion, and freedom of assembly – or do those rights only attach to American citizens? Can anyone in the country possess a firearm or only a citizen? Does anyone accused of a crime within the US get a jury trial or only citizens? The challenge is that the original Bill of Rights does not distinguish between citizens and other persons who fall within the jurisdiction of the US.

A similar challenge exists in delineating the rights of people versus the rights of states.

The clarification in Constitution II appears in Article I, Section1: Introduction to the Bill of Rights, which specifies that Constitution II establishes the rights of natural persons, citizens, and states. The subsequent sections of Article I specify the rights of Natural Persons, of Citizens, and of States.

Definition of Citizens, Natural-Born Versus Naturalized

Recent political controversies have centered on questions about the definition of citizens, and especially about the distinction between a natural-born citizen (born in the US or born of American parents while outside the US) and a naturalized citizen (an immigrant who subsequently obtained US citizenship). While the Constitution does not define any of these terms (citizen, natural-born citizen, or naturalized citizen), it does require that the President be a natural-born citizen. So the challenge is to clarify what those terms mean.

The related fix in Constitution II appears in Article I, Section 3, ¶ 3.1 Definition of Citizen

State and Local Rights and Responsibilities

States, localities, and individual citizens should have the right to act, alone or in consort with each other, on matters pertinent to their local interests. Gradually, too many rights of individuals and of states have been taken over by the federal government, usually with unsatisfactory results. Examples abound, but just a few will be cited here:

- In the natural order of things, K-12 education should be the responsibility of states, parents, and local school officials. It is difficult to argue that the federal government needs to be involved in K-12 curriculum, school policies, scheduling, financing, and so on. Does Washington really have any interest in deciding whether schools in Maryland begin after Labor Day or before, or whether Florida chooses to teach cursive writing? On the other hand, states should be able to join forces when they so choose. Common Core is an example of a state initiative to establish uniform curriculum guidelines, but then the Feds got involved by encouraging states to adopt Common Core, and the US Department of Education funded two companies to develop tests for measuring student achievement of the Common Core standards. The result, both educationally and politically, is a mess. A better result might be achieved by removing the federal government from primary and secondary education entirely while allowing states who so choose to form an association to set common standards, achieve common goals, conduct educational research, and compete for funding opportunities.

- Today most Americans agree that traffic regulations belong at the state level. Are you old enough to remember the 55 mph national speed limit? The US Department of Transportation even ran a national ad campaign, with the slogan "Stay Alive – Drive 55". As a partial response to the Arab oil embargo in 1973, the 55 mph National Maximum Speed Limit was passed in 1974 and signed by President Nixon as a way of both conserving fuel and saving lives. Congress amended the law to 65 mph in 1987 and repealed it altogether in 1995 – one of the most popular acts of the new Republican Congress elected in 1994. So why didn't the national speed limit work? The law was both ineffective and unenforceable. Too many people and too many states simply did not buy it for one simple reason: By no stretch of the imagination do drivers in New York or policy wonks in Washington have an interest in how fast trucks are permitted to drive in Montana. Period, end of story.
- Our current laws recognize that alcohol should be controlled at the state and local level. We experimented with a national prohibition on alcohol, adopted by the 18th Amendment to the Constitution in 1919, then repealed by the 21st Amendment in 1933. Yet today, having learned absolutely nothing from our failed experiment with Prohibition, we treat other intoxicants differently. We

have an abundance of conflicting state and federal laws dealing with medical marijuana, recreational marijuana, and other drugs. It's hard to see why I as a resident of Maryland should give a hoot as to whether the folks attending a Super Bowl party in Denver are getting high on pot rather than Coors Beer. If this is a matter of concern for the citizens of Denver or the state of Colorado, they can deal with it – but please leave me out of that discussion.

Most common crimes are committed locally, with local perpetrators and local victims. Therefore, in our federal system of government, most criminal laws are state laws and local ordinances. The federal government has no discernible interest in those matters. For the most part, federal crimes involve multiple state jurisdictions or international actors, such as bank fraud or smuggling or kidnapping.

Attitudes of ideologues and of party activists have long argued over states' rights versus federal prerogatives, and it's interesting to see historically how the tides and attitudes have shifted over time. In the early days of the republic, for example, slave states wanted the federal government to enforce their property rights in non-slave states by forcing those states to return fugitive slaves to their slave-state owners, while anti-slave states believed that their states had the right to prevent such extraditions. Later, as the abolitionist movement grew, the slave states became advocates for states' rights, and abolitionists thought the federal government should have the right to outlaw slavery everywhere. Though of less import than slavery in the 19th century, the same argument has occurred in our own time concerning undocumented aliens, sanctuary cities, voting rights, marijuana laws, abortion rights, gun control, and same-sex marriage. In each of these cases and many others, advocates for one side or the other have alternately claimed that federal jurisdiction should be paramount over state statutes, or that states' rights should be protected against federal intrusion – all depending on who then controls the federal government versus who controls a state government.

The federal government has an obligation to enforce the rights and privileges of all American citizens enumerated in the Constitution, including the laws Congress has passed to implement those rights. Over and above that, the question should be on the locus of control, effect, and payment: Who is in a position to control an activity, who is affected by that activity, and who must pay for it? Air traffic control, for example, must be a federal matter, since most flights go over state boundaries and conflicting state laws would be a complete mess as well as dangerous. Regulations on food and on pharmaceuticals must be national since these products inevitably involve interstate commerce. But states can handle purely local matters, such as setting standards for locally-grown and sold vegetables, high school graduation requirements, highway speed limits, and local building codes.

One challenge that always arises in these discussions is the uneven wealth among the 50 states. A solution to that challenge, occasionally employed by Congress, is federal block grants. We do some of this with Medicaid, disaster relief, and Interstate Highway System projects. But do we have enough of this type of creative funding and federal-state partnerships? Congress can set minimal guidelines that states must follow to qualify for block grants, with the dollar amount of such grants based on the unique needs of each state; but the actual regulations and procedures are left to the states. Perhaps the Constitution should spell out the authority of Congress and of the several states to act in consonance on funding solutions.

The challenge going forward will be to reconsider federal laws and regulations with a view to relegating local matters back to the states, as is mandated in principle in Amendment 10 to the Constitution, to wit: "The powers not delegated to the United States by the Constitution, nor prohibited by it to the states, are reserved to the states respectively, or to the people."

The related fix in Constitution II appears in Article I, Section 4 Bill of Rights of States.

Power of States to Secede

Some will say that we tried this once in 1861, and it did not turn out well.

In response, I would ask this question: Why should the decisions of 13 state conventions in the 1780's bind all the states and all the citizens of all those states forever? First, none of us were alive when the Articles of Confederation were adopted (which is where the notion of a "Perpetual Union" of the states was articulated). Second, 37 of the 50 states now in existence did not exist when the Constitution was adopted. Third, this perpetual union idea appears nowhere in the Constitution.

Let me repeat that: The idea that no state can secede from the Union is NOT in our Constitution.

However, this idea IS in the Articles of Confederation from 1781, written and adopted before the Revolutionary War was over. In fact, the complete title of that agreement is "Articles of Confederation and perpetual Union between the states of New Hampshire, Massachusetts-bay, Rhode Island and Providence

Plantations, Connecticut, New York, New Jersey, Pennsylvania, Delaware, Maryland, Virginia, North Carolina, South Carolina, and Georgia."

I would also posit (though I cannot demonstrate this) that leaving this "perpetual union" clause out of the Constitution was not an accident. The Constitution's Framers went over the "Articles of Confederation and perpetual Union" meticulously and retained those provisions which seemed to work well and discarded or replaced others. So why was it not included in the Constitution? Did the Framers realize that future generations might want to rethink their commitment to the Union?

This idea that the "Perpetual Union of the states" need not be perpetual has not been seriously debated since the Civil War, which for most Americans settled that matter once and for all. However, if we think about a system of empowering the people and the states, then the notion that a state might choose to opt out does have merit. The question is this: Why should the commitment to a perpetual union, made by a small, wealthy, privileged group of white men in the thirteen original states bordering the Atlantic Ocean, over two centuries ago, forever bind the people living in, for example, Texas or California (which at that time belonged to Spain), Louisiana and all the states that derived from the Louisiana Purchase of 1803 (which belonged then to France), or Alaska (which belonged to Russia)? Why should that 18th-century decision be binding on anyone in the 21st century?

Let me also interpose this thought: Once admitted to the Union, a state is vested in that Union; by the same token, the Union is vested in each state. Hence both entities, the state and the Union, must acquiesce in its dissolution.

Although we may not foresee the circumstances today that would propel the citizens of a state to make such a choice, is it fair to preclude that choice for now and forever more?

We exist as a single nation, and we function as a single entity. Among other results of our Civil War, the term "United States" became a singular noun rather than a plural noun. Clearly the ties that bind us together are strong. We depend on each other for so much, from a common military to a common currency and financial system to a fully integrated economy, transportation system, energy industry, and commercial sector.

Nevertheless, if some state or states among us conclude that they would be better off as a separate nation, then ought we not have a procedure short of civil war of allowing them to accomplish that? Secession should be difficult, much more than a passing fancy, and chosen deliberately over some period of years; and it should require acquiescence from the country as a whole as well as adequate notice to the other states to adjust – but it should be possible.

The related fix in Constitution II appears in Article I, Section 4, ¶ 4.2.

Power of the People to Initiate and Repeal Laws and to Amend the Constitution

Most states require that the citizenry approve state constitutional amendments at the ballot box, often by a super-majority. 24 states permit citizens to initiate new state laws or repeal existing laws through petitions followed by a popular referendum. We need to adopt similar measures at the federal level. Voters should approve any change to the U.S. Constitution, and citizens or states should also be able to create or repeal laws when Congress fails to act. Citizens should be able to call for a constitutional convention. The rules governing the exercise of such citizen power should make it difficult but not impossible for the citizens, through direct action, to modify our constitution or laws. We should not tinker with the Constitution or statutes on a whim, but citizens in a democracy should be able to effect change for good reason and upon due reflection.

Empowering the people to amend the Constitution will be an immense and historic step in realizing the promise of democracy. Amending our Constitution will not be easy; but if the people demand changes in the Constitution, they should have the means of achieving that result.

The political process known as "Initiative" gives citizens of a state the constitutional right to propose a state statute (and in some cases an amendment to the state constitution) through a petition, bypassing the state legislature. After a certain percentage of registered voters have signed a petition, the proposed law or constitutional amendment appears on the next general election ballot, where voters can accept or reject it. (Some states provide for an intermediate step, in which the proposal is submitted first to the legislature, where the lawmakers can deal with it, and only if the legislature ignores or rejects the proposal does it then go the voters.) Beginning with South Dakota in 1898, 24 states now include some form of Initiative in their state constitutions. The most recent state to adopt the Right of Initiative was Mississippi in 1992.

The term "referendum" simply means a ballot measure. All state constitutions include a "legislative referendum", which is a ballot measure submitted to the voters by the legislature. Typically, state constitutions require certain measures to be approved by the voters, such as constitutional amendments, bond issues, or tax increases. Some state constitutions also provide for discretionary items, in which the lawmakers just decide to punt on an issue and let the voters decide.

But a legislative referendum is not the type of referendum we are talking about here. Rather, we want to discuss another type, which could be called a "citizen referendum". Like the Initiative, a citizen referendum gives citizens the ability to circulate a petition to repeal an act of the legislature. In the typical procedure, after the legislature passes a new law, people who disapprove of that law have a limited amount of time (usually 90 days) in which they can "petition the bill to referendum". If they gain sufficient signatures on their petition, then the new law goes to the voters for an up-or-down vote at the next election, and in the meanwhile, the new law does not go into effect. 24 states have the citizen "Referendum" in their state constitutions – mostly the same states that have the "Initiative".

In sum, roughly half the states have Initiative and Referendum. States began experimenting with this more than a century ago, and nothing terrible has happened as a result. Therefore, isn't it time that we incorporate these tools of citizen empowerment into the US Constitution? We can use the rules for "Initiative and Referendum" in those states that already have such rights, encourage all states to adopt such rights, and fall back on state legislatures in those states that do not yet have such rights.

A constitutional amendment to empower citizens should replace Article V of the 1787 Constitution. This article would state:

- Citizens and states have the right to propose a federal statute, repeal a federal statute, propose a constitutional amendment, and convene a constitutional convention.

- Congress has the right to propose a constitutional amendment.

- Voters have the final decision: Voters will decide whether to enact or repeal a law brought to them through the Initiative or Referendum process; voters will ratify or reject all proposed constitutional amendments; and voters will decide whether or not to convene a constitutional convention and ratify or reject any amendments or new constitution proposed by said convention.

The Amendment on Amendments (Big Fix 3 in Part II above) gives citizens and states the power to propose Constitutional amendments and gives citizens the final say in amending the Constitution. Constitution II goes further, expanding citizen participation in the enactment and repeal of federal statutes.

The related fix in Constitution II appears in Article VII: Citizen Empowerment; Constitutional Amendments.

Convening the Constitution II Convention

To adopt a new constitution, we need to convene a constitutional convention for the purpose of creating a new constitution. We will refer to this body as the *Constitution II Convention*. The Constitution II Convention will draft the new constitution, *Constitution II*, and the **people** in each state (not the **legislatures** of each state) will then ratify it.

Two approaches to convening the Constitution II Convention present themselves. The first approach is to follow the procedures in the current Constitution. The second follows the precedent established by the Framers of the current Constitution.

Each approach can succeed only with a great deal of active citizen involvement and broad public support.

First Approach

The first approach uses the procedures in Article V of the Constitution to amend the Constitution, specifically, to replace *Article V – Amendments* with *the Amendment on Amendments*, detailed in Big Fix 3. The Amendment on Amendments gives citizens the exclusive power to approve all constitutional amendments and to propose a constitutional convention.

Article V of the Constitution spells out two procedures for proposing a constitutional amendment or constitutional convention: a) Two-thirds of the state legislatures ask Congress to call for a convention for the purpose of proposing amendments; or b) Congress itself, by a two-thirds vote in each chamber, proposes an amendment. When Congress submits a proposed constitutional amendment to the states, Congress can specify whether the amendment will be ratified by the state legislatures or by state conventions.

The American people could demand that our state legislatures petition Congress to convene a constitutional convention for the purpose of proposing the Amendment on Amendments. Or we could demand that Congress propose the Amendment on Amendments. We could further demand that Congress specify that state conventions (rather than state legislatures) will endorse the will of the people in each state, based on a ballot referendum on the Amendment on Amendments.

Under either procedure, the Amendment on Amendments is then submitted to the 50 states, where 38 states ratify it, making it part of the Constitution.

After we adopt the Amendment on Amendments, half of the states with at least half of the US population can call for a constitutional convention to rewrite the constitution.

We can expect a challenge to the constitutionality of the Amendment on Amendments since it removes the guarantee that no state will be denied its equal representation in the Senate without its consent. The counter-argument is that of James Madison: we have the authority to change our government.

If this first approach is successful, then the path will be clear to submit a rewritten constitution to the states for approval by the people, in accordance with the procedure in the Amendment on Amendments.

Second Approach

We should try the first approach first. It's clean and straightforward, and it will garner support from those who insist on following the letter of the law.

But what if it doesn't work? What if political obstructionism prevents us from replacing Article V with the will of the people, and yet public opinion polls demonstrate overwhelming public support for convening the Constitution II Convention?

In that case, we may need to follow the precedent of the guys who wrote the 1787 Constitution. That is, ignore the rules in the existing document for amending it because those rules are so prejudiced in favor of the existing power structure that we can never expect them to relinquish that power voluntarily. Instead, convene a new constitutional convention of the people, and campaign for widespread public support.

Here are specific suggested steps for convening the Constitution II Convention using the second approach:

1. The process begins with a petition, organized and circulated through any of the national civic organizations with a continuing interest in these matters, demanding a national convention for the purpose of creating a new constitution.
2. Then an existing non-partisan civic organization with a focus on politics agrees to take the lead in organizing discussions on Constitution II or helps form a new organization with this mission. The League of Women Voters, FairVote.org, Harvard University's John F. Kennedy School of Government (especially the Roy and Lila Ash Center for Democratic Governance and Innovation), the University of Virginia Center for Politics, and probably a dozen other entities would be candidates for this role. One or more state or national political leaders might see the merit in this effort and lend it credibility.
3. When citizen support for this endeavor becomes sufficiently widespread and vocal, the sponsoring organization will call together a core group of scribes to write and edit and vet the document.
4. As was the case before the 1787 Constitutional Convention, all states will be invited to participate in the process of drafting Constitution II; but this time around, direct citizen action must drive the process, rather than allowing politicians to exercise control over the process or veto power over the result.
5. The Constitution II Convention, charged with the task of drafting Constitution II, will hold its first official meeting when 60% of the states call for same and agree to send

representatives to it. A state can join the Constitution II Convention by either an action of the state legislature or by a plebiscite of its citizens.

6. And, *voila!*, the Constitution II Convention is underway. Additional states can join the process throughout the Constitution II Convention whenever they see fit to do so.

If this second approach to convening the Constitution II Convention is followed, we can expect an intense national conversation and debate about the proper method to follow for ratification.

Constitution II Convention Procedures

Technology will facilitate the participation of a wide swath of citizens in the drafting and editing process.

State governments can designate representatives if they so choose, as can Congress and the federal judiciary; all representatives can participate either electronically or in person. The Constitution II Convention can begin meeting officially when it has representatives from at least 60% of the states. Citizen opinion polls and online voting schemes can be employed to ensure citizen support for each article, section, paragraph, sentence, and clause of Constitution II. I envision a lively, months-long, highly participatory civics lesson, at the end of which the American public will be much better informed concerning their government, their constitution, and democracy – and much more supportive of all three.

When the whole document is complete, sponsors will ask each state to submit it to their voters in a public referendum. This will happen, of course, only if citizens demand it, loudly and consistently over a long period of time.

If Americans follow the first approach to convening the Constitution II Convention, then the ratification procedure will be straightforward, following the procedure in the Amendment on Amendments. Voters in two general elections (separated by at least one general election and inauguration of a new President) will accept or reject Constitution II, and if they vote twice to accept it, then this will become the new constitution and the law of the land in all 50 states.

If Americans follow the second approach to convening the Constitution II Convention, then the path to ratification is less clear. Public demands for a plebiscite in every state will be necessary to force a vote. One can hope that, if several states approve Constitution II, more states will follow, and the effort will gain momentum. Though the last few states might be a challenge, 30 states will ultimately ratify. At that point, the other 20 states will need to decide whether to join in or else lose out entirely, and hopefully all will join.

This scenario is not as far-fetched as it might seem at first glance. In any case, working to achieve it or something like it is far better than simply wringing our hands and complaining bitterly how the system is rigged against us, or how Big Money always wins, or how the entrenched politicians will remain forever entrenched and there is nothing we can do about it.

Consent of 60% of Us

Today, of course, we want our Government to be far more democratic, far more representative of the people, than the Framers of the 1787 Constitution would ever have dared dream. Therefore, this new Constitution II will come into effect only after it has been adopted (or "ratified") by a majority of voters in at least 60% of the states, including states that constitute at least 60% of the US population according to the most recent census.

The suggested 60% threshold for ratification (for both states and population) is arbitrary. Any number can be argued, both pro and con.

At one extreme, we could put the new Constitution II into effect among the states that have approved it when ratified by just nine states, making up just a majority of the US population. We could argue for this suggestion for two reasons: 1) Precedent, since that is the number of states needed to ratify the 1787 Constitution and put it into effect; and 2) Conveniently, the nine most populous states comprise 51% of the US population.

At the other extreme, we could require unanimous approval by a plebiscite in every state, perhaps with a super-majority in every state. But that would be like trying to amend the Articles of Confederation by unanimous approval of all state legislatures or trying to reconstitute the US Senate under the strictures of the existing Article V. That simply was not going to happen in 1787, and it sure ain't gonna happen now.

So 60% seems a reasonable compromise. If a majority of the voters in 60% of the states containing 60% of the nation's population think it's time for a constitutional overhaul, then perhaps we ought to just go ahead with it, and trust that the rest of the states will buy into it in due course.

Formatting Notes in Constitution II

- Most of the provisions of Constitution II are unchanged from the Constitution of 1787 as amended, which Constitution II replaces. Some provisions have been

reworded or modernized without changing the original meaning. Provisions copied or modernized from the 1787 Constitution appear in normal type along with a footnote indicating the source.
- New provisions appear in Italics. As needed, footnotes explain the new wording.
- In all cases, spelling, punctuation, and capitalization have been updated to reflect modern usage.

Finally, let me end with this: I suffer no illusion that this Constitution II is the be-all and end-all. It is merely one man's proposal and a starting point for discussions, which need to be wide-ranging, deep, extended over time, and inclusive.

And now for my *piece de resistance*, Constitution II. Read on!

Constitution II for the United States of America

Preamble

We the people of the United States, in order to form a more perfect union, establish Justice, ensure domestic tranquility, provide for the common defense, promote the general welfare, and secure the blessings of liberty to ourselves and our posterity, do ordain and establish this Constitution *II*[34] for the United States of America.[35]

This Constitution II replaces the United States Constitution of 1787, as amended.

---

[34] The revised constitution is referred to as "this Constitution II" throughout.

[35] The Preamble is copied from the 1787 Constitution, Preamble.

Stipulations

1. *All laws, treaties, responsibilities, regulations, debts, and other obligations of the United States, undertaken under the Constitution of 1787 as amended, continue in full force and effect, except where specifically contravened by this Constitution II.*[36],[37]

---

[36] The Stipulations need to be stated at the outset, though the ideas themselves are not new and in fact exist (with different wording) in the 1787 Constitution.

[37] Adapted from the 1787 Constitution, Article VI, first paragraph.

2. This Constitution II establishes a federal government consisting of three co-equal branches: the Legislative Branch, the Executive Branch, and the Judicial Branch.[38]
3. Each of the 50 states existing at the time of the creation of this Constitution II is invited to conduct a plebiscite to ratify this Constitution II within ten years of its submission to the states. This Constitution II will become effective in those states ratifying same, provided it has been ratified by a plebiscite in 30 or more states, whose total population constitutes at least 60% of the population of the United States according to the most recent decennial census.[39]
4. The first elections conducted under this Constitution II will take place in the first Presidential election year that begins at least 12 months following ratification. [40] This first election will include the President, Chancellor, Senate, and House of Representatives. (The existing President, Vice President, and Congress will continue to serve until those newly elected under this Constitution II begin their terms of office.)

---

[38] While we have always talked about the three co-equal branches of the federal government, the 1787 Constitution does not explicitly state this. Perhaps it is a good idea to stipulate that this Constitution II prescribes three co-equal branches.

[39] The procedure for ratifying the 1787 Constitution appeared in Article VII. Interestingly, the framers simply ignored the procedure for amending the Articles of Confederation, which required unanimous consent of all thirteen original states.

[40] That is, a year evenly divisible by 4.

Article I: Bill of Rights

Section 1: Introduction to the Bill of Rights

1.1 This U.S. Constitution II establishes rights of natural persons, of citizens, and of states.[41] *The federal government and the several*

---

[41] Before the Constitution of 1787 was adopted, citizens in many states stipulated that their agreement to this Constitution was dependent upon the adoption of a Bill of Rights, which became the first 10 Amendments to the Constitution. In Constitution II, these rights are built into Constitution II itself. Further, certain other rights of all persons, of American citizens, and of states deserve to be spelled out before Constitution II is adopted. Due to the preeminent importance of

states may also recognize rights of other legal entities, such as corporations, partnerships, trusts, charities, and benevolent associations; but such rights are not constitutionally guaranteed.[42]

1.2 The federal government may delegate any of its powers to the several states. A collection of states may delegate any of their powers to the federal government. A collection of states may also create a public agency to jointly execute certain state powers and may request the federal government to participate or support such public agencies, but without ceding those powers to the federal government.[43]

1.3 The enumeration in this Constitution II of certain rights shall not be construed to deny or disparage others retained by the people. [44]

---

these constitutional protections, it makes sense to state them in Article I.

[42] This provision clarifies that Constitution II guarantees the rights of persons, citizens, and states, but not of corporations or other legal entities – whose rights may be recognized by law, but are not guaranteed by this Constitution II. (By the way, the 1787 Constitution also does not mention corporations, free markets, or capitalism. It mentions private property only once: This occurs in Amendment 5 in the clause concerning eminent domain.)

[43] This notion of federalism has existed in practice for many years; this provision makes it explicit in this Constitution II.

[44] Copied from the 1787 Constitution, Amendment 9.

1.4 The powers not delegated to the United States by this Constitution II, nor prohibited by it to the states, are reserved to the states respectively or to the people.[45]

Section 2: Bill of Rights of Natural Persons

2.1 Equality of All Natural Persons[46]

All natural persons are created equal, and are born with certain inalienable rights, and among these rights are life, liberty, and the pursuit of happiness.

2.2 Freedom of Religion, Press, and Expression[47]

Congress shall make no law respecting an establishment of religion or prohibiting the free exercise thereof; or abridging the freedom of speech or of the press; or the right of the people peaceably to assemble and to petition the Government for a redress of grievances.

---

[45] Copied from the 1787 Constitution, Amendment 10.

[46] This fundamental idea, taken from the American Declaration of Independence (1776) and also incorporated in the Universal Declaration of Human Rights (1948), deserves to be a bedrock principle of Constitution II.

[47] Copied from the 1787 Constitution, Amendment 1.

2.3 Freedom from Discrimination[48]

Discrimination against any person on the basis of sex, race, ethnicity, religion, or sexual orientation is prohibited.

Discrimination against any person on the basis of age, between ages 40 and 70, is prohibited.[49]

2.4 Prohibition of Slavery[50]

Neither slavery nor involuntary servitude, except as a punishment for crime whereof the party shall have been duly convicted, shall exist within the United States or any place subject to *its*[51] jurisdiction.

2.5 Prohibition on Cruel and Unusual Punishments *and on Torture*

---

[48] This paragraph enshrines in Constitution II the basic civil liberties of the last 50 years of civil rights legislation and judicial decisions.

[49] Certain laws may require a minimum age for performing certain activities, such as signing a contract, driving a car or boat or airplane, getting married, and holding public office. Other laws may mandate a retirement age. But any laws dealing with age must not discriminate between the ages of 40 and 70.

[50] Copied from the 1787 Constitution, Amendment 13.

[51] The 1787 Constitution used the word "their" rather than "its" because, up until the Civil War, "United States" was a plural noun; since Reconstruction, "United States" became a singular noun. The United States is treated as a singular noun in Constitution II.

Excessive bail shall not be required, nor excessive fines imposed, nor cruel and unusual punishments inflicted.[52]

The United States does not practice or tolerate the use of torture. The intentional infliction of extreme pain upon any person for the purpose of obtaining information, for punishment, or for any other purpose, is prohibited.[53]

Section 3: Bill of Rights of Citizens

3.1 Definition of Citizens[54,55]

The United States recognizes two categories of American citizens: a natural-born citizen and a naturalized citizen:

- *A natural-born citizen is any person*

---

[52] Copied from the 1787 Constitution, Amendment 8.

[53] Based on all available medical and scientific evidence, torture is ineffective in producing operational intelligence, and its use as punishment has long been outlawed by the 1787 Constitution. This provision incorporates into Constitution II both American law and international conventions on the absolute prohibition of the use of torture, especially the Geneva Conventions of 1949 and Additional Protocols of 1977, treaties to which the U.S. is a signatory.

[54] American citizens enjoy certain rights, over and above the rights of all persons who come under American jurisdiction. This section spells out those additional rights, starting with a definition of American citizenship.

[55] American citizenship was not explicitly defined in the 1787 Constitution. Article I Section 3.1 of this Constitution II provides clarity on this matter.

- - o *Who was born within the United States, its territories, or possessions, or*
  - o *Whose biological mother or father was an American citizen at the time of the child's birth. To retain natural-born citizenship under this provision after one's 21st birthday, a natural-born citizen not born in the United States must notify the Secretary of State of the United States, between his/her 18th and 21st birthdays, of his/her intent to remain an American citizen.*
- *A naturalized citizen is any person who becomes an American citizen in accordance with the federal law regulating the naturalization process.*
- *With the sole exception of eligibility to hold the office of President of the United States, which requires the President to be a natural-born citizen, no distinction shall be made between natural-born and naturalized citizens.*
- *No government has the power to take American citizenship away from any American citizen.*

3.2 Right to Bear Arms[56]

---

[56] Adapted from the 1787 Constitution, Amendment 2. This version of the Second Amendment ensures that an individual citizen may own a weapon, but may be prohibited by law from owning a nuclear weapon, warship, fighter jet, fully automatic machine gun, and other military-grade weapons.

For reasons of personal safety, hunting, and/or recreation, a citizen has the right to keep and bear personal weapons, including firearms appropriate to such purposes.

3.3 Quartering of Soldiers[57]

No Soldier shall be quartered in any house in time of peace without the consent of the owner, nor in time of war but in a manner to be prescribed by law.

3.4 Search and Seizure[58]

The right of the people to be secure in their persons, houses, papers, and effects against unreasonable searches and seizures shall not be violated; and no warrants shall issue but upon probable cause, supported by oath or affirmation, and particularly describing the place to be searched and the persons or things to be seized. *This provision includes the right to privacy.*[59]

3.5 Trial and Punishment; Compensation for Takings[60]

---

[57] Copied from the 1787 Constitution, Amendment 3.

[58] Copied from the 1787 Constitution, Amendment 4, except for the final sentence, in italics.

[59] A right to privacy is inferred by the 1787 Constitution, Amendment 4, and has been so interpreted by the Supreme Court. Adding it to this provision in Constitution II makes this right explicit rather than implicit.

[60] Copied from Amendment 5, except for the final sentence, in italics.

No person shall be held to answer for a capital or otherwise infamous crime unless on a presentment or indictment of a grand jury, except in cases arising in the land or naval forces, or in the militia when in actual service in time of war or public danger; nor shall any person be subject for the same offense to be twice put in jeopardy of life or limb; nor shall any person be compelled in any criminal case to be a witness against himself, nor be deprived of life, liberty, or property, without due process of law; nor shall private property be taken for public use without just compensation. *No citizen shall be forced to surrender private property for private gain; the principle and legal process of eminent domain shall only be used to serve a demonstrated public need, and any private property gained through eminent domain shall become public property in perpetuity.*[61]

3.6 Right to Speedy Trial; Confrontation of Witnesses; Assistance of Counsel[62]

In all criminal prosecutions, the accused shall enjoy the right to a speedy and public trial by an impartial jury of the state and district wherein the crime shall have been committed, which district shall have been previously ascertained by law. The accused shall enjoy the right to be informed of the nature and cause of the accusation, to be confronted with the witnesses

---

[61] Both conservatives and liberals, from time to time, have condemned the abuse of eminent domain. This provision states clearly that eminent domain may only be used to acquire or protect a public benefit.

[62] Copied from the 1787 Constitution, Amendment 6.

against him, to have compulsory process for obtaining witnesses in his favor, and to have the assistance of counsel for his defense.

3.7 Trial by Jury in Civil Cases[63]

In suits at common law, where the value in controversy shall exceed $1000, the right of trial by jury shall be preserved; and no fact tried by a jury shall be otherwise reexamined in any court of the United States other than according to the rules of the common law.

3.8 Healthcare, Education, and Necessities of Life[64]

Citizens of all ages have a right to basic healthcare, including physicians, hospitals, medicines, medical devices, reproductive services, and mental health services.

Citizens have a right to tax-supported public education.

Citizens have a right to the basic necessities of life – food, clothing, and shelter – sufficient to prevent death from starvation and exposure to the elements.

---

[63] Copied from the 1787 Constitution, Amendment 7. However, the amount has been raised from $20 to $1000.

[64] Article I Section 3.8 guarantees to every citizen the most basic necessities of life. It enshrines in Constitution II the actual, concrete meaning of the Declaration of Independence statement about everyone's inalienable right to life, liberty, and the pursuit of happiness. It also provides a constitutional basis for all of our social support programs – Social Security, Medicare, Medicaid, veterans' healthcare, and ACA (or whatever replaces it).

The citizen rights in Section 3.8 shall be provided by the state in which each citizen resides.

3.9 Equal Protection of the Laws[65]

No state shall make or enforce any law which shall abridge the privileges or immunities of citizens of the United States; nor shall any state deprive any person of life, liberty, or property, without due process of law; nor deny to any person within its jurisdiction the equal protection of the laws.

3.10 Voting rights[66]

All citizens who have attained the age of 18 are eligible to vote in all federal and state elections and in the state in which they reside, provided that a state may temporarily disenfranchise a citizen, on a case by case basis, for reasons of mental deficiency or because, at the time of an election, the citizen is incarcerated due to a felony conviction.

Section 4: Bill of Rights of States

4.1 Voluntary Union of states

- *The United States of America is a voluntary union of those states which have ratified this Constitution II and have*

---

[65] Copied from the 1787 Constitution, Amendment 14.

[66] Voting rights are adapted from the 1787 Constitution, Amendments 1, 15, 24 and 26. Prohibitions of discrimination on the basis of ethnicity and of sexual orientation are based on Supreme Court decisions that in turn depended on those constitutional provisions.

therefore agreed to join the Union and be subject to its jurisdiction.[67]

- *In addition to the 50 states in the Union under the 1787 Constitution, the District of Columbia and the Territory of Puerto Rico also each have the right to voluntarily join the Union as states under this Constitution II, if approved by a majority vote of their citizens, held within 5 years following submission of this Constitution II to the people and states.*[68]
- New states may be admitted by the Congress into this Union. However, no new states shall be formed or erected within the jurisdiction of any other state, nor any state be formed by the junction of two or more states or parts of states, without the consent of the *voters and* legislatures of the states concerned as well as of Congress.[69]

4.2 Secession

---

[67] The idea of a voluntary union is implied by the 1787 Constitution; this provision makes it explicit.

[68] This new provision is another attempt to empower citizens of the USA – in this case, citizens of two jurisdictions who have been treated as second-class citizens for many decades. Under Constitution II, DC will lose its three Electoral Votes unless it chooses to become a state, and both DC and Puerto Rico can claim their full rights as states if they so choose. By the way, there is some precedent for including this type of provision in our foundational document: The Articles of Confederation included a provision allowing Canada to join the Confederation if it wanted to do so.

[69] Copied from the 1787 Constitution, Article IV Section 3, with the addition of a voice for voters (in italics).

A state may secede from the Union by following these steps:

1) *Any state may, by a two-thirds vote of its citizens and its legislature, give notice of its intention to secede from the Union.*

2) *At the next Presidential general election held at least two years after a state's initial vote to secede, all voters in the United States will decide whether to permit that state to secede. Permission to secede requires approval from a majority of all voters in the United States, which must include a majority of voters in each of the states bordering the state planning to secede.*

3) *If approved by two-thirds of the voters in the secessionist state in a second plebiscite, held not less than three nor more than five years after permission to secede was granted by the voters of the United States, that state shall notify the Secretary of State of the United States of its decision to secede. That state and the United States will then have three years in which to negotiate the terms and conditions of their separation, after which that state will no longer be a part of the Union.*

4.3 Each State to Honor All Others[70]

Full faith and credit shall be given in each state to the public acts, records, and judicial proceedings of every other state. Congress may by general laws prescribe the manner in which such acts, records, and proceedings shall be proved, and the effect thereof.

4.4 State Citizens, Extradition[71]

---

[70] Copied from the 1787 Constitution, Article IV.

[71] Copied from the 1787 Constitution, Article IV.

The citizens of each state shall be entitled to all privileges and immunities of citizens in the several states.

A person charged in any state with treason, felony, or other crime, who shall flee from justice and be found in another state, shall on demand of the executive authority of the state from which he fled, be delivered up, to be removed to the state having jurisdiction of the crime.

4.5 Republican Government[72]

The United States shall guarantee to every state in this Union a republican form of government and shall protect each of them against invasion and, on application of the legislature or of the executive (when the legislature cannot be convened), against domestic violence.

4.6 State Militia[73]

A well-regulated militia being necessary to the security of a free state, the right of *each state* to keep and bear arms shall not be infringed.

4.7 State Legislative Preference[74]

---

[72] Copied from the 1787 Constitution, Article IV.

[73] Adapted from the 1787 Constitution, Amendment 2. Many constitutional scholars believe that this was the original intent of the Framers of the 1787 Constitution.

[74] Advocates for states rights often argue that some federal laws and regulations improperly infringe on state prerogatives. This provision

A state statute takes precedence over a federal statute within that state, provided that the state statute

- *Does not conflict with this Constitution II,*
- *Addresses matters wholly within the state's jurisdiction,*
- *Does not adversely affect other states or citizens of other states, and*
- *Is approved by a two-thirds majority of that state's voters in a referendum on that statute, which includes the assertion that the state statute is in conflict with a federal statute but complies with all elements of this provision.*

---

would allow a state, in certain circumstances and with the concurrence of two-thirds of its citizens, to adopt a state law that supersedes a federal law.

Article II: The Legislative Branch

Section 1: The Legislature

All legislative powers herein granted shall be vested in a Congress of the United States, which shall consist of a lower chamber, known as the House of Representatives, and an upper chamber, known as the Senate.[75],[76]

Section 2: The House of Representatives

2.1 Composition

The House of Representatives shall be composed of *501* Members chosen every second year by the voters of the several states *in accordance with Article VI -- Elections.* Congress may modify the number of members by law.

Seats in the House of Representatives shall be apportioned among the states during the first year of each new decade, based on the average number of voters who voted in each state in the two most recent Presidential general elections; but each state shall have at least one Representative, and *each Representative shall have one vote.*

2.2 Eligibility[77]

---

[75] The 1787 Constitution is often confusing when using the term "House(s)", which sometimes refers to the House of Representatives and sometimes refers to either the House or the Senate, or to both of them together. To avoid that confusion in Constitution II, the term "House" always refers to the House of Representatives, the term "Senate" refers to the Senate, and the terms "body" or "chamber" is used to refer to either or both the House of Representatives and the Senate.

[76] Slightly reworded from the 1787 Constitution, Article I Section 1.

[77] Except for the term limit clause in italics, these provisions are adapted from the 1787 Constitution, Article I Section 2.

When he/she takes office, a Representative must be

- At least 25 years old;
- At least 7 years a citizen of the United States;
- *Less than 19 years a Member of the House of Representatives;[78] and*
- A resident of the state from which he/she shall have been chosen.

2.3 Vacancies[79]

When vacancies happen in the representation from any state, the executive authority thereof shall issue writs of election to fill such vacancies.

2.4 Officers

The House of Representatives shall choose their Speaker and other officers.[80] *The Speaker, who may or may not be a Member, shall have no vote unless the House be equally divided.[81]*

---

[78] This provision implements term limits for the House. Ten 2-year terms is specified as the maximum amount of time a member may remain in the House.

[79] Copied from the 1787 Constitution, Article I Section 2.

[80] Copied from the 1787 Constitution, Article I Section 2.

[81] This provision is intended to make the position of Speaker less partisan, more a maintainer of good order rather than party leader, perhaps a bit more like the Speaker in the British House of Commons.

Section 3: The Senate

3.1 Composition[82]

The Senate of the United States shall be composed of Senators from each state, chosen by the voters for a six-year term of office; and each Senator shall have one vote. The number of Senators from each state is one-fifth of the number of Representatives from that state, with fractions always rounded up, so that each state will have at least one Senator.[83] All Senators shall be elected at large by all the voters in a state.

Seats in the Senate shall be divided as equally as they may be into three classes (Class I, Class II, and Class III). For any state, the number of seats assigned to each Class shall be the same, as nearly as possible. One Class shall be elected every two years. Thus one-third of the total Senate, and one-third of the Senate seats from each state, shall be elected every two years.[84]

When, due to the decennial Congressional reapportionment, the number of Senators for any state is decreased, the next Senator

---

[82] One of the fundamental improvements of Constitution II over the 1787 Constitution is replacing the unrepresentative Original Senate with the population-based New Senate.

[83] That is, a state with 1 to 5 House seats will have one Senator; a state with 6 to 10 House seats will have two Senators; a state with 11 to 15 House seats will have three Senators; and so on.

[84] This paragraph mirrors the 1787 Constitution, Article I Section 3, except for the clause dealing with the equal distribution of Senate seats from each state across the three Senate Classes.

from that state whose term of office is expiring shall not be replaced after his term expires. When the number of Senators from any state is increased, a new Senator from that state shall be elected at the next election, and that seat will be assigned to Class I, II, or III, so that, as far as possible, one third of the Senate remains elected every two years, and one third of the Senators from each state remains elected every two years.[85]

The first election cycle following reapportionment will include separate primary and general elections for all three Senate classes. This will include elections for 6-year terms for all the seats in the class normally scheduled for elections that year, as well as elections for 4-year terms and for 2-year terms for those seats in the other two classes which do not have an incumbent.

The election of Senators shall take place in accordance with Article VI – Elections.

3.2 Eligibility[86]

When he/she takes office, a Senator must be

- At least 30 years old;
- At least 9 years a citizen of the United States;

---

[85] This provision could result in the election of a Senator to a newly-created seat for a term of only two years or four years, that is, until such time as that seat's class next comes up for election.

[86] Except for the term limit clause in italics, these provisions are adapted from the 1787 Constitution, Article I Section 3.

- *Less than 17 years a Senator;[87] and*
- *A resident of the state from which he/she shall have been chosen.*

3.3 Vacancies[88]

When vacancies happen in the representation of any state, the executive authority of such state shall issue writs of election to fill such vacancies.

3.4 Chancellor

In accordance with Article VI – Elections, voters shall elect a Chancellor to a four-year term of office in even-numbered years not evenly divisible by four. The Chancellor shall preside over the Senate. The Chancellor shall have no vote unless the Senate be equally divided.

The Chancellor must meet the same eligibility requirements as the President of the United States. A person may be elected to the office of Chancellor a maximum of two times. Whenever there is a vacancy in the office of Chancellor, the President shall nominate a Chancellor who shall take office upon confirmation by a majority

---

[87] This provision implements term limits for the Senate. Three 6-year terms is specified as the maximum amount of time a member may remain as a Senator.

[88] Adapted from the 1787 Constitution, Amendment 17. However, that Amendment gave the governor the power to make temporary appointments to fill vacancies. This Constitution II stipulates that vacancies will be filled by an election, and is exactly the same for both chambers.

vote in both chambers of Congress; this nominee must meet the eligibility requirements to become Chancellor and must also be a Member of Congress.

The Chancellor shall appoint a Chancellor Pro Tempore, with the concurrence of a majority of Senators present and voting. The Chancellor Pro Tempore shall preside over the Senate in the absence of the Chancellor, or when the Chancellor is serving as Acting President.

The Chancellor[89] (but not the Chancellor Pro Tempore) shall have power to nominate, and by and with the advice and consent of the Senate, shall appoint Associate Justices of the Supreme Court, provided two thirds of the Senators present and voting concur;[90] and he shall nominate, and by and with the advice and consent of a majority of Senators present and voting, shall appoint federal judges of inferior courts.

In all cases of Chancellor judicial nominations, if the Senate fails to approve or disapprove a nomination within 60 calendar days after the Chancellor has made the nomination, the Chancellor may appoint the nominee, and the nominee may temporarily assume the position to which he was nominated, pending Senate action on that

---

[89] An important change in Constitution II is that the Chancellor, rather than the President, makes all judicial appointments.

[90] Lifetime appointment of a Supreme Court justice is a matter that should be carefully considered and receive the approval of two-thirds of the Senate. In the past, this notion has been imposed by the use or threatened use of the filibuster, but since the filibuster is eliminated in Constitution II, it is advisable to require a two-thirds majority for Supreme Court appointments.

nomination. However, the Chancellor may not make such a temporary appointment to the Supreme Court unless the Court at the time of the appointment has fewer than 9 Justices. All temporary appointments expire when the Senate acts or when a new Congress convenes, whichever comes first.

Section 4 - Meetings

The Congress shall assemble at least once in every year, and such meeting shall commence on *the first Sunday in January unless Congress shall by law appoint a different day.*

Wednesdays through Sundays from 4 pm to 10 pm, except federal holidays, are designated as legislative days. When Congress is in session, it shall meet on designated legislative days, unless Congress adopts a different schedule.[91] *Either chamber, when it does not meet with a quorum of members present for three consecutive legislative days, shall be deemed to be in recess.*[92]

Section 5 - Membership, Rules, Journals, and Adjournment

Each chamber shall be the judge of the elections, returns, and qualifications of its own members, and a majority of each shall

---

[91] Important Congressional debates should occur in prime time and on weekends, when many more Americans could pay attention.

[92] This provision requires each chamber to be either in session or in recess. It cannot use an artificial device of meeting briefly with only a few members in order to pretend that it is still in session.

constitute a quorum to do business; but a smaller number may adjourn from day to day and may be authorized to compel the attendance of absent members, in such manner and under such penalties as each chamber may provide.[93]

All decisions taken within each chamber shall be by majority vote of members present, except for those specific items in this Constitution II requiring a two-thirds or a three-fifths vote.

Any member may make a motion to call a bill, a resolution, or a Presidential appointment to the floor for a vote; and, if a majority of members present concur, that bill, resolution, or appointment shall become the first order of business in that chamber on the next legislative day; and at that time, such bill, resolution, or appointment will, by majority vote, be either approved, disapproved, or tabled for later consideration.[94]

Each chamber may determine the rules of its proceedings, punish its members for disorderly behavior, and, with the concurrence of two-thirds, expel a member.

Each chamber shall keep a Journal of its proceedings and from time to time publish the same, excepting such parts as may in their judgment require secrecy; and the yeas and nays of the members of either chamber on any question shall, at the desire of one fifth of those present, be entered on the journal.

---

[93] Except for the two paragraphs in italics, Section 5 is copied from the 1787 Constitution, Article I Section 5.

[94] This provision allows either chamber to vote on items that a majority of the members want to vote on.

Neither chamber, during the session of Congress, shall, without the consent of the other, adjourn for more than three days, nor to any other place than that in which the two chambers shall be sitting.

In even-numbered years (that is, election years), Congress shall adjourn sine die no later than July 4. Unless called back into session by the President of the United States due to a national emergency, Congress shall not reconvene until the convening of the new Congress following the election.

Section 6 - Compensation

All Members of Congress and the Chancellor shall receive compensation for their services, to be ascertained by law, and paid out of the Treasury of the United States.[95] However, no law varying the compensation for the services of the Senators, Representatives, or Chancellor shall take effect until an election of Representatives shall have intervened.

No Senator or Representative shall, during the time for which he was elected, be appointed to any office under the authority of the United States *or any state* which shall have been created, or the emoluments whereof shall have been increased during such time;

---

[95] This section is adapted from the 1787 Constitution, Article I Section 6, and Amendment 27.

and no person holding any office under the United States shall be a member of either chamber during his continuance in office. [96]

Senators and Representatives shall in all cases, except treason, felony and breach of the peace, be privileged from arrest during their attendance at the session of their respective chambers, and in going to and returning from the same; and for any speech or debate in either chamber, they shall not be questioned in any other place.

Section 7 - Revenue Bills, Legislative Process, and Presidential Veto

All bills for raising revenue shall originate in the House of Representatives, but the Senate may propose or concur with amendments as on other bills.[97]

The earliest effective date of any bill, when enacted by Congress, shall be July 1st following the next Congressional election after passage of the bill. An earlier effective date can only be enacted if (1) the sole purpose of the bill is to repeal a bill which has not yet

---

[96] This clause has been modified from the 1787 Constitution to remove the word "civil" before the first occurrence of the word "office", and to add the phrase "or any state". The purpose of these changes is to prohibit Senators and Representatives from holding military (as well as civil) appointments while they serve in Congress, including the Armed Forces of the United States as well as any state militia.

[97] Except for the paragraph in italics, this section is copied from the 1787 Constitution, Article I Section 7.

gone into effect, or (2) an earlier date is agreed to by three-fifths of members present in both chambers upon final passage of the bill.[98]

Every Bill which shall have passed the House and the Senate, shall, before it becomes a law, be presented to the President of the United States; If he approves the bill, he shall sign it, but if not he shall return it, with his objections to that chamber in which it shall have originated, who shall enter the objections at large on their journal, and proceed to reconsider it. If after such reconsideration two-thirds of that chamber shall agree to pass the bill, it shall be sent, together with the objections, to the other chamber, by which it shall likewise be reconsidered, and if approved by two-thirds of that chamber, it shall become a law. But in all such cases the votes of both chambers shall be determined by yeas and nays, and the names of the persons voting for and against the bill shall be entered on the journal of each chamber respectively. If any bill shall not be returned by the President within ten days (Sundays excepted) after it shall have been presented to him, the same shall be a law, in like manner as if he had signed it, unless the Congress by their adjournment prevent its return, in which case it shall not be a law.

Every order, resolution, or vote to which the concurrence of the Senate and House may be necessary (except on a question of

---

[98] This provision eliminates the need for a filibuster to delay action on a bill until "the people exercise their right to weigh in". It also extends to both chambers the same privilege to pass emergency legislation with a super majority, but to enact normal legislation by a simple majority vote.

adjournment) shall be presented to the President of the United States; and before the same shall take effect, shall be approved by him, or being disapproved by him, shall be repassed by two thirds of the Senate and of the House of Representatives, according to the rules and limitations prescribed in the case of a bill.

Section 8 - Powers of Congress

The Congress shall have power as follows:[99]

To lay and collect taxes, duties, imposts, and excises, to pay the debts and provide for the common defense and general welfare of the United States; but all duties, imposts, and excises shall be uniform throughout the United States;

To lay and collect taxes on incomes, from whatever source derived, without apportionment among the several states, and without regard to any census or enumeration;[100]

To borrow money on the credit of the United States;

To regulate commerce with foreign nations, and among the several states, and with the Indian Tribes;

To establish a uniform rule of naturalization and uniform laws on the subject of bankruptcies throughout the United States;

---

[99] Except for the clauses in italics, and except also for the clauses noted individually, this entire section is adapted from the 1787 Constitution, Article I Section 8.

[100] Copied from the 1787 Constitution, Amendment 16.

To coin money, regulate the value thereof, and of foreign coin, and fix the standard of weights and measures;

To provide for the punishment of counterfeiting the securities and current coin of the United States;

To establish post offices;

To conduct a census or enumeration of the United States and to maintain estimated census figures at all times. The actual enumeration shall be made within three years after the first meeting of the Congress of the United States *under this Constitution II, and subsequently during every year evenly divisible by 10,* in such manner as they shall by law direct;[101]

To promote the progress of science and useful arts, *by conducting and sponsoring scientific research and cultural and artistic endeavors;*[102]

To secure for limited times to authors and inventors the exclusive right to their respective writings and discoveries, *provided,*

---

[101] The first sentence of this provision is adapted from the 1787 Constitution, Article I, Section 2. The second sentence is copied from the 1787 Constitution, Article I, Section 2. The italicized clause clarifies the requirement for a decennial census.

[102] This clause makes the federal role in science and the arts more explicit.

however, that copyright protection shall not exceed 50 years, and patent protection shall not exceed 25 years;[103]

To constitute tribunals inferior to the Supreme Court;

To define and punish piracies and felonies committed on the high seas, and offenses against the Law of Nations;

To declare war, *authorize privateers and other military proxies,*[104] and make rules concerning captures wherever they may occur;

To raise and support the *Armed Forces*[105] of the United States *(on land, on and under the sea, in the air, and in cyberspace)*;

---

[103] This new limitation on Congressional power is a response to Congress' abuse of that power in recent decades.

[104] The 1787 Constitution used the now-obsolete phrase "grant letters of marques and reprisal". In the 18th century, governments sometimes issued "letters of marques and reprisal", which authorized a private vessel (privateer or pirate ship) to seize and confiscate enemy ships. Constitution II substitutes the phrase "privateers and other military proxies", meaning essentially the same thing but employing modern terminology. The significance of this passage is that Congress – not the President or any sort of king – has this power.

[105] Constitution II refers to the Armed Forces of the United States rather than to just the Army and the Navy. It addresses all American forces, wherever they may be – on land, on sea, in the air, or in cyberspace. The term "Armed Forces" is preferable to naming the service branches (Army, Navy, Air Force, Marine Corps, Coast Guard), since a number of proposals have been made to merge all of the service branches into one, or to restructure them in some other way. The single term "Armed

To make rules for the government and regulation of the Armed Forces;

To provide for calling forth state militia to execute the laws of the Union, suppress Insurrections, and repel Invasions;

To provide for organizing, arming, and disciplining the state militia, and for governing such part of them as may be employed in the service of the United States, reserving to the states respectively the appointment of the officers and the authority of training the militia according to the discipline prescribed by Congress;

To protect the environment, and to provide for public health and safety by ensuring access to clean and safe water, air, energy, medicines, and the food supply;[106]

To provide financial assistance to the several states, based on the unique needs of each state, for infrastructure projects, for emergency relief from natural disasters, for fulfillment of each state's obligations under Article I Section 3.8, and for such other purposes as Congress may deem appropriate and necessary;[107]

Forces" covers all of our federal military forces, no matter how they are organized in the future.

[106] This provision ensures that Congress has the constitutional authority to pass environmental regulations.

[107] This provision ensures that Congress can issue block grants to the states to help states meet their financial obligations, taking into account the differing needs of each state.

To provide public financing for federal elections and election campaigns, to regulate and limit campaign contributions, and to mandate full disclosure of the sources and amounts of campaign contributions;[108]

To regulate all federal elections in accordance with Article VI, provided that the actual conduct of the elections is left to the states; and to modify by law any of the provisions of Article VI, provided two-thirds of members present in each chamber agree.[109]

To dispose of and make all needful rules and regulations respecting the territory or other property belonging to the United States, and nothing in this Constitution II shall be so construed as to prejudice any claims of the United States or of any particular state;[110]

To exercise exclusive legislation in all cases whatsoever over the District of Columbia *(unless the District of Columbia chooses to become a state, in accordance with Article I Section 4}*, and to exercise like authority over all places purchased by the consent of the legislature of the state in which the same shall be, for the

---

[108] This provision ensures that Congress has the constitutional authority to fund federal elections and to regulate election finances,

[109] Since the specific procedures of Article VI are new, it is wise to provide a mechanism to alter them without the more challenging procedure of amending Constitution II.

[110] Copied from the 1787 Constitution, Article IV, Section 3.

erection of forts, magazines, arsenals, dockyards, and other needful buildings;[111] And

To make all laws which shall be necessary and proper for carrying into execution the foregoing powers, and all other powers vested by this Constitution II in the Government of the United States, or in any department or officer thereof.

Section 9 - Limits on Congress

The privilege [112] of the writ of habeas corpus [113] shall not be suspended, unless when in cases of rebellion or invasion the public safety may require it.

---

[111] Copied from the 1787 Constitution, Article II Section 8, with additional wording in italics concerning Washington, DC, should it choose to become a state.

[112] Except for the clauses on liquor and other drugs, Section 9 is copied from the 1787 Constitution, Article I Section 9, although several provisions of that Section are omitted from Constitution II.

[113] A writ of *habeas corpus* is a demand issued by a court to an executive over whom the court has jurisdiction, demanding that the executive bring to the court someone whom the executive is holding in confinement, and requiring the executive to explain to the court the legal justification for continuing to confine that person. This provision, including the suspension of the privilege during a rebellion or invasion, is lifted directly from British Common Law. It is included verbatim in the 1787 Constitution, Article I, Section 9.

No bill of attainder[114] or ex post facto[115] law shall be passed.

No tax or duty shall be laid on articles exported from any state.

No preference shall be given by any regulation of commerce or revenue to the ports of one state over those of another: nor shall vessels bound to, or from, one state, be obliged to enter, clear, or pay duties in another.

The transportation or importation into any state, territory, or possession of the United States for delivery or use therein of intoxicating liquors, *marijuana, cocaine, or any other mood-altering substances,* in violation of the laws thereof, is hereby prohibited. *In states where such substances are permitted by state law, Congress shall not prohibit them. Congress shall make no national law regarding the manufacture, import, export, possession, or use of such substances.*[116]

---

[114] A bill of attainder makes a person or group guilty of treason or other capital offense without a trial, and also takes away the civil rights, property, and titles of the person "attainted".

[115] An *ex post facto* law is a law that criminalizes behavior that occurred before the law was passed.

[116] The provisions concerning intoxicating liquors are copied from the 1787 Constitution, Amendment 21. Marijuana and other drugs have been added to Constitution II. This provision ensures that the use of alcohol, marijuana, and other mind-altering substances is entirely a state matter. The federal government will neither compel nor prohibit state action in this realm.

No money shall be drawn from the Treasury but in consequence of appropriations made by law; and a regular statement and account of the receipts and expenditures of all public money shall be published from time to time.

No title of nobility shall be granted by the United States: And no person holding any office of profit or trust under them shall, without the consent of the Congress, accept any present, emolument, office, title, or *payment*, of any kind whatever, from any king, prince, foreign state, or *other public or private foreign entity*.[117]

Section 10 - Powers Prohibited of States

No state[118] shall enter into any treaty, alliance, or confederation; *authorize privateers or other military proxies for the state*[119]; print or coin money; emit bills of credit; pass any bill of attainder, ex post facto law, or law impairing the obligation of contracts; or grant any title of nobility.

---

[117] Corporations and other private commercial entities were not typically instruments of monarchical power when the 1787 Constitution was written. The added words make it clear that all such foreign payments, from whatever source, public or private, are prohibited.

[118] Section 10 is copied entirely from the 1787 Constitution, Article I Section 10,

[119] The 1787 constitution used the phrase "grant letters of marques and reprisal". The phrase "authorize privateers and other proxies for the state" is the modern equivalent.

No state shall, without the consent of Congress, lay any imposts or duties on imports or exports, except what may be absolutely necessary for executing its inspection laws: and the net produce of all duties and imposts, laid by any state on imports or exports, shall be for the use of the Treasury of the United States; and all such laws shall be subject to the revision and control of Congress.

No state shall, without the consent of Congress, lay any duty of tonnage, keep troops, or ships of war in time of peace, enter into any agreement or compact with another state, or with a foreign power, or engage in war, unless actually invaded, or in such imminent danger as will not admit of delay.

Section 11 - Transition from the 1787 Constitution to this Constitution II

After this Constitution II becomes effective, [120] and before the beginning of the year when the first elections under this Constitution II will be held, the Vice President, acting as President of the Senate, will arrange for an orderly transition from the Congress under the 1787 Constitution to the Congress under this Constitution II.

Following the procedure specified in Article II Section 2.1, the 501 seats in the House of Representatives shall be apportioned to the several states. After the apportionment of seats in the House, apportionment of seats in the Senate is automatic.

---

[120] Article II Section 12 is entirely new.

The three Senate Classes shall continue as they did in the Senate according to the 1787 Constitution, and on the same schedule.[121] *Senators currently in office will be assigned to the same Class in the Senate as they had in the Senate according to the 1787 Constitution, and will continue to serve as Senators until their current six-year terms expire, including Senators whose seats will not be renewed under the apportionment provisions of Constitution II.*

Every Senate seat will be assigned to Class I, Class II, or Class III, as follows:

a) *For states with at least three Senate seats, the same number of seats will be assigned to each Class, so that, following this initial assignment, 0, 1, or 2 seats from each of these states remain to be assigned to a Class.*
b) *For states with two Senate seats, and for states with two seats remaining to be assigned after step (a), one seat will be assigned to each of two Classes.*
c) *All remaining seats will be assigned to a Class.*
d) *The Vice President will ensure that*
    a. *The Class assignment of each incumbent Senator remains the same;*
    b. *The size of each Class in future elections is the same, or does not differ by more than one seat; and*

---

[121] Under the current Senate election schedule, Class I Senate seats are elected in 2018 and every 6 years thereafter, Class II Senate seats are elected in 2020 and every 6 years thereafter, and Class III Senate seats are elected in 2022 and every 6 years thereafter.

> c. *For each state, the number of seats in each Class also does not differ by more than one seat.*

The first Senate elections under this Constitution II will follow the procedure for the first election each decade following reapportionment, as specified in Article II Section 3.1.

The last Vice President under the 1787 Constitution will continue to serve as the first Chancellor under this Constitution II.

Article III: The Executive Branch

Section 1 - The President

1.1 The executive power shall be vested in a President of the United States of America.[122] *He/she shall hold office for a four-year term. Voters shall choose the President in years evenly divisible by four. Presidential elections shall be conducted in accordance with Article VI – Elections.*[123]

---

[122] Copied from the 1787 Constitution, Article II, Section 1.

[123] All election procedures in Constitution II appear in Article VI.

1.2 Eligibility for the office of President:[124] Upon taking office, the President must be

- At least 35 years old,
- A natural-born citizen of the United States,
- At least 14 years a resident within the United States, and
- Less than 6 years the President of the United States.

1.3 Lack of a qualified President-elect: If, at the time fixed for the beginning of the term of the President, the President-elect shall have died, the Chancellor shall become President. If a President shall not have been chosen before the time fixed for the beginning of his term, or if the President-elect shall have failed to qualify, then the Chancellor shall act as President until a President shall have qualified.[125] *If neither a President-elect nor a Chancellor shall have qualified, then the Speaker of the House of Representatives shall become the Acting President, and the first duty of the Acting President shall be to arrange for new Presidential elections as soon as practicable or to pursue whatever actions are necessary to qualify the President-elect; but the Acting President shall also carry*

---

[124] Adapted from the 1787 Constitution, Article II Section 1 and Amendment 12. Since the office of Vice President has been eliminated in Constitution II. the requirement that the President and the Vice President reside in different states has been deleted.

[125] Copied from the 1787 Constitution, Amendment 20.

out all the duties of the President until a properly-elected President shall have qualified.[126]

1.4 Vacancy in the office of President:[127]

1. In case of the removal of the President from office or of his death or resignation, the Chancellor shall become President.

2. Whenever the President transmits to the Chancellor of the Senate and the Speaker of the House of Representatives his written declaration that he is unable to discharge the powers and duties of his office, and until he transmits to them a written declaration to the contrary, such powers and duties shall be discharged by the Chancellor as Acting President.

3. Whenever the Chancellor and a majority of either the principal officers of the executive departments or of such other body as Congress may by law provide, transmit to the Chancellor Pro Tempore of the Senate and the Speaker of the House of Representatives their written declaration that the President is unable to discharge the powers and duties of his office, the Chancellor shall immediately assume the powers and duties of the office as Acting President.

Thereafter, when the President transmits to the Chancellor Pro Tempore of the Senate and the Speaker of the House of Representatives his written declaration that no inability exists, he shall resume the powers and duties of his office unless the

---

[126] This is a new provision, which provides an elected official with a national mandate (the Speaker of the House) as a caretaker President, until a properly-elected President can assume the office.

[127] The remainder of this section is copied from the 1787 Constitution, Amendment 25.

Chancellor and a majority of either the principal officers of the executive departments or of such other body as Congress may by law provide, transmit within four days to the Chancellor Pro Tempore and the Speaker their written declaration that the President is unable to discharge the powers and duties of his office. Thereupon Congress shall decide the issue, assembling within forty-eight hours for that purpose if not in session. If the Congress, within twenty-one days after receipt of the latter written declaration, or, if Congress is not in session, within twenty-one days after Congress is required to assemble, determines by two thirds vote of both chambers that the President is unable to discharge the powers and duties of his office, the Chancellor shall continue to discharge the same as Acting President; otherwise, the President shall resume the powers and duties of his office.

1.5 Compensation: At stated times the President shall receive for his/her services a compensation, which shall neither be increased nor diminished during the period for which he/she shall have been elected, and he/she shall not receive within that period any other emolument from the United States or any of them.[128]

1.6 Oath of Office[129]: Before the President enters on the execution of his office, he shall take the following oath or affirmation:

"I do solemnly swear (or affirm) that I will faithfully execute the office of President of the United States, and will to the best of my

---

[128] Copied from the 1787 Constitution, Article II Section 1.

[129] Copied from the 1787 Constitution, Article II Section 1.

ability, preserve, protect and defend this Constitution II of the United States."

Section 2 - Civilian Power over Military; the Cabinet, Pardon Power, and Appointments

The President shall be Commander in Chief of the Armed Forces of the United States, and of the militia of the several states, when called into the actual service of the United States; he may require the opinion, in writing, of the principal officer in each of the executive departments, upon any subject relating to the duties of their respective offices, and he shall have power to grant reprieves and pardons for offenses against the United States, except in cases of impeachment[130] *or of alleged offenses by the President or the Chancellor.*[131]

As Commander in Chief, the President may order the use of military force in a war properly declared by Congress in accordance with Article II Section 8. In the absence of a declaration of war, the President may employ military force to defend the United States or its allies, or for such other purposes as the President deems necessary in the national interest of the United States, *provided that the President notifies Congress within*

---

[130] This provision is copied from the 1787 Constitution, Article II Section 2.

[131] The President cannot absolve himself or those around him from alleged wrongdoing.

48 hours of the beginning of such a military operation, and provided also that Congress approves of such use within 60 days after such a military operation commences. Without a declaration of war, the President may continue a military operation into a new calendar year only if Congress, by a law enacted no more than six months before the calendar year, authorizes the continued use of military force.[132]

The President shall have Power, by and with the advice and consent of the Senate, to make treaties, provided two thirds of the Senators present concur; and he shall nominate, and by and with the advice and consent of the Senate, shall appoint ambassadors, other public ministers and consuls, and all other officers *in the Executive Branch* of the United States *Government*, whose appointments are not herein otherwise provided for, and which shall be established by law: but Congress may by law vest the appointment of such inferior officers, as they think proper, in the President alone or in the heads of departments.[133]

In all cases of Presidential nominations, if the Senate fails to approve or disapprove a nomination within 60 calendar days after the President has made the nomination, the President may appoint the nominee, and the nominee may temporarily assume the position

---

[132] This provision codifies and strengthens the Authorized Use of Military Force doctrine within Constitution II. It insures that any continuing military operation not supported by a Declaration of War will have Congressional authorization at least once every year.

[133] Except for the clause in italics, this provision is copied from the 1787 Constitution, Article II Section 2.

to which he was nominated, pending Senate action on that nomination. Such temporary appointments expire when the Senate acts or when a new Congress convenes, whichever comes first.

The President shall have power to fill up all vacancies that may happen during the recess *or adjournment* of the Senate, by granting commissions which shall expire *when the next Congress convenes.*[134]

Section 3 - State of the Union, Convening Congress, and Executive Orders

The President shall from time to time give to the Congress information on the state of the Union, and recommend for their consideration such measures as he shall judge necessary and expedient; he may, on extraordinary occasions, convene both chambers, or either of them, and in case of disagreement between them with respect to the time of adjournment, he may adjourn them to such time as he shall think proper; he shall receive ambassadors and other public ministers; he shall take care that the laws be faithfully executed, and shall commission all the *military* officers of the United States.[135]

In carrying out his responsibility to "take care that the laws be faithfully executed", the President may issue Executive Orders which have the same effect as the law upon which the Executive

---

[134] This provision is adapted from the 1787 Constitution, Article II Section 2. The words "or adjournment" were added. The expiration date for temporary appointments has been modified.

[135] Copied from the 1787 Constitution, Article II Section 3.

Order is based, provided that any Executive Order will have an effective date not less than thirty days from its issuance, and provided further that either chamber by majority vote taken during that 30-day waiting period may prevent any Executive Order from coming into effect.

Article IV: The Judicial Branch

Section 1 – The Judiciary

The judicial power of the United States shall be vested in one Supreme Court and in such inferior courts as the Congress may from time to time ordain and establish. *The Supreme Court shall consist of a Chief Justice of the United States and several Associate Justices.* The judges, both of the Supreme Court and inferior courts, shall, at stated times, receive for their services a compensation which shall not be diminished during their continuance in office.[136] All federal judges whose appointments have been confirmed by the Senate shall hold their offices during good behavior.[137]

Any current or former federal judge is eligible to be nominated to serve as an Associate Justice of the Supreme Court. When the position of Chief Justice of the United States becomes vacant, the sitting Associate Justices shall select one of their own number as the next Chief Justice.[138] No one shall serve as a Supreme Court Justice for longer than 15 years; however, after 15 years on the Supreme Court, a Justice is entitled to continue serving as a federal judge on an inferior court.[139]

All federal judges appointed to office under the 1787 Constitution shall continue their lifetime appointments under this Constitution II.[140]

---

[136] Copied from the 1787 Constitution, Article III Section 1.

[137] The 1787 Constitution, Article III Section 1, specified that "Judges of inferior courts shall hold their offices during good behavior." There is no compelling reason to exclude Supreme Court Justices from this same protection,

[138] The purpose of this provision is to encourage comity among the Justices. They will be more likely to work well together if their leader is chosen by them.

[139] The 15-year term of office provides a new check on the unfettered power of Supreme Court Justices.

[140] This sentence ensures continuity of the federal judiciary when this Constitution II goes into effect.

Section 2 – Judicial Power, Original Jurisdiction, and Jury Trials

2.1 Judicial Review. The judicial power extends to judicial review of acts of the Legislative branch, in order to judge whether such acts are in conformance with this Constitution II, and the federal courts shall have the power to invalidate any law, or any part of any law, found by the courts not to be in compliance with this Constitution II. The judicial power also extends to judicial review of all acts of the Executive branch, in order to judge whether such acts are in conformance with this Constitution II and with laws duly enacted by Congress, and the federal courts shall have the power to invalidate any such acts or parts of such acts, found by the courts not to be in compliance with this Constitution II or the laws of the United States. In conducting judicial reviews of both the Legislative and the Executive branches, federal courts may consider both the inscribed provisions of this Constitution II and laws enacted by Congress, as well as their intent. [141]

2.2 Judicial Power. The judicial power shall extend to all cases, in law and equity, arising under this Constitution II, the laws of the United States and treaties made, or which shall be made, under their authority; to all cases affecting ambassadors, other public ministers and consuls; to all cases of admiralty and maritime jurisdiction; to controversies to which the United States shall be

---

[141] This provision incorporates into this Constitution II the principle of judicial review, which has been practiced and followed under the 1787 Constitution ever since the Marbury v. Madison decision in 1803.

a party; to controversies between two or more states; between a state and citizens of another state; between citizens of different states; between citizens of the same state claiming lands under grants of different states, and between a state, or the citizens thereof, and foreign states, citizens or subjects.[142]

The Judicial power of the United States shall not be construed to extend to any suit in law or equity, commenced or prosecuted against one of the United States by citizens of another state, or by citizens or subjects of any foreign state.[143]

2.3 Original Jurisdiction. In all cases affecting ambassadors, other public ministers and consuls, and those in which a state shall be party, the Supreme Court shall have original jurisdiction. In all the other cases before mentioned, the Supreme Court shall have appellate jurisdiction, both as to law and fact, with such exceptions and under such regulations as the Congress shall make.[144]

2.4 Jury Trials. The trial of all crimes, except in cases of Impeachment, shall be by jury; and such trial shall be held in the state where the said crimes shall have been committed; but when not committed within any state, the trial shall be at such place or places as the Congress may by law have directed.[145]

---

[142] Copied from the 1787 Constitution, Article III Section 2.

[143] Copied from the 1787 Constitution, Amendment 11.

[144] Copied from the 1787 Constitution, Article III Section 2.

[145] Copied from the 1787 Constitution, Article III Section 2.

Section 3 - Treason

Treason[146] against the United States shall consist only in levying war against the United States or in adhering to the enemies of the United States, giving them aid and comfort. No person shall be convicted of treason unless on the testimony of two witnesses to the same overt act or on confession in open court. The Congress shall have power to declare the punishment of treason.

Section 4 – Misconduct by Public Officials

The President, *the Chancellor,* and all civil officers of the United States shall be removed from office on impeachment for, and conviction of, treason, bribery, or other high crimes and misdemeanors. [147]

No person or office is above the law, and no individual is indispensable. Accordingly, a person holding a public office, even while continuing to hold that office, shall nevertheless be liable and subject to indictment, trial, judgment, and punishment, according to law.[148] *Any federal official indicted for a felony or impeached by the House is suspended from office until the matter is*

---

[146] Copied from the 1787 Constitution, Article III Section 3.

[147] Copied from the 1787 Constitution, Article II, Section 4, except that the word "Chancellor: replaces "Vice President".

[148] Holding a high public office does not shield the incumbent from prosecution for any crime.

resolved through conviction or acquittal.[149] *If convicted following impeachment or indictment, the official shall be removed from office; if acquitted, the person shall resume the duties of the office.*

When alleged misconduct by the President warrants an investigation, the Chancellor shall appoint a Special Counsel to conduct that investigation. When alleged misconduct by the Chancellor warrants an investigation, the Attorney General shall appoint a Special Counsel to conduct that investigation. The Special Counsel will submit a report of his findings to the Chancellor, the Speaker, the Attorney General, and the public.[150]

The House of Representatives, *by majority vote,* shall have the sole power of impeachment.[151]

The Senate shall have the sole power to try all impeachments. When sitting for that purpose, they shall be on oath or affirmation. When the President of the United States *or the*

---

[149] Defending oneself in a criminal proceeding or impeachment trial is so time-consuming and onerous that an official in that situation cannot give proper attention to his official duties. Therefore, the public interest demands that such an official temporarily step aside until the matter is resolved.

[150] A high public official such as a President or a Chancellor should not investigate himself.

[151] Copied from the 1787 Constitution, Article I, Section 2. The phrase "by majority vote" is added for clarity.

Chancellor of the Senate[152] is tried, the Chief Justice shall preside: And no person shall be convicted without the concurrence of two thirds of the members present. [153]

Judgment in cases of impeachment shall not extend further than to removal from office and disqualification to hold and enjoy any office of honor, trust or profit under the United States.[154]

---

[152] The Chancellor, were he/she impeached by the House, should not preside over his/her own trial. Therefore, the Chief Justice should carry that responsibility.

[153] This entire paragraph, except for the phrase in italics, is copied from the 1787 Constitution, Article I, Section 3.

[154] Copied from the 1787 Constitution, Article I, Section 3.

Article V: Debts, Supremacy, and Oaths

All debts contracted and engagements entered into before the adoption of this Constitution II shall be as valid against the United

States under this Constitution II as under the 1787 Constitution.[155],[156]

The notion of a "national debt ceiling" has no meaning or merit whatsoever. When Congress legislates expenditures from the United States Treasury and the Treasury borrows money to make those expenditures, then the resulting debts are a sovereign debt of this nation and must be repaid.[157]

This Constitution II and the laws of the United States which shall be made in pursuance thereof and all treaties made or which shall be made under the authority of the United States shall be the supreme law of the land; and the judges in every state shall be bound thereby, anything in the constitution or laws of any state to the contrary notwithstanding.

The Senators and Representatives before mentioned, and the members of the several state legislatures, and all executive and judicial officers, both of the United States and of the several states, shall be bound by oath or affirmation, to support this Constitution II; but no religious test shall ever be required as a qualification to any office or public trust under the United States.

---

[155] The first two paragraph of this article are new; the last two paragraphs are copied from the 1787 Constitution, Article VI.

[156] The 1787 Constitution contained basically the same idea in the first paragraph of Article VI, but in that case it referred to the validity of debts of the United States entered into under the Articles of Confederation.

[157] This provision simply makes it clear that, when the United States borrows money, the debt must be repaid.

Article VI: Elections

Section 1. General Provisions
1.1 Voter registration

Congress[158] shall establish a National Voter Registration Authority, which will

---

[158] Article VI is entirely new, though it preserves certain fundamental principles of the 1787 Constitution, federal law, and traditional practices, especially the guarantee of a secret ballot, proportional representation in Congress, and elections conducted by the states.

- *create a national database of registered voters, to be shared with all authorized election officials in all jurisdictions,*
- *prevent the national database of registered voters from unauthorized disclosure or access from unauthorized entities,*
- *ensure that the national database of registered voters is used for no other purpose than voter registration, authentication, and authorization,*
- *assign to each voter a unique Voter Identifier which remains with that voter for life. This unique Voter Identifier cannot be used for any purpose other than voting,*
- *ensure that every registered voter has only one unique Voter Identifier,*
- *maintain for each voter both their legal (voting) address and current contact information,*
- *accept and process voter registration applications from all eligible citizens,*
- *automatically register each citizen to vote upon their 18th birthday,*
- *automatically register each citizen to vote, or verify his/her earlier registration, whenever a citizen interacts with a state or federal government entity,*
- *remove a voter who has deceased, and*
- *establish appropriate means of voter authentication and authorization to vote.*

1.2 Ranked Choice Voting

Ranked Choice Voting (RCV) is mandatory for all federal elections.

VOTING: *For each office being contested, voters will be able to rank their choices, selecting a 1st choice, a 2nd choice, and a 3rd choice.*

For elections for more than three positions, voters may select additional 3rd choices, so that the total candidates selected does not exceed the number of positions to be filled.

COUNTING BALLOTS:

- *For an election with a single winner:*[159]

    1. *Count the 1st choice votes for each candidate, and rank order the results. Repeat steps 2 through 4 until one candidate has a majority of the 1st choice votes.*

    2. *Eliminate the candidate with the fewest votes.*

    3. *Reassign each vote for the eliminated candidate to each voter's next highest choice for a candidate not yet eliminated.*

    4. *If a ballot for the eliminated candidate contains no choice for a candidate not yet eliminated, then that ballot is exhausted and is no longer counted as part of the 1st choice votes.*

- *For a primary election for a single seat in Congress, three primary winners qualify for the general election:*

    1. *Count the 1st choice votes for each candidate, and rank order the results. Repeat steps 2 through 4 until only three candidates remain, or until three candidates each exceed 25% of the 1st choice votes.*

---

[159] This includes the primary and general elections for President and for Chancellor, in which votes are tabulated and a single winner declared in each Congressional District. This also includes the general election for a single seat in Congress (House or Senate).

2. Eliminate the candidate with the fewest votes.

3. Reassign each vote for the eliminated candidate to each voter's next highest choice for a candidate not yet eliminated.

4. If a ballot for the eliminated candidate contains no choice for a candidate not yet eliminated, then that ballot is exhausted and is no longer counted as part of the 1st choice votes.

- *For elections for two or more positions.*

    1. For both the primary and the general election, calculate the weighted vote for each candidate, which equals 3 X the voter's 1st choice votes + 2 X the 2nd choice votes + the 3rd choice votes. Rank order the results. Winners are at the top of this list.

    2. In the primary, the number of candidates who qualify for the general election equals two more than the number of positions to be filled.

    3. In the general election, the number of winners equals the number of positions to be filled.

1.3 Conduct of elections

All elections are conducted by the several states and by any other United States territories or possessions so authorized by

Congress.[160] *A secret ballot is guaranteed. Every vote must be recorded on a paper ballot, retained for subsequent audit for 10 years. Votes may be cast by mail provided such votes are received by the first weekday of the election; votes may also be cast in person for nine days, beginning on a Saturday, except that a state may choose to conduct its entire election by mail.*[161] *A state may authorize a citizen, with reasonable cause, to cast an emergency absentee ballot during the nine-day voting period. By law, Congress may authorize other methods of voting.*

Election officials shall count, tabulate, and announce the first-choice results of every election by midnight after polls close each day during the in-person voting period. Such totals will include votes cast by absentee ballot. After applying RCV procedures, election officials shall announce and certify election results within one week after the end of the in-person voting period.

Congress shall have the power to refine the procedures in Sections 1.2 and 1.3 of this Article.

1.4 Open primaries

Open primaries are mandatory for all federal elections (for President, Chancellor, and both chambers of Congress). Open primaries are non-partisan; the party affiliation of a candidate, if any, will be indicated on the ballot. All registered voters are eligible

---

[160] The current, well-established system gives the responsibility for conducting elections to the states. There is no compelling reason to change this.

[161] This provision establishes mail-in voting, early voting, and in-person voting for all federal elections.

to vote in every primary and general election within the jurisdiction where they legally reside.

Any eligible candidate may compete in any open primary, subject to state rules for qualifying for the ballot. The results of the primaries determine the candidates whose names will appear on the general election ballot. Those eligible to compete in the general election may withdraw within one week after they have been certified to appear on the general election ballot.

1.5 Fundraising and transparency

No candidate for a federal office may personally engage in fundraising nor appear at a fundraising event while Congress is in session.

To appear on a primary ballot, a candidate must authorize the US Treasury to release, two weeks after the National Primary, the five most recent tax returns of that candidate and his or her spouse, if that candidate qualifies for the general election, and if that candidate does not withdraw as a candidate before such tax returns are released. To appear on a general election ballot, each candidate must also release, on the same schedule, a statement of net worth, showing his/her complete assets and liabilities and those of his/her spouse, including details concerning creditors, investors, and customers.[162]

---

[162] This provision requires all general election candidates to be completely transparent with respect to their personal finances.

By the Sunday after the National Primary, any candidate who has qualified to appear on any general election ballot may withdraw as a candidate.

Section 2. Elections for President and for Chancellor

2.1 Direct Election of the President and of the Chancellor

The President and the Chancellor shall be elected directly by the voters. [163] *Votes for President and for Chancellor in both the primary and general elections shall be cast and counted by Congressional District (CD). In counting ballots, RCV procedures are used to determine the single winner in each CD.*

Congress shall establish a National Vote Tabulation Authority, whose responsibility is to collect from the states the results of the primary and general elections for President and for Chancellor, to tabulate and summarize the results, and announce the winners.

2.2 Primary Elections for President

The total Nominating Votes for President equals the number of seats in the House of Representatives plus the Nominating Votes in non-state jurisdictions.

- *Each CD has the same number of Nominating Votes as it has seats in the House of Representatives.*

---

[163] One of the most important democratic improvements of Constitution II is the direct election of the President by the voters.

- *Congress may authorize certain non-state jurisdictions to participate in Presidential primaries. All such jurisdictions taken together are considered one Non-State Primary Election District. For each 1 million inhabitants or portion thereof, this Non-State Primary Election District is awarded one Nominating Vote.*
- *The primary election shall be held at large in each CD and in the one Non-State Primary Election District, and the winner of the primary election shall be awarded all of that jurisdiction's Nominating Votes.*

The candidates for President who qualify for the general election ballot are determined through three rounds of primary elections, including four states in Round 1, ten states in Round 2, and all other states and non-state jurisdictions in Round 3.

Unless Congress adopts a different scheme for selecting the states for Rounds 1 and 2, Round 1 primaries will occur in New Hampshire, Iowa, South Carolina, and New Mexico; and Round 2 primaries will occur in 10 states who volunteer for that duty. If more than 10 states apply, random selection will be used to select 10 of them; if fewer than 10 apply, random selection from the remaining states will be used to round out the 10.

Any candidate who meets a state's requirements to appear on the primary ballot for President will appear on the primary ballot in that state. In addition, any candidate who earns at least one Nominating Vote in a Round 1 or a Round 2 Presidential primary automatically qualifies to appear on the ballot in all remaining Presidential primaries.

At the conclusion of the three rounds of Presidential primaries, any candidate who has received at least 15% of the total Nominating Votes qualifies for the general election ballot for President in all states. If fewer than three candidates achieve the 15% threshold, then the three candidates with the most Nominating Votes qualify for the general election ballot in all states. In addition, any candidate who has won at least one Nominating Vote in any state qualifies for the general election ballot in all CDs in that state. No other candidate will appear on the general election ballot for President in any state.

Any candidate who withdraws as a Presidential candidate within one week after Round 2 of the Presidential primaries may become a candidate for the Senate or for the House. A person can be a candidate for only one federal office at a time.

2.3. Primary Election for Chancellor

The total Nominating Votes for Chancellor equals the total Nominating Votes for President, determined in the same manner.

The candidates for Chancellor who qualify for the general election ballot are determined through three rounds of primary elections, including four states in Round 1, ten states in Round 2, and all other states and non-state jurisdictions in Round 3. Unless Congress adopts a different scheme, the states that held Round 1 and Round 2 primaries in the most recent Presidential election year shall also hold Round 1 and Round 2 Chancellor primaries.

Any candidate who meets a state's requirements to appear on the primary ballot for Chancellor will appear on the primary ballot in that state. In addition, any candidate who earns at least one Nominating Vote in a Round 1 or a Round 2 Chancellor primary automatically qualifies to appear on the ballot in all remaining Chancellor primaries.

At the conclusion of the three rounds of Chancellor primaries, any candidate who has received at least 15% of the total Nominating Votes qualifies for the general election ballot for Chancellor in all states. If fewer than three candidates achieve the 15% threshold, then the three candidates with the most Nominating Votes qualify for the general election ballot in all states. In addition, any candidate who has won at least one Nominating Vote in any state qualifies for the general election ballot in all CDs in that state. No other candidate will appear on the general election ballot for Chancellor in any state.

Any candidate who withdraws as a Chancellor candidate within one week after Round 2 of the Chancellor primaries may become a candidate for the Senate or for the House. A person can be a candidate for only one federal office at a time.

2.4 Local-State-National (L-S-N) general election voting system for President and for Chancellor

General elections for President and for Chancellor will take place on the date specified for the General Election for all federal offices. The winner of each election is determined by Electoral Votes. The total Electoral Votes for President and for Chancellor equals the number of seats in the House of Representatives, plus twice the number of states.

The L-S-N voting system determines the winner at each level – local, state, and national. Using the RCV procedure for an election with one winner, the winner within each CD will be awarded all the Electoral Votes for that CD; in each state, the statewide winner will be awarded one additional Electoral Vote; and the winner of the national popular vote will be awarded one additional Electoral Vote for each state in the Union.[164]

If one candidate has earned a majority of all Electoral Votes, that candidate will be declared the winner and will become the President-elect or Chancellor-elect.

If no candidate has a majority of the Electoral Votes, then all but the top two candidates will be eliminated, and a final round of ballot counting using the RCV procedure for a single winner will take place, in order to determine the voters' preference among the two remaining candidates. When the Electoral Votes are reassigned to the two remaining candidates, the one with a majority of all Electoral Votes will be the winner. If these last two candidates are tied, then the winner of the national popular vote will be the winner.[165]

Section 3. Elections for Members of Congress

Elections for Congress shall occur in even-numbered years. In each such election cycle, all Members of the House shall be elected for two-year terms, and one Class of the three Senate Classes shall be elected for six-year terms.

---

[164] For example, with 50 states, there would be 601 electoral votes: 501 for the seats in the House, 50 for the winner of each state, and 50 for the winner of the national popular vote.

[165] As long as the number of seats in the House is an odd number, an Electoral Vote tie between the last two candidates is impossible.

If a state has fewer than four House seats, then all House members will be elected at-large, that is, in one Congressional District (CD). For states with four or more House seats, the state shall be divided into 3-seat CDs as far as possible, leaving one 1-seat or 2-seat CD if necessary.

Congress shall establish a rule-based procedure for drawing CD boundaries without human decision-making, based solely on the two principles of equalizing populations per House seat and keeping communities together in the same CD.

All Senators within a state are elected at large.

Section 4. Dates of Primary and General Elections, Convening of Congress, and Inauguration

Federal elections for Congress occur in even-numbered years; Presidential elections occur in years evenly divisible by four; Chancellor elections occur in even-numbered years not evenly divisible by four. For each primary or general election, the nine-day period for in-person voting begins on the following days:

Presidential or Chancellor Primary Round 1: First Saturday in August

Presidential or Chancellor Primary Round 2: First Saturday in September

National Primary (which includes Presidential Primary Round 3, Chancellor Primary Round 3, and Congressional Primary for House and Senate): First Saturday in October

General Election: First Saturday in December

Convening the new Congress and Inauguration of the Chancellor: Noon on the first Sunday in January following their election

Inauguration of the new President: Noon on the second Sunday in January following the election.

Section 5. Continuance in Office

To continue in office, all federal elected officials, by October 1 of each year, must authorize the US Treasury to release the five most recent tax returns of that official and his or her spouse. Each official must also release, on the same schedule, a statement of net worth, showing his/her complete assets and liabilities and those of his/her spouse.

Every federal elected official is prohibited from hiring, nominating, or appointing any member of his/her immediate family to any position within the federal government.

Article VII: Citizen Empowerment; Constitutional Amendments

Section 1. Enacting and Repealing Federal Statutes

Any citizen or state may initiate a PROPOSAL to adopt a new federal statute or repeal an existing federal statute.[166] *Each of the several states may endorse the PROPOSAL either through ordinary*

---

[166] Section 1 extends citizens' power of Initiative and Referendum, currently available in 24 states with respect to state statutes, to the citizens of the United States with respect to Federal statutes.

state legislation or through its own state procedures for initiative and voter-approved referendum. When half of the states comprising half of the population have endorsed the PROPOSAL, the PROPOSAL will appear on the ballot throughout the United States at the next general election.

Adoption of the PROPOSAL requires the approval of 1) a majority of all votes cast, and 2) a majority of votes cast in 50% of the states containing 50% of the population.

Section 2. Proposing an Amendment

This section prescribes two methods for proposing an amendment to the Constitution:

- ***Method 1.*** *The Congress, whenever a majority of both chambers shall deem it necessary, shall propose an amendment to this Constitution.*[167]

- ***Method 2.*** *Each of the several states may propose a Constitutional amendment by approving the amendment according to the procedures of each state for amending their own state constitutions. When at least half of the states comprising at least half of the US population propose such*

---

[167] Article VII grants citizens the exclusive power to approve all Constitutional amendments. It seems unreasonable to allow one-third of the House or Senate the power to block an amendment desired by a majority. Hence in Constitution II a mere majority (rather than 2/3) of each chamber is necessary for the Congress to propose a Constitutional amendment.

an amendment, then this amendment becomes a proposed Constitutional amendment.

When an amendment to this Constitution has been proposed according to either method specified in this Section, that amendment shall be valid to all intents and purposes as part of this Constitution, when ratified by the people as specified in Section 4.

Section 3. Constitutional Convention

This section prescribes two methods for calling a Constitutional Convention charged with the task of drafting a New Constitution:

- ***Method 1.** On the application of the legislatures of two-thirds of the several states, Congress shall call a Constitutional Convention.*

- ***Method 2.** Each of the several states may propose a Constitutional Convention by approving the call for a Constitutional Convention according to the procedures of each state for amending their own state constitutions. When at least half of the states comprising at least half of the US population propose a Constitutional Convention in this manner, Congress shall call a Constitutional Convention.*

When states have called for a Constitutional Convention according to either method specified in this Section, Congress shall convene said convention. The product of said convention shall be the Proposed New Constitution, which shall be valid and will replace this Constitution when ratified by the people as specified in Section 4.

Section 4. Ratification

The power to amend or replace the Constitution of the United States rests solely with the people of the United States. This section prescribes the only method for ratification of a proposed Constitutional amendment or a proposed New Constitution.

- ***Two General Elections.*** *Ratification requires the approval of voters in two general elections. Between these two general elections, at least one other general election must have taken place and a new person must hold the office of President.*

- ***Ratification Threshold.*** *In both of these two general elections, ratification requires the approval of 1) a majority of all votes cast, and 2) a majority of votes cast in 60% of the states containing 60% of the population.*

Appendix 1. RCV Procedures

This book proposes the use of Ranked Choice Voting (RCV) in all elections in the United States. The specific RCV procedure differs depending on several factors, including the number of positions being contested and whether this is a primary or a general election. Common to all RCV elections is that voters choose multiple candidates for each office and rank their choices.

Some critics have suggested that this will not really work because few voters will opt to make a 2nd or 3rd choice. But experience with RCV around the world does not support that conclusion. Voters do learn fairly quickly that RCV really does give them a greater voice in the outcome. It allows them to vote for their preferred candidate first, knowing that their vote will be reassigned to their 2nd choice if no candidate has a majority and their 1st choice is eliminated.

RCV also allows a voter to select an independent or third-party candidate as their 1st choice, without fearing that they are thereby "throwing away their vote" on a candidate with zero chance of winning. Under RCV, if the independent or third-party candidate (as expected) fails to win, and if neither major party candidate earns a majority, then that voter's vote will be reassigned to his 2nd choice and later if needed. His 3rd choice.

RCV Categories

This appendix summarizes the RCV procedures for federal elections conducted in accordance with the reforms I have proposed in this book. Specific procedures obtain in each of these categories:

- An election with a single winner. This is the most common election category and includes:
    - A general election for a single seat in Congress (Senate or House) or
    - A primary or general election for President or for Chancellor conducted in each Congressional District
- An open primary election (with three winners) for a single seat in Congress (Senate or House)
- A primary or general election for two to four seats in the Senate or the House.

RCV Voting

- For any primary or general election which will fill fewer than four positions, voters select a 1st choice, a 2nd choice, and a 3rd choice.
- For any primary or general election which will fill four positions, voters select a 1st choice, a 2nd choice, and two 3rd choices.

RCV Counting of Ballots

- For an election with a single winner, the objective is that the winning candidate should demonstrate some level of support from a majority of the electorate:
    1. Count the 1st choice votes for each candidate, and rank order the results. Repeat steps 2 through 4 until one candidate has a majority of 1st choice votes.

2. Eliminate the candidate with the fewest votes.

3. Reassign each vote for the eliminated candidate to each voter's next highest choice for a candidate not yet eliminated. (That is to say, the voter's 2nd choice becomes that voter's 1st choice among the remaining candidates.)

4. If a ballot for the eliminated candidate contains no choice for a candidate not yet eliminated, then that ballot is exhausted and is no longer counted as part of the 1st choice votes. [Note that, as candidates are eliminated, the share of the 1st choice votes for each remaining candidate can only grow, never shrink.]

- For an open primary election for a single position, the objective is that all voters can participate in choosing the candidate of their choice, and ¾ or more of all voters will choose one of the three candidates who qualify for the general election:

    1. Count the 1st choice votes for each candidate, and rank order the results. Repeat steps 2 through 4 until only three candidates remain, or until three candidates each exceed 25% of the 1st choice votes. (Note: it is mathematically impossible for four candidates to exceed 25%.)

    2. Eliminate the candidate with the fewest votes.

    3. Reassign each vote for the eliminated candidate to each voter's next highest choice for a candidate not yet eliminated.

    4. If a ballot for the eliminated candidate contains no choice for a candidate not yet eliminated, then that

ballot is exhausted and is no longer counted as part of the 1st choice votes.

- Elections for two to four positions.

    1. The objective in multi-winner elections is that the candidates with the greatest collective support among voters become winners. This system gives greater weight to the voter's 1st choice over their 2nd choice, and greater weight to their 2nd choice over their other (3rd) choices, while still allowing voters to participate in choosing all contested positions.

    2. For all primary elections for two or more positions, the number of candidates who qualify for the general election equals two more than the number of positions to be filled. Thus the general election will result in the election of all but two of the candidates on the general election ballot.

    3. In a general election for three positions, this system ensures that the minority party has an opportunity to win one seat. Specifically, if a candidate is the 1st choice of 41% of the voters, that candidate is assured of winning.

    4. In a general election for three or four positions, a voter who votes for all positions to be filled will have voted for at least one winner. This ensures that every voter has at least one elected representative.

    5. Procedure: For both the primary and the general election, calculate the weighted vote for each

candidate, which equals 3 X the candidate's 1st choice votes + 2 X the 2nd choice votes + the 3rd choice votes. Rank order the results.

While the RCV procedure suggested here is less than ideal, it has the advantage of being easy to understand and to implement, and it does result in much-improved representation of minority views. For example, in a three-winner contest, if Party A has a 59% to 41% majority over Party B, Party B can guarantee victory for one candidate if all its voters select the same candidate as their 1st choice.

FairVote.org's Procedure for Multi-Winner Elections

FairVote.org is an organization that advocates for free and fair elections, and it has sponsored and campaigned for a number of reforms. FairVote was instrumental in Maine's adoption of Ranked Choice Voting, for example. The procedure proposed in this book for counting ballots in single-winner elections is the same procedure recommended by FairVote.

FairVote also proposes a procedure for counting ballots in multi-winner elections. The procedure is complex and difficult to understand at first reading, and some will find the underlying math challenging. Even though the FairVote procedure produces better results than the procedures I have proposed, I opted for a simpler procedure, easier to understand and easier to implement. Nevertheless, the FairVote procedure should be part of our discussion.

RCV procedure for counting ballots when an election has multiple winners:

The objective in an election with multiple winners is to ensure that all views held by a significant portion of the electorate are represented by at least some of the winners. Essentially, the way this is accomplished is that the number of votes needed to guarantee victory is calculated (called the Actual Threshold (AT)). For example, if an election will have two winners, then the AT will be one-third of the total votes cast, plus one vote. That amount guarantees victory because it is mathematically impossible for two other people to also have that many votes. When a candidate's vote total exceeds the Actual Threshold, the procedure involves calculating what portion of each vote for the winning candidate was needed to reach that threshold, and then reassigning the excess portion of each voter's vote to each voter's next highest choice among all candidates not yet elected or eliminated. If this procedure still results in too few winners, then the candidate with the fewest votes is eliminated, and all of that candidate's votes are reassigned to each voter's next highest choice.

Admittedly the math here is a bit daunting. Hopefully you can follow it. You can also see a visual demonstration of these procedures by visiting FairVote.org, open the Fair Representation Act page, and click on Demo.

- Definition of variables:
  - N = number of winners for an election with multiple winners.
  - Threshold Percent (T%) Plus One Vote (T%+1): The share of the total vote that guarantees a candidate's victory. The formula for T%+1 is 100%/(N+1), + 1 vote. For example, if a general

election will elect three members of Congress, then T%+1 = 100%/4 or 25% of the total vote, plus one vote. This is because, if one candidate reaches that threshold, it is mathematically impossible for three other candidates to also have 25% + 1 vote. T%+1 can be calculated at any time and is always the same for any election with a given number of winners.
- Actual Threshold (AT): The number of votes needed to win a particular election, defined as the total votes cast multiplied by T%, plus one vote. This can only be calculated after the election when the total votes cast is known. For example, in an election with three winners and 1000 votes cast, the AT is 251. Any candidate with at least 251 votes is elected.
- Winner's Votes (WV): The number of votes earned by a winning candidate.
- Winner's Percent (W%): For a winning candidate, the portion of each voter's vote needed to reach the Actual Threshold. It is calculated as AT/WV. For example, if 251 is the Actual Threshold, a candidate who earns exactly 251 votes is elected but needs 100% of every vote to reach the AT. But if that candidate had 400 votes, then only 62.75% of each voter's vote would be needed to meet the threshold.
- Excess Percent (E%): For a winning candidate, the portion of each voter's vote that can be reassigned to each voter's next highest choice. It is calculated as 100% − W%. Continuing the same example,

where W% was calculated as 62.75%, E% would be 37.25%.
- If N or fewer candidates were on the ballot, all candidates are winners and the election is done.
- The first step in applying RCV is to calculate T% and AT for this election.
- If more than N candidates were on the ballot, any candidate whose 1st choice votes meet or exceed the AT is a winner. If N candidates meet the AT, then all these candidates are winners and the election is done.
- If fewer than N candidates meet the AT, then the following steps are repeated until N candidates meet the AT or only N candidates remain:
  - For any candidate who has won, W% is calculated, and then E% is calculated. E% of each of the winning candidate's voter's vote is then reassigned to that voter's next highest choice (among candidates neither elected nor eliminated).
  - The candidate with the fewest votes is eliminated, and all the votes for that candidate are reassigned to each voter's next highest choice (among candidates neither elected nor eliminated).

Appendix 2. Maryland Redistricting

Let's apply this scheme to Maryland as our test case. I chose Maryland as my first sample state for three reasons:

1) With eight congressional districts, Maryland's population is about average.
2) Maryland has two major metro areas (Baltimore and the Maryland suburbs of Washington, DC) and two large rural areas (western Maryland and the Eastern Shore, the area east of the Chesapeake Bay). Maryland is one of the most weirdly shaped states in the nation. Hence, a redistricting scheme that can work for this oddly-shaped and unevenly-populated state might well work for them all.
3) I live here! So I'm partial to my home state. In addition, Maryland is seriously gerrymandered in favor of Dems, and even though I myself am a Democrat, I consider our own gerrymandering shameful, so I'd like to come up with a scheme to fix this.

We begin with a map of Maryland's 23 counties plus Baltimore City:

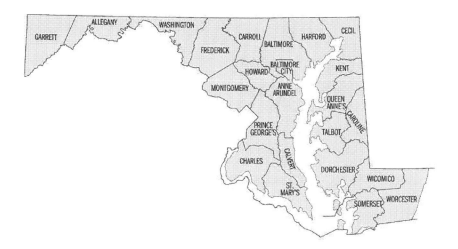

Statewide Data: Significant data points for drawing Congressional Districts based on the 2010 Census include the following:

- Total state population
- Number of House seats apportioned to the state
- Average population per CD (AVG), that is, total population divided by the number of House seats
- Minimum population (MIN) that will be split off from LAST County or LAST ZCTA when deciding whether or not to partition LAST County or LAST ZCTA to complete any CD. The MIN (or "allowable variation") for a state is defined as 5% of AVG.

Statewide Data	
State	Maryland
Population	5773552

Seats	8
AVG	721694
MIN	36085

Maryland Congressional District 1

Next, let us create Maryland's 1st congressional district. We begin by drawing the Reference Line connecting Maryland's two most widely separated points. We determine the Starting Point as the westernmost point on the Reference Line, and we draw the Scan Line perpendicular to the Reference Line, like this:

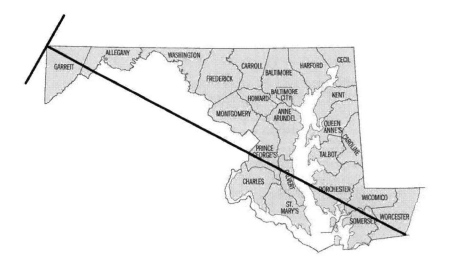

After creating the initial Reference Line and Scan Line, we drag the Scan Line from the Starting Point along the Reference Line, keeping its slope constant. As the Scan Line encounters each county, we add that county to CD 1 – both its land area and its population. This takes us through Garrett, Allegany, Washington, Frederick, and Carroll counties and into Montgomery. But we cannot add all of Montgomery County to Maryland Congressional District 1, because CD 1 would then have way too many people. We also cannot leave Montgomery completely out of CD 1, because then the CD would have too few people. Therefore, we must partition Montgomery (termed LAST County in MD CD 1). Continuing with the Scan Line perpendicular to the Reference Line, we scan ZCTA's across Montgomery until the CD is complete – assigning ~7% of Montgomery's population to CD 1. Here is the resulting map (showing the CD boundaries) and spreadsheet (showing the county populations):

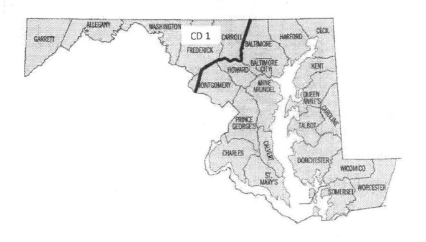

Maryland Congressional District 1 (MD CD 1) includes Garrett, Allegany, Washington, Carroll, and Frederick Counties and Part 1 of Montgomery.

Master Congressional District Table - Maryland									
		County Population				Running Aggregates			
		Available	Assigned to this CD	Pt	Left Over	State Total	This CD	Total Target	Diff
CD#	County								
1	Previous State Total and New Target for This CD					0	0	721694	721694
1	Garrett	30097	30097			30097	30097	721694	691597
1	Allegany	75087	75087			105184	105184	721694	616510
1	Washington	147430	147430			252614	252614	721694	469080
1	Frederick	233385	233385			485999	485999	721694	235695
1	Carroll	167134	167134			653133	653133	721694	68561
1	Montgomery	971777	68561	1	903216	721694	721694	721694	0

*Column Definitions:

- **CD#:** Congressional District number
- **County:** Name of county, city, or other political jurisdiction
- **County Population:**
  - **Available:** The county population available to be assigned to this CD. In most cases this is the total county population. However, if this county was previously partitioned, then the available population equals the amount left over after the previous partition(s).
  - **Assigned to this CD:** The amount of the Available population assigned to the current CD. In most cases, all of the Available population is Assigned to the current CD. However, if this county is LAST County in the current CD and is partitioned, then the Assigned population will be less than the Available population.
  - **Pt:** Partition #. If a county is partitioned among CDs, the number in this field is the consecutive partition number.
  - **Left Over:** If a county is partitioned, the amount Left Over equals Available less Assigned.

- **Running Aggregates:**
  - **State Total:** The running total of the population assigned to all CDs so far.
  - **This CD:** The running total of the population assigned to the current CD so far.
  - **Total Target:** The target total population assigned to all CDs upon completion of the current CD. This is defined as AVG multiplied by CD#.
  - **Diff:** The Difference between Total Target and State Total. The number represents the population remaining to be assigned to the current CD. (When Diff becomes negative, the current CD exceeds Total Target.)

Partitioning LAST County

Whenever we need to partition a county, we will also need a detailed map of that county's ZCTA's (Maryland has 546). For purposes of the demos in this paper, I did not obtain the detailed maps of ZCTA's in each partitioned county. However, since ZCTA's are simply zip codes with boundaries, and since every zip code defines a collection of mail delivery routes, we can expect each ZCTA to contain a relatively compact and contiguous land area. Therefore, we know that we can scan the county and add ZCTA's as we encounter them until the requisite population for the CD is attained. The partitions in these demos are based only on the needed population to complete the current CD.

Special note on partitioning LAST County: In some cases the total CD population may differ from AVG by less than MIN. That is, the CD population falls within 5% (MIN) of the average population for one CD (AVG) either by adding or by excluding LAST County. In such a case (which does not occur in the Maryland example), we can add or exclude the entire county, so that there is no LAST County.

To complete the current CD, we scan LAST County using the map of ZCTA's for that county along with population data for all ZCTA's in LAST County. (ZCTA maps and ZCTA population data are available from the Census Bureau.) We add ZCTA's to the current CD until the addition of one more ZCTA would cause the target population to be exceeded. We then add or do not add this LAST ZCTA to the current CD depending on whether the addition of LAST ZCTA would or would not bring the aggregate population closer to target.

"Partition" and "Left Over" Definitions

In the tables shown in this demo, we add a county to a CD either in whole or in part when the Scan Line touches that county. If we assign the entire county, then the Pt and Left Over columns are left blank. However, If we assign only part of a county to the current CD, then we show the consecutive county Partition # in the Pt column and the population not yet assigned to any CD in the Left Over column. Note the following:

- Pt 1 designates the LAST County in a CD. The Left Over amount will be available for PT 2 in a subsequent CD.
- For any partitioned county, a Left Over amount of 0 designates a county whose entire remaining (that is, previously Left Over) population is assigned to the current CD.
- A Left Over amount > 0 designates a county which still contains some population available to a subsequent CD.

Could the LAST ZCTA in LAST County Be Too Large?

At this point, before deciding that the current CD is complete, we must check the CDs population to ensure that it falls within 5% of the target population for a CD in this state. Though technically possible, exceeding this ±5% criterion is most unlikely, based on the following logic:

1. Based on the 2010 Census figures, there were 709,747 residents per House member (that is, total US population divided by 435). Hence that is the average Target per House seat across the country. 5% of this target is 35,487. We either add or do not add LAST ZCTA to the congressional district, depending on whether or not the addition of LAST ZCTA brings the total congressional district population closer to Target or not. Hence to exceed the 5% threshold, LAST ZCTA would have to have more than 70,974 residents, and the breakpoint would have to be such that the smaller portion would have to exceed 35,487. (To apply this principle to any particular state, we calculate 5% of the average population per House seat in that state. This amount is the allowable variance when deciding whether or not to partition LAST County or LAST ZCTA.)

2. Of the 33,092 ZCTA's in the United States, only 126 have a population over 70,974. (The average population per ZCTA is 9330.)

3. The greatest population ZCTA in the country (ZCTA 60629, near Chicago's Midway Airport) had 113,916 residents in 2010. If that ZCTA happens to be the last ZCTA added or not added to complete a congressional district,

and if the target was exactly in the middle of that ZCTA, then that CD would miss Target by a maximum of that ZCTA's population divided by 2, or 56,958, which is about 9% of AVG for Illinois. Technically possible, but not likely.

In short, when following the procedure for assigning LAST County and LAST ZCTA, the likelihood of creating a congressional district whose population is too small or too large is tiny. But if such an event were to occur, we can split LAST ZCTA into two parts by census tracts, which contain ~4000 people per tract. Just use the same Scan Line to scan the census tracts within LAST ZCTA, and stop adding census tracts when Target is reached.

Subdividing LAST County for This Demo

For this exercise I did not obtain detailed ZCTA maps of Maryland's counties. I am simply pointing out that someone can scan the ZCTA map for a county and add ZCTA's to the congressional district quite readily, if that someone has in hand the requisite ZCTA maps and ZCTA population data.

I took a shortcut for this demonstration: I added to the CD the population from LAST County needed to complete that CD. I calculated the percentage of LAST County's population assigned to that CD and drew an approximate boundary line based on the same percentage of land mass. This shortcut is less than precise but seems adequate for demo purposes.

Maryland CDs 2 Through 8.

With Maryland's CD 1 complete, we can proceed to the other CDs. In each case, we draw a new Reference Line connecting the two most distant points in the state not yet assigned to a CD. We select the Starting Point at the western end of the Reference Line, and we draw the Scan Line perpendicular to the Reference Line and through the Starting Point. We then drag the Scan Line along the Reference Line, adding counties as we go, and adding ZCTA's as needed in LAST County. For each Maryland CD from CD 2 through CD 8, this section displays the map of the Reference and Scan Lines, the map of the resulting CD, and the table of counties and populations that make up the CD.

MD CD 2:

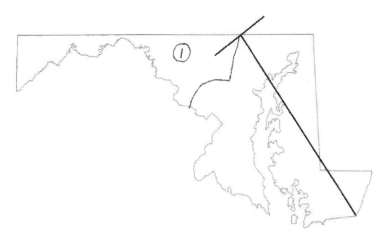

The CD 2 Reference Line connects the two most widely separated points in the state not yet assigned to a CD. The Scan Line runs perpendicular to the Reference Line and through the Starting Point.

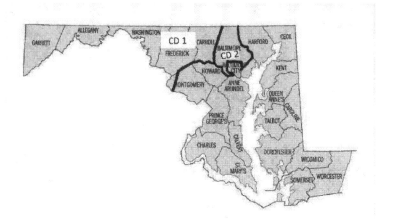

MD CD 2 consists entirely of Part 1 of Baltimore County.

For each CD after CD 1, the first data row in the Master Congressional District Table displays the aggregate state population after completing the previous CD, along with the new target and difference for the current CD.

		Master Congressional District Table						
		County Population			Running Aggregates			
CD#	County	Available	Assigned to this CD	Pt	Left Over	State Total	This CD	Total Target	Diff
2	Previous State Total and New Target for This CD					721694	0	1443388	721694
2	Baltimore County	805029	721694	1	83335	1443388	721694	1443388	0

MD CD 3:

Reference & Scan Lines for CD 3

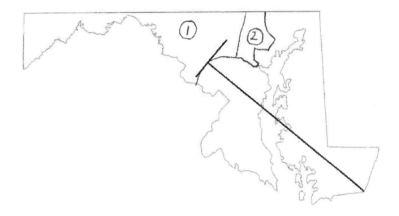

MD CD 3 contains Part 2 of Montgomery County.

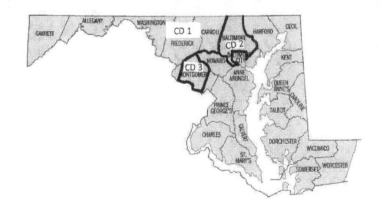

		Master Congressional District Table							
		County Population			Running Aggregates				
CD#	County	Available	Assigned to this CD	Pt	Left Over	State Total	This CD	Total Target	Diff
3	Previous State Total and New Target for This CD					1443388	0	2165082	721694
3	Montgomery	903216	721694	2	181522	2165082	721694	2165082	0

MD CD 4:

Reference & Scan Lines for CD 4

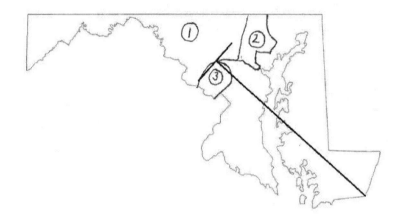

MD CD 4: Howard County, Part 3 of Montgomery, and Part 1 of Baltimore City

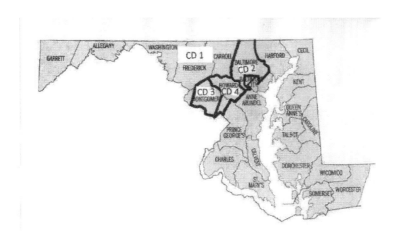

Looking at the map of Maryland CD 4, note that this CD is not entirely contiguous. A small slice of Baltimore County (just under five miles wide) separates the portion of the CD in Baltimore City from the portion in Howard and adjoining Montgomery counties. If we apply the proposed scheme consistently, a few such non-contiguous CDs will occur, so you should know that it can and does occur. Allowing this to occur is far better than artificially fixing it with a narrow corridor connecting the two parts. Contiguity is a desirable characteristic, but it is not essential to having fair districts.

[Note this special rule on contiguity: If the proposed scheme results in a CD with non-contiguous portions, and if those portions are more than 30 miles apart, the portion with the smaller population is skipped for the current CD.]

		Master Congressional District Table							
		County Population				Running Aggregates			
CD#	County	Available	Assigned to this CD	Pt	Left Over	State Total	This CD	Total Target	Diff
4	Previous State Total and New Target for This CD					2165082	0	2886776	721694
4	Howard	287085	287085			2452167	287085	2886776	434609
4	Montgomery	181522	181522	3	0	2633689	468607	2886776	253087
4	Baltimore City	620961	253087	1	367874	2886776	721694	2886776	0

MD CD 5:

Reference & Scan Lines for CD 5

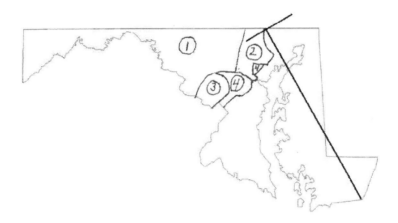

MD CD 5: Harford and Cecil Counties, Part 2 of Baltimore County, and Part 2 of Baltimore City

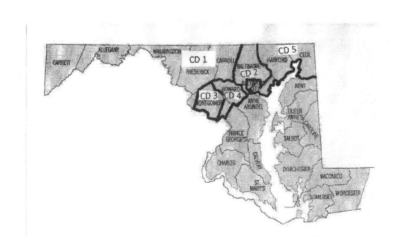

Master Congressional District Table								
	County Population				Running Aggregates			
CD#	County	Available	Assigned to this CD	Pt	Left Over	State Total	This CD	Total Target	Diff
5	Previous State Total and New Target for This CD					2886776	0	3608470	721694
5	Harford	244826	244826			3131602	244826	3608470	476868
5	Cecil	101108	101108			3232710	345934	3608470	375760
5	Baltimore County	83335	83335	2	0	3316045	429269	3608470	292425
5	Baltimore City	367874	292425	2	75449	3608470	721694	3608470	0

MD CD 6:

Reference & Scan Lines for CD 6

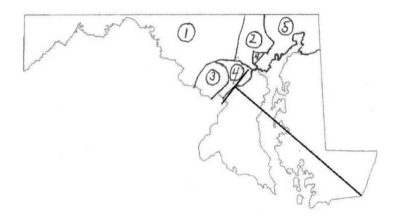

MD CD 6 contains Part 1 of Prince George's County.

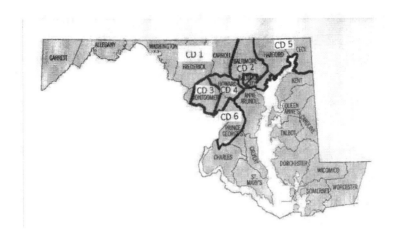

		County Population			Running Aggregates			
			Assigned		State		Total	
CD#	County	Available	to this CD	Pt	Left Over	State Total	This CD	Total Target	Diff
6	Previous State Total and New Target for This CD					3608470	0	4330164	721694
6	Prince George's	863420	721694	1	141726	4330164	721694	4330164	0

Master Congressional District Table

MD CD 7

Reference & Scan Lines for CD 7

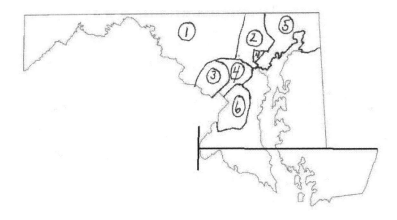

MD CD 7 contains Charles and St. Mary's Counties, Part 2 of Prince George's, and Part 1 of Anne Arundel.

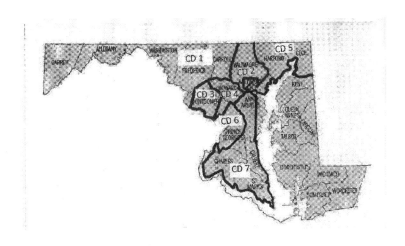

| | | Master Congressional District Table ||||||||
| | | County Population ||| Running Aggregates |||
CD#	County	Available	Assigned to this CD	Pt	Left Over	State Total	This CD	Total Target	Diff
7	Previous State Total and New Target for This CD					4330164	0	5051858	721694
7	Charles	146551	146551			4476715	146551	5051858	575143
7	Prince George's	141726	141726	2	0	4618441	288277	5051858	433417
7	St. Mary's	105151	105151			4723592	393428	5051858	328266
7	Anne Arundel	537656	328266	1	209390	5051858	721694	5051858	0

MD CD 8:

We do not need a Reference Line and Scan Line for the last CD in a state, because, by definition, any area/population not yet assigned to a CD must be assigned to the last one.

MD CD 8 contains Kent, Calvert, Caroline, Queen Anne's, Somerset, Talbot, Wicomico, Dorchester, and Worcester Counties, Part 3 of Baltimore City, and Part 2 of Anne Arundel.

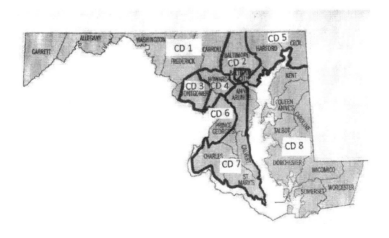

Master Congressional District Table								
		County Population				Running Aggregates		
CD#	County	Available	Assigned to this CD	Pt	Left Over	State Total	This CD	Total Target	Diff
8	Previous State Total and New Target for This CD					5051858	0	5773552	721694
8	Anne Arundel	209390	209390	2	0	5261248	209390	5773552	512304
8	Baltimore City	75449	75449	3	0	5336697	284839	5773552	436855
8	Kent	20197	20197			5356894	305036	5773552	416658
8	Calvert	88737	88737			5445631	393773	5773552	327921
8	Caroline	33066	33066			5478697	426839	5773552	294855
8	Queen Anne's	47798	47798			5526495	474637	5773552	247057
8	Somerset	26470	26470			5552965	501107	5773552	220587
8	Talbot	37782	37782			5590747	538889	5773552	182805
8	Wicomico	98733	98733			5689480	637622	5773552	84072
8	Dorchester	32618	32618			5722098	670240	5773552	51454
8	Worcester	51454	51454			5773552	721694	5773552	0

All 8 Maryland CDs

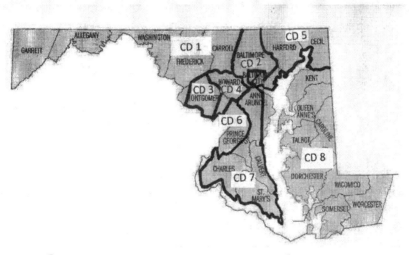

Avoiding Future Gerrymanders

One more item is necessary to complete this redistricting scheme: Once adopted, how do we prevent the manipulation of county and ZCTA boundaries in an effort to gerrymander? The answer is that we adopt the county and ZCTA boundaries used for the 2010 census in perpetuity, updated by population data from the census every 10 years. (By the way, this does not mean that states cannot change county boundaries or that the Postal Service cannot add or alter zip codes; what it does mean is that, for purposes of drawing CD boundaries for the next Congress, the Census Bureau will count the people in each county and each ZCTA using the boundaries from the 2010 Census.)

Technical note: *These maps of Maryland congressional districts are approximations. I used county population data for whole counties and for portions of counties as needed to complete each congressional district. The lines are adequate for demo purposes, but they are not exact. I did not attempt to allocate individual ZCTAs to each district's LAST County.*

Appendix 3. Pennsylvania Redistricting

I used Pennsylvania as a second sample state. Pennsylvania is a good candidate to see how the proposed solution works in a large state with a regular shape. Pennsylvania is among the states with the largest congressional delegations – 18. Pennsylvania is also very much in the news since the State Supreme Court mandated redistricting across the entire state due to gerrymandering in advance of the 2018 midterm elections. Here are the detailed maps and county listings.

We start with a map of Pennsylvania showing all 67 counties:

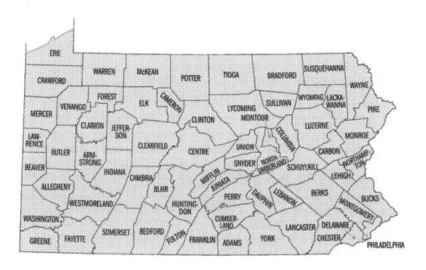

Statewide Data	
State	Pennsylvania
Population	12702379
Seats	18
AVG	705688
MIN	35284

Given these statewide data plus the population figures for each county, we can draw Pennsylvania's 18 CDs.

The following pages display, for each congressional district in Pennsylvania, a) a map showing the Reference Line and Scan Line, b) a map of the completed CD, and c) a table showing the allocation of county populations to the CD.

Note that, throughout this example, we have not actually partitioned LAST County by ZCTA's. Rather, in the table, we have listed the portion of LAST County's population assigned to this CD, and on the map, we have drawn in a portion of the county roughly equal to this same percentage of territory. Let us simply stipulate that the actual redistricting process includes scanning of LAST County and assignment of ZCTA's to the current CD until target is reached.

Pennsylvania Congressional District 1

Reference Line and Scan Line for drawing PA CD 1

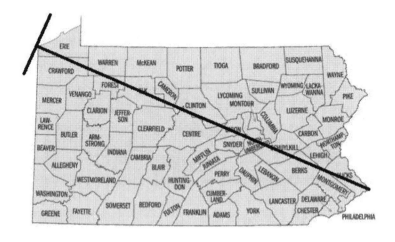

Completed PA CD 1

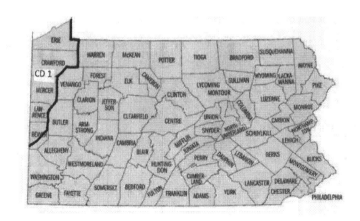

Master Congressional District Table								
		County Population			Running Aggregates			
CD#	County	Available	Assigned to this CD	Pt Left Over	State Total	This CD	Total Target	Diff
1	Erie PA	280566	280566		280566	280566	705688	425122
1	Crawford PA	88765	88765		369331	369331	705688	336357
1	Mercer PA	116638	116638		485969	485969	705688	219719
1	Lawrence PA	91108	91108		577077	577077	705688	128611
1	Beaver PA	170539	128611	1 41928	705688	705688	705688	0

Pennsylvania Congressional District 2

Reference Line and Scan Line for drawing PA CD 2

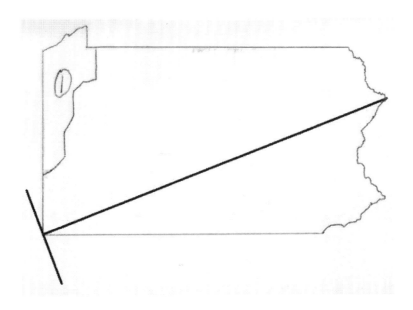

Complete PA CD 2

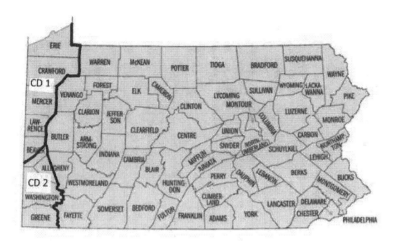

Master Congressional District Table							
		County Population			Running Aggregates		
CD#	County	Available	Assigned to this CD	Pt	Left Over	State Total	This CD	Total Target	Diff
2	Previous State Total and New Target for This CD					705688	0	1411376	705688
2	Greene PA	38686	38686			744374	38686	1411376	667002
2	Washington PA	207820	207820			952194	246506	1411376	459182
2	Beaver	41928	41928	2	0	994122	288434	1411376	417254
2	Allegheny PA	1223348	417254	1	806094	1411376	705688	1411376	0

Pennsylvania Congressional District 3

Reference Line and Scan Line for drawing PA CD 3

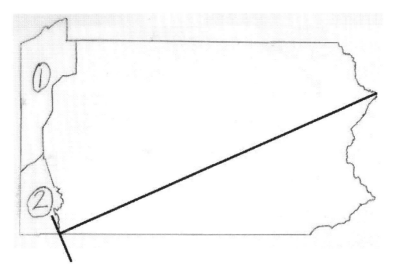

Completed PA CD 3

Note that Pennsylvania CD 3 is one of the rare districts whose land area is not entirely contiguous.

Master Congressional District Table								
		County Population			Running Aggregates			
CD#	County	Available	Assigned to this CD	Pt	Left Over	State Total	This CD	Total Target	Diff
3	Previous State Total and New Target for This CD					1411376	0	2117064	705688
3	Fayette PA	136606	136606			1547982	136606	2117064	569082
3	Allegheny PA	806094	569082	2	237012	2117064	705688	2117064	0

Pennsylvania Congressional District 4

Reference Line and Scan Line for drawing PA CD 4

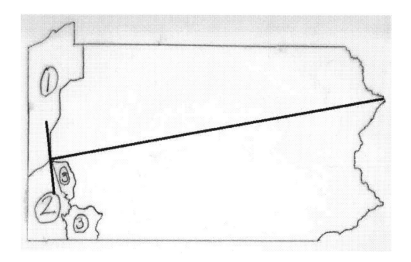

Completed PA CD 4

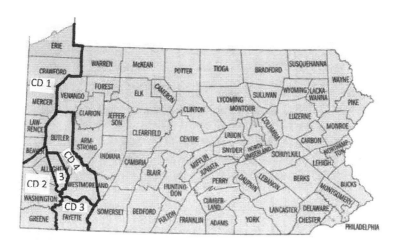

	Master Congressional District Table							
		County Population				Running Aggregates		
			Assigned			State		Total	
CD#	County	Available	to this CD	Pt	Left Over	Total	This CD	Target	Diff
4	Previous State Total and New Target for This CD					2117064	0	2822752	705688
4	Butler PA	183862	183862			2300926	183862	2822752	521826
4	Allegheny PA	237012	237012	3	0	2537938	420874	2822752	284814
4	Westmoreland P.	365169	284814	1	80355	2822752	705688	2822752	0

Pennsylvania Congressional District 5

Reference Line and Scan Line for drawing PA CD 5

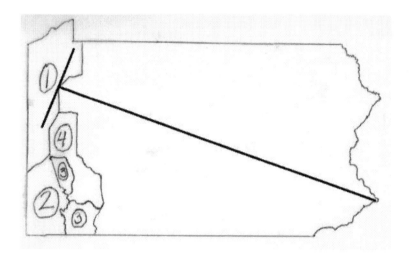

Complete PA CD 5

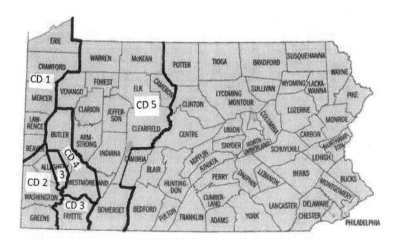

Master Congressional District Table

		County Population				Running Aggregates			
CD#	County	Available	Assigned to this CD	Pt	Left Over	State Total	This CD	Total Target	Diff
5	Previous State Total and New Target for This CD					2822752	0	3528440	705688
5	Venango PA	54984	54984			2877736	54984	3528440	650704
5	Warren PA	41815	41815			2919551	96799	3528440	608889
5	Forest PA	7716	7716			2927267	104515	3528440	601173
5	Clarion PA	39988	39988			2967255	144503	3528440	561185
5	Armstrong PA	68941	68941			3036196	213444	3528440	492244
5	Jefferson PA	45200	45200			3081396	258644	3528440	447044
5	Mc Kean PA	43450	43450			3124846	302094	3528440	403594
5	Elk PA	31946	31946			3156792	334040	3528440	371648
5	Indiana PA	88880	88880			3245672	422920	3528440	282768
5	Westmoreland P,	80355	80355	2	0	3326027	503275	3528440	202413
5	Clearfield PA	81642	81642			3407669	584917	3528440	120771
5	Somerset PA	77742	77742			3485411	662659	3528440	43029
5	Cameron PA	5085	5085			3490496	667744	3528440	37944
5	Cambria PA	143679	37944	1	105735	3528440	705688	3528440	0

Pennsylvania Congressional District 6

Reference Line and Scan Line for drawing PA CD 6

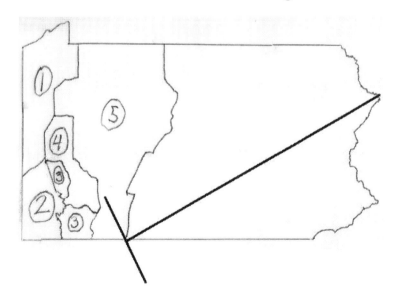

Complete PA CD 6

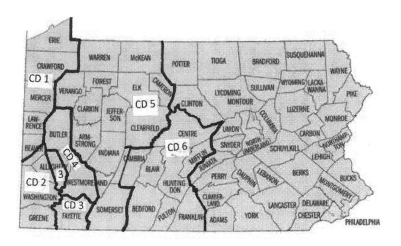

		County Population				Running Aggregates			
			Assigned			State		Total	
CD#	County	Available	to this CD	Pt	Left Over	Total	This CD	Target	Diff
6	Previous State Total and New Target for This CD					3528440	0	4234128	705688
6	Bedford PA	49762	49762			3578202	49762	4234128	655926
6	Cambria PA	105735	105735	2	0	3683937	155497	4234128	550191
6	Fulton PA	14845	14845			3698782	170342	4234128	535346
6	Blair PA	127089	127089			3825871	297431	4234128	408257
6	Franklin PA	149618	149618			3975489	447049	4234128	258639
6	Huntingdon PA	45913	45913			4021402	492962	4234128	212726
6	Centre PA	153990	153990			4175392	646952	4234128	58736
6	Mifflin PA	46682	46682			4222074	693634	4234128	12054

Master Congressional District Table

Note that the last Diff value of 12054 is less than Pennsylvania's MIN 0f 35284. Therefore, we do not partition LAST County. Rather, we allow CD 6 to be less than the target population by 12504. This overage will be made up in the next CD, as CD 7 will be over target by the same amount.

Pennsylvania Congressional District 7

Reference Line and Scan Line for drawing PA CD 7

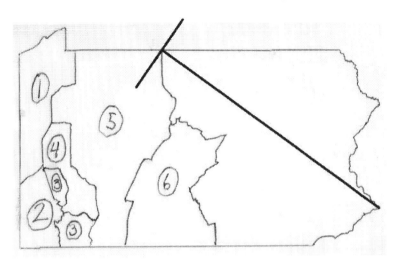

Complete PA CD 7

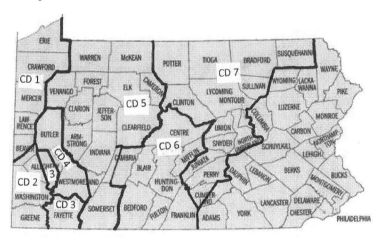

| | | Master Congressional District Table |||||||
| | | County Population ||| Running Aggregates |||
CD#	County	Available	Assigned to this CD	Pt	Left Over	State Total	This CD	Total Target	Diff
7	Previous State Total and New Target for This CD					4222074	0	4939816	717742
7	Potter PA	17457	17457			4239531	17457	4939816	700285
7	Tioga PA	41981	41981			4281512	59438	4939816	658304
7	Clinton PA	39238	39238			4320750	98676	4939816	619066
7	Lycoming PA	116111	116111			4436861	214787	4939816	502955
7	Bradford PA	62622	62622			4499483	277409	4939816	440333
7	Sullivan PA	6428	6428			4505911	283837	4939816	433905
7	Union PA	44947	44947			4550858	328784	4939816	388958
7	Snyder PA	39702	39702			4590560	368486	4939816	349256
7	Juniata PA	24636	24636			4615196	393122	4939816	324620
7	Susquehanna PA	43356	43356			4658552	436478	4939816	281264
7	Perry PA	45969	45969			4704521	482447	4939816	235295
7	Northumberland	94528	94528			4799049	576975	4939816	140767
7	Montour PA	18267	18267			4817316	595242	4939816	122500
7	Cumberland PA	235406	122500	1	112906	4939816	717742	4939816	0

Pennsylvania Congressional District 8

Reference Line and Scan Line for drawing PA CD 8

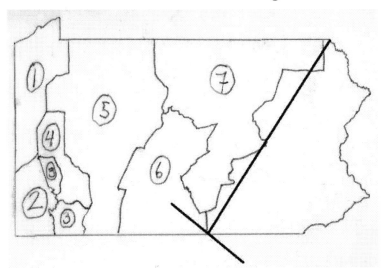

Complete PA CD 8

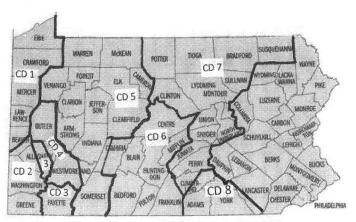

Master Congressional District Table

CD#	County	County Population				Running Aggregates			
		Available	Assigned to this CD	Pt	Left Over	State Total	This CD	Total Target	Diff
8	Previous State Total and New Target for This CD					4939816	0	5645504	705688
8	Adams PA	101407	101407		0	5041223	101407	5645504	604281
8	Cumberland PA	112906	112906	2	0	5154129	214313	5645504	491375
8	York PA	434972	434972			5589101	649285	5645504	56403
8	Lancaster PA	519445	56403	1	463042	5645504	705688	5645504	0

Pennsylvania Congressional District 9

Reference Line and Scan Line for drawing PA CD 9

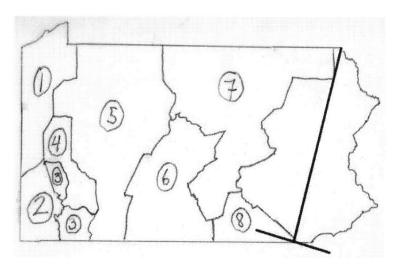

Complete PA CD 9

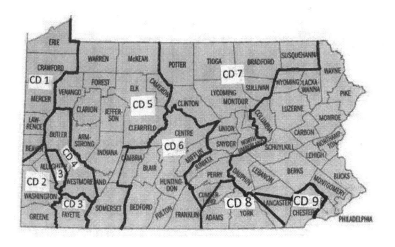

Master Congressional District Table

		County Population			Running Aggregates			
CD#	County	Available	Assigned to this CD	Pt Left Over	State Total	This CD	Total Target	Diff
9	Previous State Total and New Target for This CD				5645504	0	6351192	705688
9	Chester	498886	498886		6144390	498886	6351192	206802
9	Lancaster PA	463042	206802	2 256240	6351192	705688	6351192	0

Pennsylvania Congressional District 10

Reference & Scan Lines for drawing PA CD 10

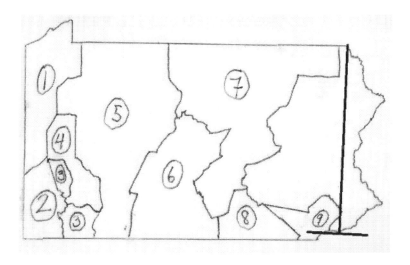

Complete PA CD 10

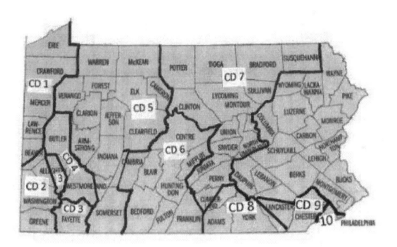

		Master Congressional District Table							
		County Population				Running Aggregates			
CD#	County	Available	Assigned to this CD	Pt	Left Over	State Total	This CD	Total Target	Diff
10	Previous State Total and New Target for This CD					6351192	0	7056880	705688
10	Delaware	558979	558979			6910171	558979	7056880	146709
10	Philadelphia	1526006	146709	1	1379297	7056880	705688	7056880	0

378

Pennsylvania Congressional District 11

Reference & Scan Lines for drawing PA CD 11

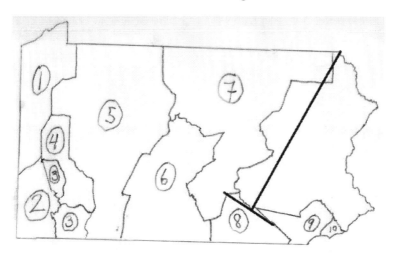

Complete PA CD 11

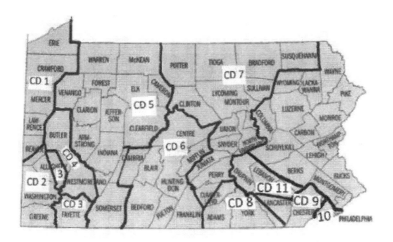

Master Congressional District Table								
		County Population				Running Aggregates		
CD#	County	Available	Assigned to this CD	Pt	Left Over	State Total	This CD	Total Target	Diff
11	Previous State Total and New Target for This CD					7056880	0	7762568	705688
11	Lancaster PA	256240	256240	3	0	7313120	256240	7762568	449448
11	Dauphin	268100	268100			7581220	524340	7762568	181348
11	Lebanon	133568	133568			7714788	657908	7762568	47780
11	Berks	411442	47780	1	363662	7762568	705688	7762568	0

Pennsylvania Congressional District 12

Reference & Scan Lines for drawing PA CD 12

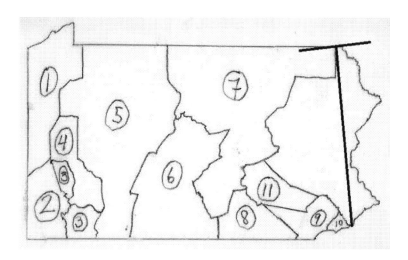

Complete PA CD 12

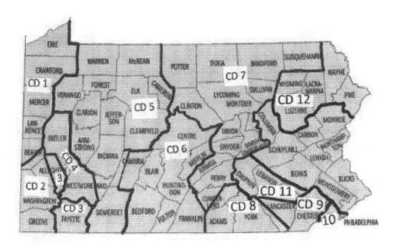

		Master Congressional District Table						
		County Population			Running Aggregates			
			Assigned		State		Total	
CD#	County	Available	to this CD	Pt Left Over	Total	This CD	Target	Diff
12	Previous State Total and New Target for This CD				7762568	0	8468256	705688
12	Wayne	52822	52822		7815390	52822	8468256	652866
12	Lackawanna	214437	214437		8029827	267259	8468256	438429
12	Wyoming	28276	28276		8058103	295535	8468256	410153
12	Pike	57369	57369		8115472	352904	8468256	352784
12	Luzerne	320918	320918		8436390	673822	8468256	31866

Pennsylvania Congressional District 13

Reference & Scan Lines for drawing PA CD 13

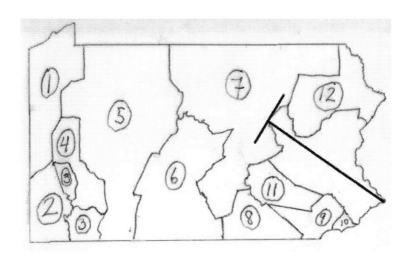

Complete PA CD 13

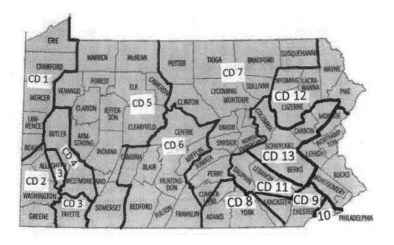

Master Congressional District Table

CD#	County	County Population			Running Aggregates			
		Available	Assigned to this CD	Pt Left Over	State Total	This CD	Total Target	Diff
13	Previous State Total and New Target for This CD				8436390	0	9173944	737554
13	Columbia	67295	67295		8503685	67295	9173944	670259
13	Schuylkill	148289	148289		8651974	215584	9173944	521970
13	Berks	363662	363662	2 0	9015636	579246	9173944	158308
13	Carbon	65249	65249		9080885	644495	9173944	93059
13	Monroe	169842	93059	1 76783	9173944	737554	9173944	0

Pennsylvania Congressional District 14

Reference & Scan Lines for drawing CD 14

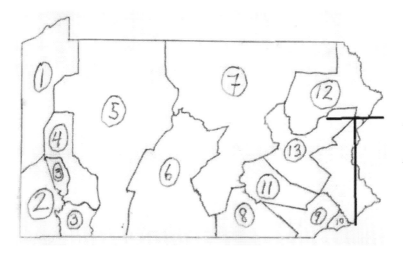

Complete PA CD 14

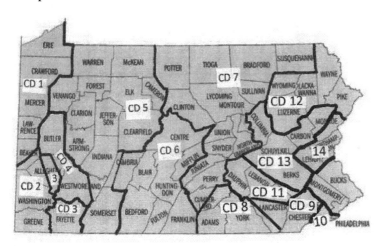

| | | Master Congressional District Table |||||||
| | | County Population ||| Running Aggregates |||
CD#	County	Available	Assigned to this CD	Pt	Left Over	State Total	This CD	Total Target	Diff
14	Previous State Total and New Target for This CD					9173944	0	9879632	705688
14	Monroe	76783	76783	2	0	9250727	76783	9879632	628905
14	Northampton	297735	297735			9548462	374518	9879632	331170
14	Lehigh	349497	349497			9897959	724015	9879632	-18327

384

Pennsylvania Congressional District 15

Reference & Scan Lines for drawing PA CD 15

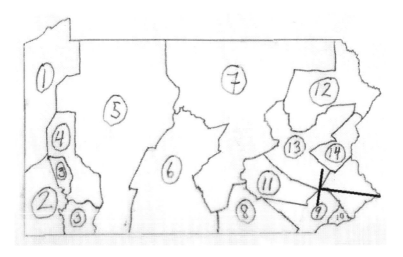

Complete PA CD 15

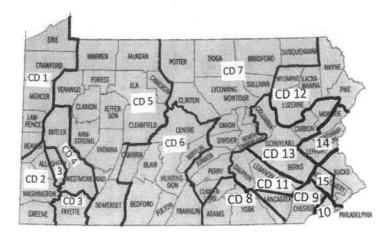

Master Congressional District Table								
		County Population				Running Aggregates		
CD#	County	Available	Assigned to this CD	Pt	Left Over	State Total	This CD	Total Target	Diff
15	Previous State Total and New Target for This CD					9897959	0	10585320	687361
15	Montgomery	799874	687361	1	112513	10585320	687361	10585320	0

Pennsylvania Congressional District 16

Reference & Scan Lines for drawing PA CD 16

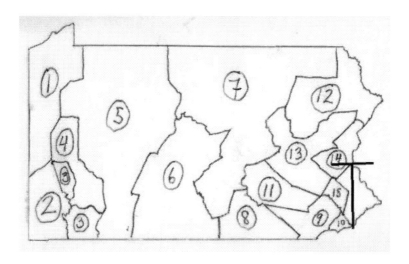

Complete PA CD 16

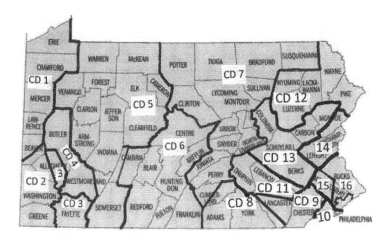

| | | Master Congressional District Table ||||||||
| | | County Population ||| Running Aggregates ||||
CD#	County	Available	Assigned to this CD	Pt	Left Over	State Total	This CD	Total Target	Diff
16	Previous State Total and New Target for This CD					10585320	0	11291008	705688
16	Bucks	625249	625249			11210569	625249	11291008	80439
16	Montgomery	112513	112513	2	0	11323082	737762	11291008	-32074

Pennsylvania Congressional District 17

Reference & Scan Lines for drawing PA CD 17

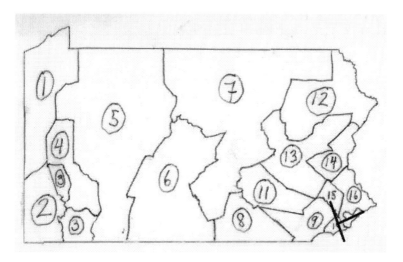

Complete PA CD 17

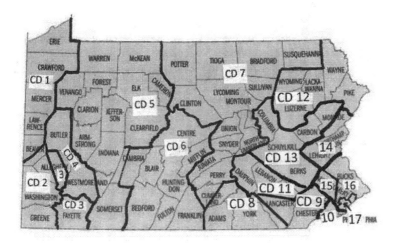

Master Congressional District Table									
		County Population				Running Aggregates			
CD#	County	Available	Assigned to this CD	Pt	Left Over	State Total	This CD	Total Target	Diff
17	Previous State Total and New Target for This CD					11323082	0	11996696	673614
17	Philadelphia	1379297	673614	2	705683	11996696	673614	11996696	0

Pennsylvania Congressional District 18

Reference & Scan Lines are not needed for the last CD since everything not yet assigned to an earlier CD must necessarily be assigned to this one.

Complete PA CD 18

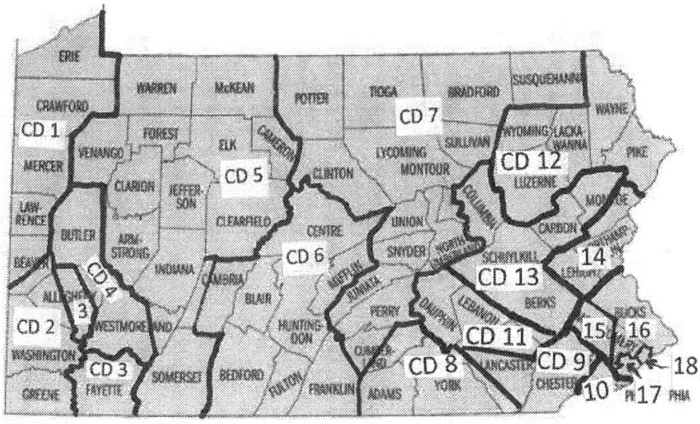

Master Congressional District Table								
		County Population			Running Aggregates			
CD#	County	Available	Assigned to this CD	Pt	State Total	This CD	Total Target	Diff
18	Previous State Total and New Target for This CD				11996696	0	12702384	705688
18	Philadelphia	705683	705683	3	12702379	705683	12702384	5

All 18 Pennsylvania CDs

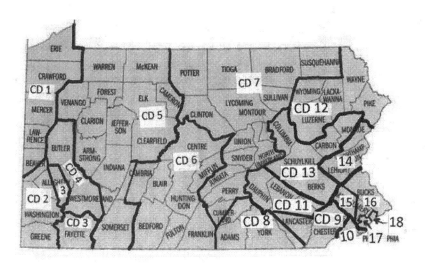

Appendix 4. North Carolina Redistricting

For the third sample state, I used North Carolina, which has 13 seats in the House of Representatives. We start with a map of North Carolina showing all 100 counties and a table showing the population of each county.

Statewide Data	
State	North Carolina
Population	9535483
Seats	13
AVG	733499
MIN	36675

The next pages display North Carolina's 13 CDs following the proposed scheme.

North Carolina Congressional District 1

For CD 1, we display the individual steps.

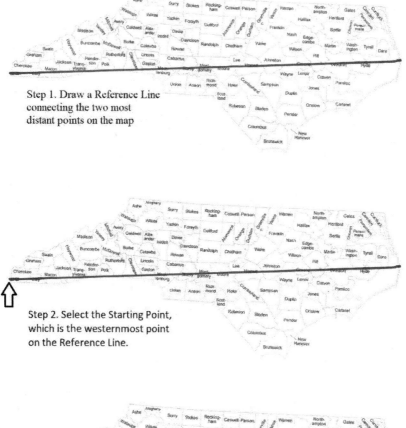

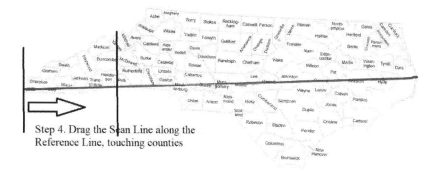

- Step 5. Add each touched county to CD 1

- Step 6. Stop adding counties when one more county ("LAST County") would put too many people in CD 1.

- Step 7. Scan LAST County with the same Scan Line, adding Zip Code Tabulation Areas (ZCTA's) until the CD target is reached.

- For NC CD 1, LAST County is McDowell. 76% of McDowell's population is assigned to CD 1. Here is the completed CD 1.

Complete NC CD 1

Master Congressional District Table									
		County Population			Running Aggregates			
CD#	County	Available	Assigned to this CD	Pt	Left Over	State Total	This CD	Total Target	Diff
1	Previous State Total and New Target for This CD					0	0	733498	733498
1	Cherokee	27444	27444			27444	27444	733498	706054
1	Clay	10587	10587			38031	38031	733498	695467
1	Graham	8861	8861			46892	46892	733498	686606
1	Swain	13981	13981			60873	60873	733498	672625
1	Macon	33922	33922			94795	94795	733498	638703
1	Jackson	40271	40271			135066	135066	733498	598432
1	Haywood	59036	59036			194102	194102	733498	539396
1	Transylvania	33090	33090			227192	227192	733498	506306
1	Madison	20764	20764			247956	247956	733498	485542
1	Buncombe	238318	238318			486274	486274	733498	247224
1	Henderson	106740	106740			593014	593014	733498	140484
1	Yancey	17818	17818			610832	610832	733498	122666
1	Polk	20510	20510			631342	631342	733498	102156
1	Rutherford	67810	67810			699152	699152	733498	34346
1	McDowell	44996	44996			744148	744148	733498	-10650

Note that the last Diff value, -10650, is within MIN of target. Hence, we do not partition LAST County, McDowell.

North Carolina Congressional District 2

Draw a new Reference Line for CD 2, connecting the two most distant points in that portion of the state not yet assigned to a CD.

Pick the Starting Point, the westernmost point on the Reference Line. Then draw the Scan Line perpendicular to the Reference Line and through the Starting Point.

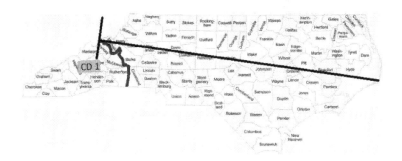

Complete NC CD 2

| Master Congressional District Table ||||||||
| CD# | County | County Population ||| Running Aggregates |||
		Available	Assigned to this CD	Pt Left Over	State Total	This CD	Total Target	Diff
2	Previous State Total and New Target for This CD			744148	0	1466996	722848
2	Mitchell	15579	15579		759727	15579	1466996	707269
2	Avery	17797	17797		777524	33376	1466996	689472
2	Burke	90912	90912		868436	124288	1466996	598560
2	Watauga	51079	51079		919515	175367	1466996	547481
2	Caldwell	83029	83029		1002544	258396	1466996	464452
2	Ashe	27281	27281		1029825	285677	1466996	437171
2	Cleveland	98078	98078		1127903	383755	1466996	339093
2	Wilkes	69340	69340		1197243	453095	1466996	269753
2	Alleghany	11155	11155		1208398	464250	1466996	258598
2	Catawba	154358	154358		1362756	618608	1466996	104240
2	Lincoln	78265	78265		1441021	696873	1466996	25975
2	Alexander	37198	37198		1478219	734071	1466996	-11223

North Carolina Congressional Districts 3 through 12

The next pages demonstrate the creation of North Carolina CDs 3 through 12. For each CD, you see the Reference and Scan Lines drawn on top of the map of the CDs previously created, then the updated map showing the new CD, and the table of counties and county populations that make up the new CD.

North Carolina Congressional District 3

Reference & Scan Lines for drawing NC CD 3

Complete NC CD 3

		Master Congressional District Table							
		County Population				Running Aggregates			
			Assigned			State		Total	
CD#	County	Available	to this CD	Pt	Left Over	Total	This CD	Target	Diff
3	Previous State Total and New Target for This CD					1478219	0	2200494	722275
3	Gaston	206086	206086			1684305	206086	2200494	516189
3	Iredell	159437	159437			1843742	365523	2200494	356752
3	Mecklenburg	919628	356752	1	562876	2200494	722275	2200494	0

North Carolina Congressional District 4

Reference & Scan Lines for drawing NC CD 4

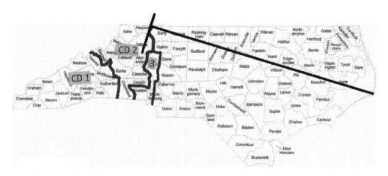

Complete NC CD 4

		Master Congressional District Table						
		County Population			Running Aggregates			
CD#	County	Available	Assigned to this CD	Pt Left Over	State Total	This CD	Total Target	Diff
4	Previous State Total and New Target for This CD				2200494	0	2933992	733498
4	Surry	73673	73673		2274167	73673	2933992	659825
4	Yadkin	38406	38406		2312573	112079	2933992	621419
4	Davie	41240	41240		2353813	153319	2933992	580179
4	Stokes	47401	47401		2401214	200720	2933992	532778
4	Rowan	138428	138428		2539642	339148	2933992	394350
4	Forsyth	350670	350670		2890312	689818	2933992	43680
4	Cabarrus	178011	43680	1 134331	2933992	733498	2933992	0

North Carolina Congressional District 5

Reference & Scan Lines for drawing NC CD 5

Complete NC CD 5

Master Congressional District Table								
		County Population				Running Aggregates		
CD#	County	Available	Assigned to this CD	Pt	Left Over	State Total	This CD	Total Target	Diff
5	Previous State Total and New Target for This CD					2933992	0	3667490	733498
5	Mecklenburg	562876	562876	2	0	3496868	562876	3667490	170622
5	Union	201292	201292			3698160	764168	3667490	-30670

North Carolina Congressional District 6

Reference & Scan Lines for drawing NC CD 6

Complete NC CD 6

Master Congressional District Table								
		County Population			Running Aggregates			
CD#	County	Available	Assigned to this CD	Pt	Left Over	State Total	This CD	Total Target	Diff
6	Previous State Total and New Target for This CD					3698160	0	4400988	702828
6	Cabarrus	134331	134331	2	0	3832491	134331	4400988	568497
6	Stanly	60585	60585			3893076	194916	4400988	507912
6	Davidson	162878	162878			4055954	357794	4400988	345034
6	Anson	26948	26948			4082902	384742	4400988	318086
6	Montgomery	27798	27798			4110700	412540	4400988	290288
6	Richmond	46639	46639			4157339	459179	4400988	243649
6	Randolf	141752	141752			4299091	600931	4400988	101897
6	Guilford	488406	101897	1	386509	4400988	702828	4400988	0

North Carolina Congressional District 7

Reference & Scan Lines for drawing NC CD 7

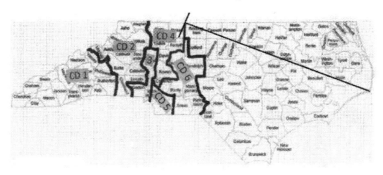

Complete NC CD 7

Master Congressional District Table								
		County Population				Running Aggregates		
CD#	County	Available	Assigned to this CD	Pt	Left Over	State Total	This CD	Total Target	Diff
7	Previous State Total and New Target for This CD					4400988	0	5134486	733498
7	Rockingham	93643	93643			4494631	93643	5134486	639855
7	Guilford	386509	386509	2	0	4881140	480152	5134486	253346
7	Caswell	23719	23719			4904859	503871	5134486	229627
7	Alamance	151131	151131			5055990	655002	5134486	78496
7	Chatham	63505	63505			5119495	718507	5134486	14991

The CD 7 Scan Line touches Moore County before touching Chatham. However, Moore would have been LAST County in CD 7, and Chatham would not have been included. Since the distance from Moore to the rest of CD 7 exceeds 30 miles, Moore County was skipped

North Carolina Congressional District 8

Reference & Scan Lines for drawing NC CD 8

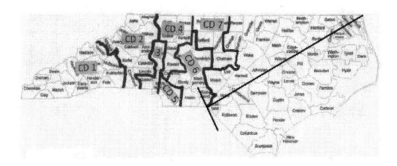

Complete NC CD 8

		County Population			Running Aggregates			
			Assigned		State		Total	
CD#	County	Available	to this CD	Pt Left Over	Total	This CD	Target	Diff
8	Previous State Total and New Target for This CD				5119495	0	5867984	748489
8	Scotland	36157	36157		5155652	36157	5867984	712332
8	Robeson	134168	134168		5289820	170325	5867984	578164
8	Moore	88247	88247		5378067	258572	5867984	489917
8	Columbus	58098	58098		5436165	316670	5867984	431819
8	Hoke	46952	46952		5483117	363622	5867984	384867
8	Brunswick	107431	107431		5590548	471053	5867984	277436
8	Bladen	35190	35190		5625738	506243	5867984	242246
8	Cumberland	319431	242246	1 77185	5867984	748489	5867984	0

Master Congressional District Table

North Carolina Congressional District 9

Reference & Scan Lines for drawing NC CD 9

Complete NC CD 9

Master Congressional District Table

		County Population				Running Aggregates			
CD#	County	Available	Assigned to this CD	Pt	Left Over	State Total	This CD	Total Target	Diff
9	Previous State Total and New Target for This CD					5867984	0	6601482	733498
9	Lee	57866	57866			5925850	57866	6601482	675632
9	Harnett	114678	114678			6040528	172544	6601482	560954
9	Cumberland	77185	77185	2	0	6117713	249729	6601482	483769
9	Wake	900993	483769	1	417224	6601482	733498	6601482	0

North Carolina Congressional District 10

Reference & Scan Lines for drawing NC CD 10

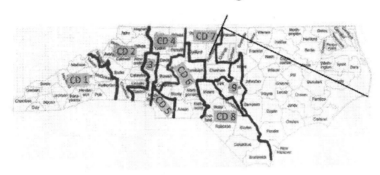

Complete NC CD 10

| Master Congressional District Table ||||||||||
| CD# | County | County Population ||| Running Aggregates ||||
		Available	Assigned to this CD	Pt	Left Over	State Total	This CD	Total Target	Diff
10	Previous State Total and New Target for This CD					6601482	0	7334980	733498
10	Person	39464	39464			6640946	39464	7334980	694034
10	Orange	133801	133801			6774747	173265	7334980	560233
10	Durham	267587	267587			7042334	440852	7334980	292646
10	Granville	59916	59916			7102250	500768	7334980	232730
10	Wake	417224	232730	2	184494	7334980	733498	7334980	0

North Carolina Congressional District 11

Reference & Scan Lines for drawing NC CD 11

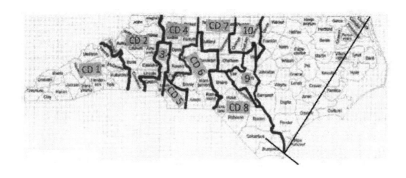

Complete NC CD 11

		County Population			Running Aggregates			
		Available	Assigned to this CD	Pt Left Over	State Total	This CD	Total Target	Diff
CD#	County							
11	Previous State Total and New Target for This CD				7334980	0	8068478	733498
11	New Hanover	202667	202667		7537647	202667	8068478	530831
11	Pender	52217	52217		7589864	254884	8068478	478614
11	Sampson	63431	63431		7653295	318315	8068478	415183
11	Duplin	58505	58505		7711800	376820	8068478	356678
11	Onslow	177772	177772		7889572	554592	8068478	178906
11	Johnston	168878	168878		8058450	723470	8068478	10028

Master Congressional District Table

North Carolina Congressional District 12

Reference & Scan Lines for drawing NC CD 12

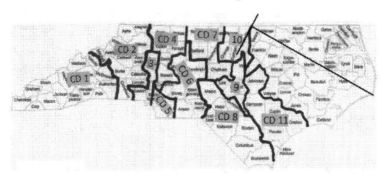

Complete NC CD 12

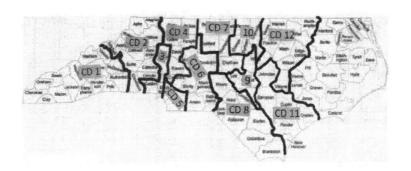

		County Population				Running Aggregates			
			Assigned			State		Total	
CD#	County	Available	to this CD	Pt	Left Over	Total	This CD	Target	Diff
12	Previous State Total and New Target for This CD					8058450	0	8801976	743526
12	Vance	45422	45422			8103872	45422	8801976	698104
12	Warren	20972	20972			8124844	66394	8801976	677132
12	Franklin	60619	60619			8185463	127013	8801976	616513
12	Wake	184494	184494	3	0	8369957	311507	8801976	432019
12	Northampton	22099	22099			8392056	333606	8801976	409920
12	Halifax	54691	54691			8446747	388297	8801976	355229
12	Nash	95840	95840			8542587	484137	8801976	259389
12	Wilson	95840	95840			8638427	579977	8801976	163549
12	Wayne	95840	95840			8734267	675817	8801976	67709
12	Edgecombe	95840	95840			8830107	771657	8801976	-28131

North Carolina Congressional District 13

We do not need to draw Reference and Scan Lines for the last CD in a state since everything not yet assigned to another CD must necessarily be assigned to the last CD.

Complete NC CD 13

Master Congressional District Table

CD#	County	County Population			Running Aggregates			
		Available	Assigned to this CD	Pt Left Over	State Total	This CD	Total Target	Diff
13	Previous State Total and New Target for This CD				8830107	0	9535474	705367
13	Beaufort	47759	47759		8877866	47759	9535474	657608
13	Bertie	21282	21282		8899148	69041	9535474	636326
13	Camden	9980	9980		8909128	79021	9535474	626346
13	Carteret	66469	66469		8975597	145490	9535474	559877
13	Chowan	14793	14793		8990390	160283	9535474	545084
13	Craven	103505	103505		9093895	263788	9535474	441579
13	Currituck	23547	23547		9117442	287335	9535474	418032
13	Dare	33920	33920		9151362	321255	9535474	384112
13	Gates	12197	12197		9163559	333452	9535474	371915
13	Greene	21362	21362		9184921	354814	9535474	350553
13	Hertford	24669	24669		9209590	379483	9535474	325884
13	Hyde	5810	5810		9215400	385293	9535474	320074
13	Jones	10153	10153		9225553	395446	9535474	309921
13	Lenoir	59495	59495		9285048	454941	9535474	250426
13	Martin	24505	24505		9309553	479446	9535474	225921
13	Pamlico NC	13144	13144		9322697	492590	9535474	212777
13	Pasquotank NC	40661	40661		9363358	533251	9535474	172116
13	Perquimans NC	13453	13453		9376811	546704	9535474	158663
13	Pitt NC	168148	168148		9544959	714852	9535474	-9485
13	Tyrrell NC	4407	4407		9549366	719259	9535474	-13892
13	Washington NC	13228	13228		9562594	732487	9535474	-27120

Because we allow any CD to differ from the target population for a CD by any amount less than MIN, it is entirely possible that one of the CDs that misses target is the last CD in the state. In this case, North Carolina CD 13 has 27,120 more people than the average CD for the state.

All 13 North Carolina CDs

Here is the final map, showing all 13 CDs in North Carolina:

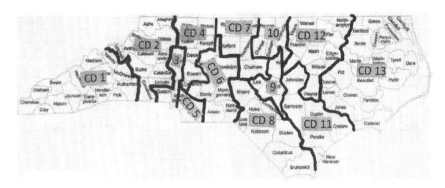

Appendix 5. The Rules in Excruciating Detail

Try following these step-by-step procedures for drawing congressional districts for your home state. Better yet, write the computer program to do it! (A programmer familiar with Geographical Information System applications software could create it.)

General Principles

- Equal population among congressional districts (CDs)
- Geographic proximity
- A rule-determined process
- The same process in every state
- No human-decision-making

Summary Procedures

Draw each congressional district (CD) following these steps:

1. Draw a Reference Line connecting the two most widely separated points on a map of the parts of the state not yet assigned to a CD.

2. Select the Starting Point at the western end of this Reference Line.

3. Draw the Scan Line perpendicular to the Reference Line and through the Starting Point.

4. Drag the Scan Line along the Reference Line. As the Scan Line touches a county, add that county to the CD. Stop adding counties when one more county (called LAST County) would make the CDs population too large.

5. Scan the ZCTA's in LAST County using the same Scan Line, adding ZCTA's to the CD until the target population is reached.

Detailed Procedures

Note: These detailed procedures assume that you are drawing single-seat CDs. If you are drawing multi-seat CDs, these procedures require several minor modifications.

Obtain your state's source data:

State summary data

- Download the state's total population according to the 2010 Census;

- Find the Number (N) of House seats apportioned to this state. Congressional districts will be numbered consecutively as CD 1, CD 2, CD 3, ..., CD N-1, CD N;

- Calculate the Average population per House seat (AVG), that is, total population divided by N; and

- Calculate the minimum population (MIN) that will be split off from LAST County if LAST County is partitioned to complete any CD, or that will be split off from LAST ZCTA if LAST ZCTA is partitioned to complete any CD. The MIN for a state is defined as 5% of AVG. (You might also refer to MIN as the "allowable variance". That is, in the interest of keeping a county's entire population in the same congressional district, we will allow a CDs population to be over or under the target as long as the variance is less than MIN.)

Here is a sample for Maryland:

Statewide Data	
State	Maryland
Population	5773552
Seats	8
AVG	721694
MIN	36085

County data

- Download the list of the state's counties and county populations according to the 2010 Census; and

- Obtain a map of the state's counties showing county boundaries as of the 2010 Census.

ZCTA data

- Download the list of the state's ZCTA's and ZCTA populations according to the 2010 Census; and

- Obtain a map of the state's 2010 ZCTA's, showing both county as well as ZCTA boundaries.

Replicate these steps for each CD from CD 1 to CD N-1:

Draw the Reference Line

Draw a Reference Line between the two most widely separated points within the portion of the state not yet assigned to a congressional district. (Initially, the unassigned portion is the entire state.)

If two or more candidate lines are tied as longest, then the Reference Line is the one whose slope is closest to a northwest to southeast diagonal. If two candidate lines are still tied (both are closest to a northwest to southeast diagonal), then the Reference Line is the candidate line whose northernmost point is farthest to the north; and, if two lines are still tied (that is, they have the same northernmost point), then the Reference Line is the candidate line whose westernmost point is farthest to the west.

Select the Starting Point

The Starting Point is the westernmost point on the Reference Line. Special case: if the Reference Line is exactly vertical (meaning there is no single westernmost point), then the Starting Point is the northernmost point.

Scan Line and Scanning

The Scan Line is a line perpendicular to the Reference Line and passing through the Starting Point. Scanning occurs by dragging the Scan Line from the Starting Point along the Reference Line while keeping the Scan Line perpendicular to the Reference Line.

Build the Congressional District
Addition of Counties

When the Scan Line first touches a county not yet assigned to a CD (or a portion of a county left over from a previously-assigned CD), then we add that entire county or county portion to the current CD, including the county's land mass and population. The process of adding a county while dragging the Scan Line across the state continues until the addition of the next county would cause the target population to be exceeded.

The target population is defined as the total population which should be assigned to all CDs in the state up to and including the current CD. This definition is preferable to simply defining target as AVG (the average population per seat in the state). By defining target to include all CDs constructed so far, the excess or shortage of population in each CD will be self-corrected in subsequent CDs. If we use AVG as the target for each CD, then, in a given state, every CD from CD 1 to CD N-1 might end up a little over (or a little under) AVG, meaning that the final CD in the state will miss AVG by a whole lot.

Designate the county that would cause the target to be exceeded as LAST County. We handle LAST County in one of four ways:

  a. If the CD population without LAST County is under the target by less than MIN, then the CD is complete without adding LAST County.

  b. If the CD population with LAST County added is over the target by less than MIN, then we make the CD complete by adding LAST County.

c. If both (a) and (b) are true, then we either add or do not add LAST County to the CD, depending on which of these actions brings the CD closer to the target.

d. If both (a) and (b) are not true, then we will need to partition LAST County by ZCTA's.

LAST County – Scanning ZCTA's

If we need to partition LAST County to complete the current CD, we scan LAST County using the map of ZCTA's for that county along with population data for all ZCTA's in LAST County. We add ZCTA's to the current CD until the addition of one more ZCTA would cause the target population to be exceeded. This LAST ZCTA in LAST County is then either added or not added to the current CD, depending on whether the addition of this ZCTA would or would not bring the aggregate population closer to target.

LAST ZCTA in LAST County

Before concluding that the CD is now complete, we must ensure that the total CD population varies from the target by less than MIN. In the most unlikely event that this criterion is not met, we split LAST ZCTA into two parts by census tracts, which contain ~4000 people per tract. Just use the same Scan Line to scan the census tracts within LAST ZCTA, and add census tracts until the target is reached.

Contiguity

Note that this method of constructing CDs will result in a small number of CDs with non-contiguous areas. This is the rule for handling a non-contiguous CD:

- If the non-contiguous portions are more than 30 miles apart and the current CD is not the last CD in the state, then the portion with the smaller population is skipped for the current CD.

- If the current CD is the last CD in the state, then no corrective action is needed.

- If the non-contiguous portions of the CD are separated by less than 30 miles, then no corrective action is needed.

- If application of this rule results in any anomaly, then no corrective action is needed.

Last CD in a State (CD N)

When we have drawn all CDs in a state save one, then all remaining land area and population must comprise the final CD. You will not need a Reference Line, Scan Line, or Starting Point.

Resources and Tools

You can obtain county and ZCTA population data tables for any state from the Missouri Census Data Center. Look for county and ZCTA boundary maps from free Internet sources or from your state's planning department. To manually construct the CDs in any state, use a spreadsheet program – I used Excel for the examples shown here

Data source: Missouri Census Data Center

From the Missouri Census Data Center you can obtain the necessary 2010 Census population data for any state, including the total state population, the list of counties and population of each county, and the list of ZCTA's sorted by county and showing the population of each ZCTA. Here is how you get that data:

The Missouri Census Data Center has created a series of data products using 2010 Census data from the U.S. Census Bureau. One of these products is called the Geographic Correspondence Engine. This example shows you how to get the county and ZCTA populations for any state.

1. Visit http://mcdc.missouri.edu/websas/geocorr14.html

2. Select a state to process. (In this example, I used my home state of Maryland.)

3. In both the SOURCE (left-hand) and the TARGET (right-hand) Geocodes columns, select "County 2010" and "5-digit ZIP/ZCTA: Zip Census Tab Area 2010". (You do this in each column by clicking "County 2010" and then Ctrl-Click "5-digit ZIP/ZCTA: Zip Census Tab Area 2010".)

4. Scroll down below the two geocode columns. Select "Population (2010 Census)" as the Weighting Variable.

5. Below the list of Weighting Variables, click the "Run Request" button.

6. When processing is complete, the output screen shows that two files have been created, a Listing (report format) and a Comma Delimited ("csv") file.

7. Click on Listing (report format). This displays the extracted data. The output is sorted by county and, within county, by ZCTA. The output appears in six columns.

8. The six columns in the report are as follows:

a. County: This number uniquely identifies every county and county-like entity in the United States. (A county-like entity is a place that is not a county but is treated as a county for census purposes. This includes cities that are not part of any county, such as the City of Baltimore, Maryland, or Alexandria, Virginia.) We will not need this numeric identifier for our purposes, and so we will delete this column.

b. Cntyname: This is the name of the county and state. Both the county and state names are needed, along with the 5-digit ZCTA, to uniquely identify a ZCTA. This is because ZCTA's are based on 5-digit zip codes, which the US Postal Service created to group mail delivery routes around a post office. Political subdivisions were not part of the equation. Therefore, a single zip code sometimes serves people in more than one county or more than one state. In creating Zip Code Tabulation Areas (ZCTA's) from 5-digit zip codes, the Census Bureau drew boundaries that do respect county and state borders. Hence, a given 5-digit ZCTA in County A may be repeated in County B or in an adjoining state. The Census Bureau counted the population in each jurisdiction.

c. ZIP Census Tabulation Area: The 5-digit ZCTA will be the basis for partitioning LAST County into the ZCTA's assigned to the current CD and the ZCTA's Left Over for later assignment to a subsequent CD. Very importantly, we propose using the 2010 ZCTA's in perpetuity, precisely because they are forever fixed and no one can manipulate them. In each congressional district, 5-digit ZIP Code

Tabulation Areas, or ZCTA's, will be the basis for subdividing LAST County.

   d. Zipname: This is the name of the place (city or town) associated with this ZCTA. We do not need this information for our purposes, so we will delete this column.

   e. Total Pop. 2010 Census: This is the population of the ZCTA according to the 2010 Census. If this proposal is adopted, the Census Bureau will be mandated to calculate the population of each 2010 ZCTA following each succeeding decennial census.

   f. ZCTA5 to ZCTA5 Allocation Factor: Since ZCTA5 was both a Source and a Target Geocode, this factor is always 1. We can eliminate this column.

9. The other output file, geocorr14.csv, is easily adapted to processing either in Excel or in a computer program. At this point, create a folder on your computer to hold the files related to redistricting for your selected state. I called my sample folder "Maryland Redistricting". Download geocorr14.csv to this folder, and rename the file so that it includes the state abbreviation and ZCTAs ("XX ZCTAs.csv"). In my sample, the filename is "MD ZCTAs.csv". This is the Source File for your state's ZCTA's.

Now follow the same procedure to get the 2010 population data for each county in your selected state. The only differences are these:

- In step 3, select only "County 2010" as the SOURCE (left column) and TARGET (right column).

- As before, we will delete the first column (county numeric identifier) and last column (county to county allocation factor). After those deletions, the output looks like this:

cntyname	pop10
County name	Total population (2010)
Allegany MD	75087
Anne Arundel MD	537656
Baltimore MD	805029
Calvert MD	88737
Caroline MD	33066
Carroll MD	167134
Cecil MD	101108
Charles MD	146551
Dorchester MD	32618
Frederick MD	233385
Garrett MD	30097
Harford MD	244826
Howard MD	287085
Kent MD	20197
Montgomery MD	971777

Prince Georges MD	863420
Queen Annes MD	47798
St. Marys MD	105151
Somerset MD	26470
Talbot MD	37782
Washington MD	147430
Wicomico MD	98733
Worcester MD	51454
Baltimore City MD	620961

- Save the output file grocorr14.csv to your computer. Then rename the file to include the state abbreviation and "counties". In my case, the filename is "MD Counties.csv".

Master Congressional District Workbook for <state name> using Excel

Here are instructions and definitions for building an Excel Workbook for any state.

Create the Excel Workbook and Load Source Data

Open a new Excel workbook. Save the workbook (that is, the Excel file) as "<state abbreviation> Master CDs.xlsx". My state table for Maryland is "MD Master CDs.xlsx". Within this workbook, create and name three spreadsheets:

- **County Pop:** This spreadsheet contains an alphabetical list of the counties in the target state along with the population of each county. As you assign counties to a CD, you will update this spreadsheet to show which CDs receive the population of each county. Setup the headers like this (a few sample data rows are also included here):

Maryland Population by County		CD Assignments			
County	Population	CD #	Pct	Assigned	Left Over
A	B	C	D	E	F
Allegany MD	75087	1			
Anne Arundel MD	537656	7	1	328266	209390
		8	2	209390	0
Baltimore County MD	805029	2	1	721694	83335
		5	2	83335	0
Calvert MD	88737	8			

| Caroline MD | | 33066 | 8 | | | |

Populate columns A and B of this spreadsheet with the county population data from the Missouri Census Data Center, contained in your file "<state> County.csv". You will fill out columns C thru F later as you build the CDs. The CD# field (column C) will identify the CD number. If the entire county is assigned to one CD, columns D, E, and F are left blank. If you assign only a portion of the county's population to a CD, then you will fill in the Partition # (Pt), Assigned Population (Assigned), and Left Over fields.

- **ZCTA Pop:** This spreadsheet contains the list of ZCTA's in the state, sorted by county and then by ZCTA within county. You will use this spreadsheet as the source for the list of ZCTA's in LAST County assigned to the current CD, and for the list of left-over ZCTA's assigned to one or more subsequent districts. Column headers and sample data rows:

MD ZCTA's by County			CD Assignments		
county	zcta	population	CD#	Pt	Total
A	B	C	D	E	F
Sample MD	20765	169	1	1	169
Sample MD	20670	298	1	1	467
Sample MD	20672	45	1	1	512
Sample MD	20761	255	1	1	767
Sample MD	20829	27642	1	1	28409
Sample MD	20815	29082	1	1	57491

Sample MD	20816		16208	3	2	16208	
Sample MD	20763		9768	3	2	25976	

Populate columns A, B, and C of this spreadsheet with the ZCTA population data from the Missouri Census Data Center, contained in your file "<state> ZCTAs.csv". You will fill out columns D, E, and F later as you build the CDs; you will only fill these columns for a county that you partition.

- **Master CD Table:** This is the master table for building congressional districts. Set this table up as shown below:

		Master Congressional District Table - Maryland							
		County Population				Running Aggregates			
CD#	County	Available	Assigned to this CD	Pt	Left Over	State Total	This CD	Total Target	Diff
A	B	C	D	E	F	G	H	I	J
1	Previous State Total and New Target for This CD					0	0	721694	721694
1	Garrett	30097	30097			30097	30097	721694	691597
1	Allegany	75087	75087			105184	105184	721694	616510
1	Washington	147430	147430			252614	252614	721694	469080
1	Frederick	233385	233385			485999	485999	721694	235695
1	Carroll	167134	167134			653133	653133	721694	68561
1	Montgomery	971777	68561	1	903216	721694	721694	721694	0

Column Definitions and Instructions:

CD# (Column A): Enter the number of the congressional district you are building. Start by entering 1 in the CD# field in the first data row. Enter a formula in the second data row to copy the contents from the first data row, and populate this formula to the rest of the data rows. In this way, every data row will be assigned to the same CD# as the row above. They will all be 1 until you enter 2, after which all remaining rows will become 2 until you change a CD to 3. As you drag the scan line across the state, you will add counties to the current CD. You will continue to add counties to the current CD until the addition of one more county would cause the Running Aggregate – State Total (column G) to exceed the Running Aggregate – Total Target (column I).

County (Column B): Enter the name of the county you are adding to the CD# shown in column A. Exception: The first row within each CD contains this entry in Column B: "Previous State Total and New Target for This CD", along with the appropriate entries in columns G through J.

To identify the county, use the map to drag the Scan Line along the reference Line, touching counties as you go. Each touched county is entered in Column B, and the county's population is found in the County Pop spreadsheet. Find the county name in that spreadsheet, and enter the CD# in column C of that spreadsheet.

County Population (Columns C through F): These columns contain data concerning the population of the county shown in column B.

County Population – Available (Column C): Enter the population of this county available for assignment. The first time you enter a county, this will be the population of the entire county taken from column B of the County Pop spreadsheet. If you previously assigned part of a county to another CD, then the amount entered here is taken from the Left Over field (Column F) of the County Pop spreadsheet.

County Population – Assigned to this CD (Column D): Add each county to the current CD with the assumption that the entire available population of that county will be assigned to the current CD. Ultimately this will not be the case, because Diff (column K) will become negative and the current county will become LAST County for the current CD. Therefore, the default formula for column D is to copy the population from column C. Enter a formula in column D in the first data row that copies the contents from column C. Populate this formula to the rest of column D.

When Diff becomes negative, and if you end up partitioning this county, then at that point you will delete the formula in column D, because you will assign only a portion of the available county population to the current CD. Instead, you will follow the instructions below for "Partitioning LAST County".

County Population – Pt (that is, Partition #) (Column E): If you are assigning the entire county population to this CD when the Scan Line first touches this county, then leave columns E and F blank. If this county is partitioned, then enter the Partition # in column E. Notes:

- o The first partition of a county (Partition # 1) occurs only when that county is LAST County for the current CD.

- o Partitions 2, 3, and so on can only occur in a county which was partially assigned previously to another CD.

County Population – Left Over (column F): If this county is partitioned, Left Over = Available (column C) minus Assigned to this CD (column D}.

Running Aggregates (Columns G through J): These columns are all based on calculations derived from information previously entered. You will enter a formula in the top row of each field and populate that formula to the rest of the table.

Running Aggregates - State Total (Column G): The running total of the state's population that has been assigned to all congressional districts so far. The formula for the current row is the sum of the previous total (column G of the previous row) plus the population assigned in the current row (column D of the current row). Populate this formula to the rest of column G.

Running Aggregates - This CD (Column H): The running total of the population assigned to the current congressional district. The formula for the current row is the sum of the previous total (column H of the previous row) plus the population assigned in the current row (column D of the current row). Populate this formula to the rest of column H. (Note that, for CD# 1, the data displayed in columns G and H will be the same.)

Total Target (Column I): This column displays the total state population which should be assigned to all CDs when the current CD is complete. Enter a formula to calculate Total Target, defined as AVG * CD# (column A). Populate this formula to the entire column.

Note that the Total Target for each congressional district is the aggregate target for all congressional districts completed so far, rather than just the AVG for one congressional district. This technique ensures that the accumulated differences from one congressional district to the next tend to even out. Initially, every row will display the target for CD 1. However, when the CD# (column A) changes to 2, the figure in the Total Target field (column I) will automatically update.

Difference (Diff) (Column J): This column displays the population still needed to complete the current CD, defined as Total Target (Column I) less the running aggregate for the state (Column G). In the first data row, insert a formula to calculate this Difference. Then populate that formula to the entire column.

As you begin building each CD, Difference is large, meaning a large population still needs to be assigned to complete the current CD. As you assign counties to the current CD, Difference decreases. Finally, Difference becomes negative. At that point, the county named in column B is LAST County for the current CD.

Instructions for LAST County:

- **Determine if you can complete the CD without partitioning a county.** There are three possibilities:
    - **Diff** in the row before LAST County is less than MIN and is as close or closer to 0 than the absolute value of **Diff** in the LAST County row. In this case, delete LAST County; the CD is complete without LAST County. This CD will have a population slightly smaller than AVG.
    - The absolute value of **Diff** in the LAST County row is less than MIN and is closer to 0 than the **Diff** in the row before LAST County. In this case, add LAST County to this CD and assign all of its available

population to this CD. If this is the first time you have scanned LAST County, do not partition it; if you have partitioned this county previously, then enter the next sequential partition # for this county in the Pt column, and enter 0 in the Left Over column. This CD will have a population slightly larger than AVG.

- o Both the **Diff** in the row before LAST County and the absolute value of **Diff** in the LAST County row are greater than MIN. In this case, you must partition LAST County. In the LAST County row, delete the entry in column D (County Population – Assigned to this CD).

- **Partitioning LAST County:** This procedure uses all three spreadsheets in your workbook, that is, **County Pop, ZCTA Pop,** and **Master CD Table**.

  - o Switch to the **County Pop** spreadsheet. Find LAST County. If this county has not been previously partitioned, you are now creating Partition 1. If the county has been previously partitioned, you are now creating the next consecutive partition number for that county, and you must enter a new row to contain the new partition number population assigned, and population left over. Enter the Partition # in the Pt column.

  - o In the **Master CD Table** spreadsheet, in the LAST County row, delete the entry for "County Population – Assigned to this CD" (column D). At this point, columns G, H, I, and J display the same data as the previous row. Make a note of the **Diff** field: this is the population needed to complete the current CD.

- Switch to the **ZCTA Pop** spreadsheet. Find LAST County. Also refer to the map of ZCTA's in LAST County. Scan LAST County on that map, using the same Scan Line slope as you have been using for adding counties to this CD. As you scan the county, add ZCTA's to the current CD until the total population of ZCTA's added to the current CD exceeds **Diff**. (To accomplish this In the spreadsheet, use Cut & Paste to move each ZCTA to the top of the list of ZCTA's in that county. Put the CD# and Pt# in columns D and E respectively. Use a formula in column F to keep track of the running total population assigned to this CD.) Stop adding ZCTA's when **Diff** (noted earlier from the **Master CD Table**) is exceeded. The last ZCTA encountered may or may not be the Last ZCTA in this CD. Either include this ZCTA in the current CD or do not include this ZCTA, based on whether or not the inclusion of this ZCTA brings the running total from this county closer to **Diff**. Make a note of the county population assigned to the current CD.

- Switch to the **County Pop** spreadsheet and scroll to LAST County and the current partition row:
    - Enter in column E the population assigned to the current CD from this county, which you had noted in the ZCTA Pop spreadsheet.
    - Enter a formula in column F to calculate the "Left Over" population that remains to be assigned to a subsequent CD:

- - If this is Pt 1, then Left Over = Column B (County Population) less Column E (Assigned Population).
  - If Pt is greater than 1, then Left Over = the Left Over amount from the row above less the Assigned Population in the current row.
  - Note the amounts in columns D, E, and F, which you will copy to the Master CD Table.

- Switch to the **Master CD Table** spreadsheet and scroll to the county you are now partitioning. Enter the data you noted from the County Pop spreadsheet, namely, Column D (Assigned Population), Column E (Pt), and Column F (Left Over). Columns G, H, and J should automatically update.

- Ensure that the total population assigned to this CD is within 5% (±) of AVG. If this limit is exceeded, return to the ZCTA Pop spreadsheet and make the requisite adjustment. It may be necessary to partition the Last ZCTA by census tracts (which is possible but highly unlikely): add or subtract census tracts (~4000 people per tract) in order to get the total CD population as near as possible to AVG. The Missouri Census Data Center may be able to help you find a map of census tracts within a particular ZCTA.

Appendix 6. Three-Seat CDs in Louisiana

Here is a map of all Louisiana parishes. In 2010 Louisiana had a total population of 4,533,372 and was apportioned 6 seats in the House of Representatives, which we will partition into two CDs each containing 3 seats. The AVG population per House seat is 755,562, so the population for each CD should be 2,266,686.

Louisiana Congressional District 1 (LA CD 1)

Louisiana CD 1 will elect 3 House members.

LA CD 1 Reference Line and Scan Line:

Dragging the Scan Line from northwest to southeast, we add parishes to CD 1 as shown in this table:

Master Congressional District Table -- Louisiana

		Parish Population			Running Aggregates			
CD#	Parish	Available	Assigned to this CD	Pt Left Over	State Total	This CD	Total Target	Diff
1	Previous State Total and New Target for This CD				0	0	2266686	2266686
1	Caddo	254969	254969		254969	254969	2266686	2011717
1	Bossier	116979	116979		371948	371948	2266686	1894738
1	Webster	41207	41207		413155	413155	2266686	1853531
1	De Soto	26656	26656		439811	439811	2266686	1826875
1	Claiborne	17195	17195		457006	457006	2266686	1809680
1	Red River	9091	9091		466097	466097	2266686	1800589
1	Bienville	14353	14353		480450	480450	2266686	1786236
1	Sabine	24233	24233		504683	504683	2266686	1762003
1	Lincoln	46735	46735		551418	551418	2266686	1715268
1	Union	22721	22721		574139	574139	2266686	1692547
1	Natchitoches	39566	39566		613705	613705	2266686	1652981
1	Jackson	16274	16274		629979	629979	2266686	1636707
1	Winn	15313	15313		645292	645292	2266686	1621394
1	Ouachita	153720	153720		799012	799012	2266686	1467674
1	Vernon	52334	52334		851346	851346	2266686	1415340
1	Grant	22309	22309		873655	873655	2266686	1393031
1	Caldwell	10132	10132		883787	883787	2266686	1382899
1	Richland	20725	20725		904512	904512	2266686	1362174
1	West Carroll	11604	11604		916116	916116	2266686	1350570
1	Morehouse	27979	27979		944095	944095	2266686	1322591
1	Beauregard	35654	35654		979749	979749	2266686	1286937
1	Rapides	131613	131613		1111362	1111362	2266686	1155324
1	La Salle	14890	14890		1126252	1126252	2266686	1140434
1	Calcasieu	192768	192768		1319020	1319020	2266686	947666
1	East Carroll	7759	7759		1326779	1326779	2266686	939907
1	Franklin	20767	20767		1347546	1347546	2266686	919140
1	Madison	12093	12093		1359639	1359639	2266686	907047
1	Catahoula	10407	10407		1370046	1370046	2266686	896640
1	Allen	25764	25764		1395810	1395810	2266686	870876
1	Cameron	6839	6839		1402649	1402649	2266686	864037
1	Tensas	5252	5252		1407901	1407901	2266686	858785
1	Jefferson Davis	31594	31594		1439495	1439495	2266686	827191
1	Avoyelles	42073	42073		1481568	1481568	2266686	785118
1	Evangeline	33984	33984		1515552	1515552	2266686	751134
1	Concordia	20822	20822		1536374	1536374	2266686	730312
1	Acadia	61773	61773		1598147	1598147	2266686	668539
1	St. Landry	83384	83384		1681531	1681531	2266686	585155
1	Vermilion	57999	57999		1739530	1739530	2266686	527156
1	West Feliciana	15625	15625		1755155	1755155	2266686	511531
1	Pointe Coupee	22802	22802		1777957	1777957	2266686	488729
1	Lafayette	221578	221578		1999535	1999535	2266686	267151
1	St. Martin	52160	52160		2051695	2051695	2266686	214991
1	Iberville	33387	33387		2085082	2085082	2266686	181604
1	East Feliciana	20267	20267		2105349	2105349	2266686	161337
1	Iberia	73240	73240		2178589	2178589	2266686	88097
1	West Baton Rouge	23788	23788		2202377	2202377	2266686	64309
1	East Baton Rouge	440171	64309	1 375862	2266686	2266686	2266686	0

Louisiana CD 2

Because Louisiana has only two 3-seat CDs, all the remaining counties belong to CD 2, so we can list those counties and populations and then draw one map of the two CDs in the whole state. Note that East Baton Rouge is the only parish in the whole state that we need to partition. Dramatically reducing the number of partitioned counties is another advantage of 3-seat CDs:

		Master Congressional District Table -- Louisiana						
		Parish Population			Running Aggregates			
CD#	Parish	Available	Assigned to this CD	Pt	Left Over	State Total	This CD	Total Target	Diff
2	Previous State Total and New Target for This CD					2266686	0	4533372	2266686
2	East Baton Rouge	375862	375862	2	0	2642548	2642548	4533372	1890824
2	Ascension	107215	107215			2749763	2749763	4533372	1783609
2	Assumption	23421	23421			2773184	2773184	4533372	1760188
2	Jefferson	432552	432552			3205736	3205736	4533372	1327636
2	Lafourche	96318	96318			3302054	3302054	4533372	1231318
2	Livingston	128026	128026			3430080	3430080	4533372	1103292
2	Orleans	343829	343829			3773909	3773909	4533372	759463
2	Plaquemines	23042	23042			3796951	3796951	4533372	736421
2	St. Bernard	35897	35897			3832848	3832848	4533372	700524
2	St. Charles	52780	52780			3885628	3885628	4533372	647744
2	St. Helena	11203	11203			3896831	3896831	4533372	636541
2	St. James	22102	22102			3918933	3918933	4533372	614439
2	St. John the Baptist	45924	45924			3964857	3964857	4533372	568515
2	St. Mary	54650	54650			4019507	4019507	4533372	513865
2	St. Tammany	233740	233740			4253247	4253247	4533372	280125
2	Tangipahoa	121097	121097			4374344	4374344	4533372	159028
2	Terrebonne	111860	111860			4486204	4486204	4533372	47168
2	Washington	47168	47168			4533372	4533372	4533372	0

Louisiana's completed CDs, based on 3-seat CDs:

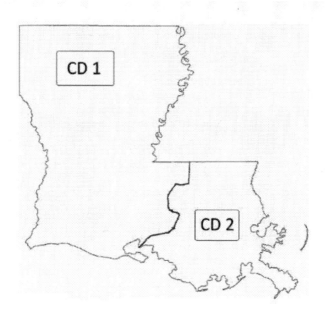

Appendix 7. Three-Seat CDs in Minnesota

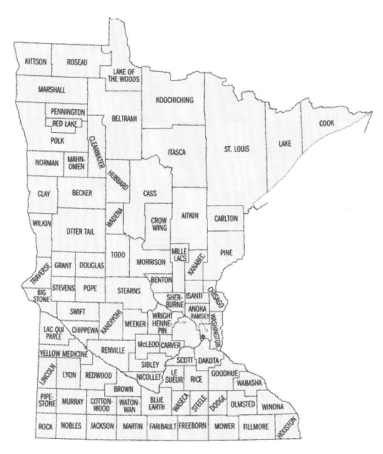

Here is a map of all Minnesota counties. According to the 2010 Census, Minnesota had a total population of 5,303,925 and was apportioned 8 seats in the House of Representatives, which we will partition into three CDs: Two CDs each containing 3 seats plus one CD containing 2 seats. The AVG population per House seat is 662,991, so the population for each 3-seat CD should be

1,988,972, and the population for the one 2-sea CD should be 1,325,981.

Statewide Data	
State	Minnesota
Population	5303925
Seats	8
3 CDs (2 with 3 seats, 1 with 2 seats)	
AVG	662991
MIN	33150

Minnesota Congressional District 1 (MN CD 1)

Minnesota CD 1 will elect 3 House members.

MN CD 1 Reference Line and Scan Line

Dragging the Scan Line from northwest to southeast, we add the counties to CD 1 as shown in this table:

Master Congressional District Table

		County Population			Running Aggregates			
		Available	Assigned to this CD	Pt Left Over	State Total	This CD	Total Target	Diff
CD#	County							
1	Previous State Total and New Target for This CD				0	0	1988972	1988972
1	Kittson MN	4552	4552		4552	4552	1988972	1984420
1	Marshall MN	9439	9439		13991	13991	1988972	1974981
1	Roseau MN	15629	15629		29620	29620	1988972	1959352
1	Polk MN	31600	31600		61220	61220	1988972	1927752
1	Pennington MN	13930	13930		75150	75150	1988972	1913822
1	Lake of the Woods	4045	4045		79195	79195	1988972	1909777
1	Beltrami MN	44442	44442		123637	123637	1988972	1865335
1	Red Lake MN	4089	4089		127726	127726	1988972	1861246
1	Norman MN	6852	6852		134578	134578	1988972	1854394
1	Koochiching MN	13311	13311		147889	147889	1988972	1841083
1	Clearwater MN	8695	8695		156584	156584	1988972	1832388
1	Clay MN	58999	58999		215583	215583	1988972	1773389
1	Mahnomen MN	5413	5413		220996	220996	1988972	1767976
1	Becker MN	32504	32504		253500	253500	1988972	1735472
1	Wilkin MN	6576	6576		260076	260076	1988972	1728896
1	Itasca MN	45058	45058		305134	305134	1988972	1683838
1	St. Louis MN	200226	200226		505360	505360	1988972	1483612
1	Hubbard MN	20428	20428		525788	525788	1988972	1463184
1	Otter Tail MN	57303	57303		583091	583091	1988972	1405881
1	Cass MN	28567	28567		611658	611658	1988972	1377314
1	Wadena MN	13843	13843		625501	625501	1988972	1363471
1	Traverse MN	3558	3558		629059	629059	1988972	1359913
1	Grant MN	6018	6018		635077	635077	1988972	1353895
1	Big Stone MN	5269	5269		640346	640346	1988972	1348626
1	Lake MN	10866	10866		651212	651212	1988972	1337760
1	Douglas MN	36009	36009		687221	687221	1988972	1301751
1	Crow Wing MN	62500	62500		749721	749721	1988972	1239251
1	Todd MN	24895	24895		774616	774616	1988972	1214356
1	Stevens MN	9726	9726		784342	784342	1988972	1204630
1	Aitkin MN	16202	16202		800544	800544	1988972	1188428
1	Cook MN	5176	5176		805720	805720	1988972	1183252
1	Pope MN	10995	10995		816715	816715	1988972	1172257
1	Morrison MN	33198	33198		849913	849913	1988972	1139059
1	Swift MN	9783	9783		859696	859696	1988972	1129276
1	Lac qui Parle MN	7259	7259		866955	866955	1988972	1122017
1	Stearns MN	150642	150642		1017597	1017597	1988972	971375
1	Carlton MN	35386	35386		1052983	1052983	1988972	935989
1	Chippewa MN	12441	12441		1065424	1065424	1988972	923548
1	Mille Lacs MN	26097	26097		1091521	1091521	1988972	897451
1	Yellow Medicine	10438	10438		1101959	1101959	1988972	887013
1	Kandiyohi MN	42239	42239		1144198	1144198	1988972	844774
1	Benton MN	38451	38451		1182649	1182649	1988972	806323
1	Lincoln MN	5896	5896		1188545	1188545	1988972	800427
1	Pine MN	29750	29750		1218295	1218295	1988972	770677
1	Kanabec MN	16239	16239		1234534	1234534	1988972	754438
1	Lyon MN	25857	25857		1260391	1260391	1988972	728581
1	Meeker MN	23300	23300		1283691	1283691	1988972	705281
1	Renville MN	15730	15730		1299421	1299421	1988972	689551
1	Sherburne MN	88499	88499		1387920	1387920	1988972	601052
1	Pipestone MN	9596	9596		1397516	1397516	1988972	591456
1	Isanti MN	37816	37816		1435332	1435332	1988972	553640
1	Wright MN	124700	124700		1560032	1560032	1988972	428940
1	Redwood MN	16059	16059		1576091	1576091	1988972	412881
1	Murray MN	8725	8725		1584816	1584816	1988972	404156
1	Chisago MN	53887	53887		1638703	1638703	1988972	350269
1	McLeod MN	36651	36651		1675354	1675354	1988972	313618
1	Rock MN	9687	9687		1685041	1685041	1988972	303931
1	Anoka MN	330844	330844		2015885	2015885	1988972	-26913

Minnesota's completed CD 1:

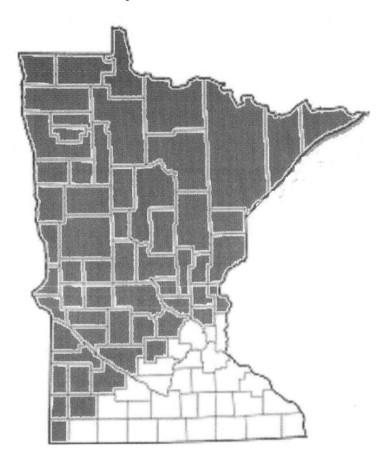

MN CD 2

Minnesota CD 2 will elect 3 House members.

MN CD 2: Reference & Scan Lines

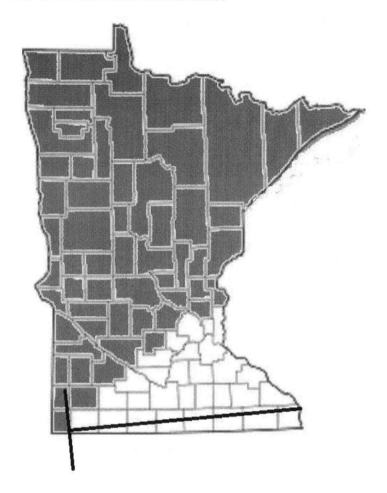

The table for CD 2:

		County Population				Running Aggregates			
			Assigned			State		Total	
CD#	County	Available	to this CD	Pt	Left Over	Total	This CD	Target	Diff
2	Previous State Total and New Target for This CD					2015885	0	3977944	1962059
2	Nobles MN	21378	21378			2037263	21378	3977944	1940681
2	Jackson MN	10266	10266			2047529	31644	3977944	1930415
2	Cottonwood MN	11687	11687			2059216	43331	3977944	1918728
2	Brown MN	25893	25893			2085109	69224	3977944	1892835
2	Martin MN	20840	20840			2105949	90064	3977944	1871995
2	Watonwan MN	11211	11211			2117160	101275	3977944	1860784
2	Nicollet MN	32727	32727			2149887	134002	3977944	1828057
2	Sibley MN	15226	15226			2165113	149228	3977944	1812831
2	Blue Earth MN	64013	64013			2229126	213241	3977944	1748818
2	Faribault MN	14553	14553			2243679	227794	3977944	1734265
2	Le Sueur MN	27703	27703			2271382	255497	3977944	1706562
2	Carver MN	91042	91042			2362424	346539	3977944	1615520
2	Scott MN	129928	129928			2492352	476467	3977944	1485592
2	Waseca MN	19136	19136			2511488	495603	3977944	1466456
2	Freeborn MN	31255	31255			2542743	526858	3977944	1435201
2	Hennepin MN	1152425	1152425			3695168	1679283	3977944	282776
2	Rice MN	64142	64142			3759310	1743425	3977944	218634
2	Steele MN	36576	36576			3795886	1780001	3977944	182058
2	Dakota MN	398552	182058	1	216494	3977944	1962059	3977944	0

MN CD 3

Minnesota CD 3 will elect 2 House members.

Any populations left over after completing CDs 1 and 2 must be assigned to CD 3, so we can show one map for CD 2 and CD 3, which follows the table of counties assigned to CD 3:

		Master Congressional District Table						
		County Population				Running Aggregates		
			Assigned			State		Total	
CD#	County	Available	to this CD	Pt	Left Over	Total	This CD	Target	Diff
3	Previous State Total and New Target for This CD					3977944	0	5303925	1325981
3	Dakota MN	216494	216494	2	0	4194438	216494	5303925	1109487
3	Dodge MN	20087	20087			4214525	236581	5303925	1089400
3	Fillmore MN	20866	20866			4235391	257447	5303925	1068534
3	Goodhue MN	46183	46183			4281574	303630	5303925	1022351
3	Houston MN	19027	19027			4300601	322657	5303925	1003324
3	Mower MN	39163	39163			4339764	361820	5303925	964161
3	Olmsted MN	144248	144248			4484012	506068	5303925	819913
3	Ramsey MN	508640	508640			4992652	1014708	5303925	311273
3	Wabasha MN	21676	21676			5014328	1036384	5303925	289597
3	Washington MN	238136	238136			5252464	1274520	5303925	51461
3	Winona MN	51461	51461			5303925	1325981	5303925	0

The completed map for all three Minnesota CDs:

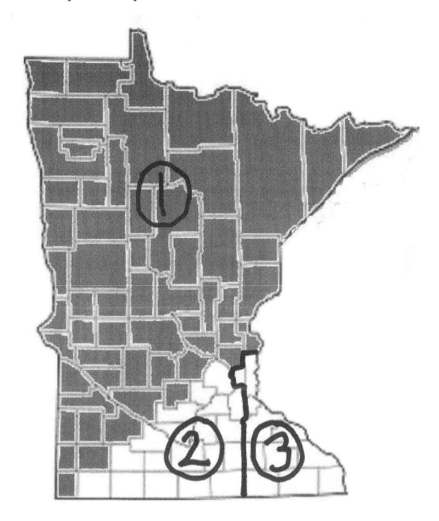

Sources/Citations

Articles of Confederation (1781). Downloaded from https://www.govinfo.gov/content/pkg/SMAN-107/pdf/SMAN-107-pg935.pdf

Ballotpedia (2019). Multiple articles containing election results. https://ballotpedia.org/Main_Page

Baltimore Sun (2016). "Senator proposes two-state solution on redistricting reform" (February 6). https://www.baltimoresun.com/news/maryland/politics/blog/bal-senator-proposes-twostate-solution-on-redistricting-reform-20160209-story.html [accessed on May 10, 2019].

Brennan Center for Justice (2019). "The National Popular Vote, Explained". https://www.brennancenter.org/blog/national-popular-vote-explained [accessed on May 10, 2019].

Common Cause (http://www.commoncause.org/issues/money-in-politics/)

Common Cause (http://www.commoncause.org/issues/voting-and-elections/)

Constitution of the United States (1787); aka "1787 Constitution". Downloaded from https://www.govinfo.gov/content/pkg/CDOC-110hdoc50/pdf/CDOC-110hdoc50.pdf

Curiel, J. and T. Steelman, "How to measure the impact of partisan gerrymandering". Paper presentation at *Reason, Reform & Redistricting Conference*, Duke University, January 2019.

End Citizens United (http://endcitizensunited.org/)

EveryVoice.org (http://everyvoice.org/)

FairVote (2017). "Why James Madison wanted to change the way we vote for President". http://www.fairvote.org/why-james-madison-wanted-to-change-the-way-we-vote-for-President. [Accessed on June 16, 2017.]

FairVote. https://www.fairvote.org/

Gallup (May 8, 2019). "Party Affiliation" (public opinion poll). https://news.gallup.com/poll/15370/party-affiliation.aspx [accessed on May 8, 2019].

League of Women Voters (http://lwv.org/issues/protecting-voters)

League of Women Voters (https://www.lwv.org/voting-rights/money-politics)

Louisiana Secretary of State: Voting and Elections (2019). https://www.sos.la.gov/ElectionsAndVoting/Pages/default.aspx

Machiavelli, N. (1513). *The Prince*. Downloaded from the Maryland Digital eLibrary Consortium. https://maryland.overdrive.com/media/283602?utm_campaign=searchfeed&utm_source=google [accessed on May 10, 2019].

Madison, J (1793). "Helvidius No. 3" (September 7). https://founders.archives.gov/documents/Madison/01-15-02-0066 [accessed on May 10, 2019].

Maryland State Board of Elections (2019). https://elections.maryland.gov/

MAYDAY.US (https://mayday.us/)

Minnesota Secretary of State: Elections and Voting (2019), https://www.sos.state.mn.us/elections-voting/

Missouri Census Data Center (2019). "Geocorr 2014: Geographic Correspondence engine. http://mcdc.missouri.edu/applications/geocorr2014.html [accessed on May 2, 2019].

MoveToAmend.org (https://movetoamend.org/)

New Republic (Nov. 8, 2012). "Welcome to America's Most Gerrymandered District". https://newrepublic.com/article/109938/marylands-3rd-district-americas-most-gerrymandered-congressional-district [accessed on May 9, 2019].

New York Times (August 1, 2016). "Only 9% of America Chose Trump and Clinton as the Nominees". https://www.nytimes.com/interactive/2016/08/01/us/elections/nine-percent-of-america-selected-trump-and-clinton.html?_r=0 [accessed on June 15, 2017].

North Carolina State Board of elections (2019). https://www.ncsbe.gov/index.html

Paine, T. (1776). *Common Sense.* Downloaded from https://archive.org/details/commonsense00painrich

Pennsylvania Department of State, Bureau of Commissions, Elections, and Legislation (2019). https://www.dos.pa.gov/VotingElections/Pages/default.aspx

Roosevelt, F. (1932). Commencement Address at Oglethorpe University, May 22, 1932. *The Atlanta Constitution*, May 23, 1932.

Singh, R.S. (2019). *In Defense of the United States Constitution*. Routledge (New York).

Tweed, W (n.d.). "Top 6 Quotes from Boss Tweed", *AZ Quotes*, http://www.azquotes.com/author/14885-Boss_Tweed [accessed on June 15, 2017].

US News & World Report (https://www.usnews.com/news/articles/2015/12/01/redistricting-reform-gains-steam) [accessed on July 1, 2019].

Wikipedia (2017). "United States Presidential Election, 1788-89." https://en.wikipedia.org/wiki/United_States_Presidential_election,_1788-89 [accessed on June 6, 2017].

Wikipedia (2019). "Electoral system of Australia". https://en.wikipedia.org/wiki/Electoral_system_of_Australia [accessed on May 10, 2019].

Wikipedia (2019). "Instant-runoff voting". https://en.wikipedia.org/wiki/Instant-runoff_voting [accessed on May 10, 2019].

Wolf-PAC (http://www.wolf-pac.com/)

Made in the USA
Middletown, DE
02 August 2019